LRUZ

FROM THE WINGS

FROM THE WINGS

Joseph Harmatz

The Book Guild Ltd
Sussex, England

This book is sold subject to the condition that it shall not, by way of trade or otherwise, be lent, re-sold, hired out, photocopied or held in any retrieval system or otherwise circulated without the publisher's prior consent in any form of binding or cover other than that in which this is published and without a similar condition including this condition being imposed on the subsequent purchaser.

The Book Guild Ltd.
25 High Street,
Lewes, Sussex

First published 1998
© Joseph Harmatz

Set in Garamond
Typesetting by Acorn Bookwork, Salisbury, Wiltshire

Printed in Great Britain by
Bookcraft (Bath) Ltd, Avon

A catalogue record for this book is
available from the British Library

The preparation and publication of this volume was made possible by a grant
from the Memorial Foundation for Jewish Culture.

ISBN 1 85776 340 8 (cased)
ISBN 1 85776 392 0 (paperback)

In memory of my late wife, Gina – a survivor
and
For my two sons, Zvi and Ronel-Efraim
and their families – to remember

CONTENTS

ACKNOWLEDGEMENTS	x
INTRODUCTION – From the Wings	xi
I LITHUANIA	1
Rokishkis 1994	1
The Valley of Death	5
Childhood Revisited	10
Massacre at Byorai	13
Memories and Memorials	19
Kaunas	21
II ESTONIA	27
Night Train to Tallin	27
Klooga	29
3835 – My Little Brother	36
III LATVIA	39
Riga 1994	39
Josef and Sanna Levin	41
Mother: Kaiserwald – Stutthof	52
Irena and Shimon Lusky	63
IV VILNA	67
Vilna 1994	67
The Vilna Ghetto	70
Father	73
FPO – Veraynigte Partisaner Organisatzye	75

Escape through the Sewers	80
The Rudnitski Forests	83
Tevya Rubin	87
Ponar – Motl Zeidel	92
Sonia	98
Vilna Liberated	100
Time to Leave	105
V FROM VILNA TO PALESTINE	**107**
Heading South	107
Bucharest	112
Remnants of our People	114
The Jewish Brigade – A Historic Meeting	116
The Reckoning	119
Manik's Tale: A Leap from the Train	120
Crime and Punishment	130
Letter from Sorrento	143
To the Promised Land	148
Abba	152
VI ISRAEL 1947–1956	**161**
The Palestine Electric Corporation	161
Gina	166
Settling New Immigrants	171
VII BACK TO EUROPE 1956–1960	**177**
Geneva	177
Cutting the Mast – The Charlton Star	181
Vitek	187

Horses from Transylvania	192
The Straits of Gibraltar	199
The Treasurer	202
Marcel	205
A Helping Hand	212
VIII ISRAEL 1960	217
Back to School	217
Shipping	221
Index of People	225
Index of Place Names and Organisations	227

ACKNOWLEDGEMENTS

This book has been written as the personal story of one individual, to illustrate the depth of pain and suffering endured by the millions who lived and died during the disastrous period of our contemporary history, known as the Holocaust.

Reference to millions is an abstract quantum, and places the facts beyond human comprehension. I believe that focusing on individual people and their life-stories puts the tragedy into some kind of perspective.

At the same time, I wanted to pay tribute and mourn all members of my family, and close friends, who perished or fell in battle defending their countries and the dignity of the Jewish people.

* * *

This book would not have been written without the help of Kitty Brod, who for years persisted in persuading me to put pen to paper and chronicle these stories. She followed this through with determination and stubborn enthusiasm by writing, translating, and editing copious amounts of material. My appreciation goes also to her family who stood by with patience and understanding during this period.

I was also encouraged over the years to bring this book to fruition by the late Abba Kovner, Vitka Kovner, and Pasha Avidov, who travelled the same long journey as I.

Grateful thanks go to Barbie Harshav for her vital and constructive endeavours in editing the final manuscript.

INTRODUCTION

From the Wings

> *'One's real life is so often the life one does not lead'*
>
> Oscar Wilde

In the autumn years of my life, after what many would term a rich and colourful life, but one which I would probably prefer to call complex, troubled and disrupted, like so many lives in those tormented times of the 1930s/1940s, I resolved to take my two sons on a nostalgic trip back to my home town in North-Eastern Lithuania. It was something I had planned for a long time – I wanted to show them their heritage – but the opportunity did not present itself until I retired from the organisation I had headed for the previous 14 years and which had claimed my undivided attention while I still held office. Once retired and having returned to Israel from my London base, I spent a while re-establishing myself and set off for the former Soviet Union, with my younger son only. The account of our trip forms the first section of this book.

At the end of this return to our roots tour across the Baltics, and before flying home to Israel, we paid a visit to Moscow. It was on June 22, 1994, ironically 53 years to the day since the German army had invaded the Soviet Union, a date which changed our lives so dramatically, that friends managed to obtain tickets for us to see Giselle at the Bolshoi. It had always been difficult to get tickets for the ballet in Moscow but we were determined to enjoy the experience and were not too disappointed to discover that our seats were in a third tier balcony box. As if to add insult to injury, they were right on the far side of the auditorium and notwithstanding the fact that they were the front row seats in the box, we had to perform elaborate acrobatics leaning right over the balcony, in order to see something. All we saw was just half the stage, and even though Giselle is always a pleasure and I'd seen it so often before, we had, after all, paid our friends 70,000 roubles for 700 rouble tickets, one hundred times more than the price for locals.

Before we entered the auditorium, ascending the grand staircase towards our seats, I turned my head and whom should I see but Mikhail

Gorbachev and his wife Raisa, a distinguished looking couple milling amongst the crowds. Later, I looked for him in the auditorium, assuming he would be seated in what is known as the Imperial Tsar's box; but no, he was not to be seen. The box meanwhile was empty. A few minutes later, there followed a commotion as a party ceremonially entered the Tsar's box. A special announcement in English and in Russian made us aware that we were all privileged to be in the presence of honoured guests in the Imperial box: Professor Maior, Director General of UNESCO, with his wife and an enormous entourage. On a loudspeaker, warm thanks and appreciation were extended to UNESCO for their assistance in the refurbishment of the Bolshoi.

Not a word about the Gorbachevs. He was, after all, the father of modern-day Russia. It was he who gave birth to perestroika, leading ultimately to the collapse of the communist world in 1990, an event universally acknowledged as unattainable before his courageous stand. There they were, seated just like anyone else with Mr and Mrs Public, without any recognition whatsoever. I very much hope that they were at least able to see the whole ballet from their seats.

Meanwhile, there was I with my son, Ronny, up in the gods still straining to see at least half the stage and it struck me that life is often like that; it is only perhaps the Gorbachevs and the Maiors who are given the opportunity of seeing the whole picture – a full frontal view, while for the rest of us, it is prescribed that we should see life just as we saw Giselle that evening, only a partial view, a side view, a view from the wings. I really would like to meet the person or persons sitting in the gallery opposite us so that I could ask them how they found their half of the performance, the part we could not see. If you, dear reader, ever come across anyone who sat up there, you might perhaps ask him or her how things looked – then we might get a complete picture.

The stories which follow in this book are recounted just like that: without any pretensions or ambitions of being seen from the front seat; on the contrary, they are all viewed from the wings; they do not give the whole picture, but one from a certain, perhaps limited, yet personal aspect and point of view.

I have, over the years, lived many varied chapters, met people from all walks of life, some of whom I remember, many of whom I do not, but of those that I do, there are some whose particular story I have always wanted to tell. It had, as I said, to wait until I made the transition from one phase of my life to another, from a hectic working life to more leisurely retirement, when I was no longer weighed down by reports, budgets, and the burden of responsibility. By now, it is possible that time has distorted the memory but while the names of the characters are sometimes fictitious, the personalities in the stories which follow are very real, entirely genuine, the salt of the earth, and above all people whom I was privileged to know.

I

LITHUANIA

Rokishkis 1994

> *No man will cure*
> *nor heaven*
> *the offence of your scalding silence*
>
> Abba Kovner

On June 8, 1994, I embarked with my younger son, Ronny, on a long-planned journey to Eastern Europe, taking in the Baltic States of Lithuania, Estonia and Latvia, St Petersburg and Moscow. I had hoped that both my sons would accompany me on this journey to our roots, but just a few days before we left, my older son Zvi suffered a vicious kidney stone attack and his doctors advised him not to travel. I had wanted to show them both the town where I was born in January 1925, where I grew up, and where I probably spent the happiest years of my life; the town where I went to school, where I lived in the warmth of my family – my parents, my two brothers and my grandparents – until the German army invaded Lithuania in June 1941, and changed all our lives.

I had been there twice since – once in 1944, immediately after the liberation, curious to see who or what was left. The front was still nearby and Schauliai was still occupied by the Germans, so I had to take a train to Latvia (to Dvinsk, to be precise) and from there I travelled to Rokishkis. It was night when I got off at the railway station, a few kilometres from the village; and so I walked into my former hometown.

I had arrived in uniform – or so-called uniform – for there was nothing uniform about it. We partisans had to assemble our clothes as best we could, using whatever we could find. I wore the khaki jacket of a Lithuanian officer, the breeches of a German cavalry soldier, which were held up by the *pièce de résistance* – a belt I had pinched from one of my German victims. The brass buckle proudly displayed the

German emblem of an eagle surrounded by the words *'Gott mit uns'* – God is with us – which clearly did not apply to that particular German soldier as indicated by the bullet hole right in the centre of the 'mit'. The only items which would have been recognisable to the Russian soldier who greeted me, were my sturdy Russian leather boots: fortunately for me these boots were parachuted in from Moscow, for I had had endless problems with my feet in the sodden swamps of the forests where our partisan brigade was located.

As I made my way into the town, a soldier on patrol suddenly called out of the darkness.

'Password!'

Of course, I had none, so I remained silent.

'Approach,' he shouted, 'and drop your gun.'

'I will not drop my gun,' said I, 'but I am coming'.

After what we had experienced during the last three years in the ghetto, in the forest and after the liberation, the idea of dropping a gun was quite out of the question, an alien concept. I went to him, told him who I was, presented my identity papers, and explained why I had come back to my hometown. His reaction was to cart me off immediately to the police station. It was three o'clock in the morning.

Nobody knew me, and certainly no-one would vouch for me, so they gave me a wooden bench were I slept until morning. The next day, one of the locals who had known my family identified me and I was released. As I wandered around the village, I met a soldier who had been serving in the 16th Lithuanian Division. Shimshon Shmushkevitch was a younger brother of General Shmushkevitch, one of the heroes of the Red Army at that time and Chief Inspector of the Soviet Aviation authority. Shmushkevitch was still in uniform and he was the first to tell me the bitter truth that my older brother had fallen in battle, fighting in the Red Army.

Zvi Hirsch Harmatz was killed on February 24, 1943, in the battle of Oriol, one of the grim winter battles for Moscow.

Before the war, Zvi had been studying at a teachers college in Wilkomir. Like so many youngsters from our town and the surrounding villages, he had fled to the Soviet Union and joined the Red Army to fight the Germans. Many others who tried to escape, however, were detained at the Russian frontier by the border police and, with the lightning advance of the German army, were caught and sent back to where they came from – straight into the hands of their German and Lithuanian murderers.

After my visit with Ronny in 1994, I realised how little I knew of the details of those terrible times. Although those years between 1941 and 1945 were probably the longest, most difficult and terrifying years of my life, I had no real knowledge of the circumstances surrounding the fate that befell my close relatives. In recent years, I have had more time to reflect on my past, and the opportunity to research the facts to recount how things were, what happened, how all the Jews of my home town perished during the German occupation; what happened to my older brother Zvi, how he was killed in the Soviet Army, near the village of Alexeievka in the region of Oriol, while his battalion defended Moscow against the Germans, then mounted an attack. How my younger brother Ephraim was incarcerated and finally murdered in the concentration camp of Klooga in Estonia after the liquidation of the Vilna Ghetto in September 1943; how my mother suffered and mercifully survived, against all odds, in the concentration camp in Riga and later in Stutthof; and how my father and all four of my grandparents perished.

I feel it my duty to tell all this, first in memory of those who died; but also as a legacy to future generations. Thus I started searching for background material: I read books, and questioned friends, especially those who stayed in Lithuania long after I left in 1945. Many of them emigrated in the early 1970s, and had visited our birthplace, the places we had lived in Vilna, before and during the ghetto; they questioned neighbours, researched the archives which were unearthed after the war, and erected memorials to the thousands who had been annihilated throughout Lithuania and elsewhere.

From this extensive research I learned much about this period, and I am grateful to Meir Kark, Fay Rief, and Colonel Ze'ev Wilensky for filling in the gaps in my knowledge of those grim years.

Above all, it has helped me remember my brother, Zvi Hirsch.

The 16th Lithuanian Division of the Soviet Army, established at the beginning of 1942 in Balachna, on the Volga in the Gorky region, spent the summer in military training. Many of the recruits were Jewish youngsters who had managed to escape to the Soviet Union and who had no military knowledge or experience whatsoever. Towards the end of the year they were given winter clothes and in January 1943 were dispatched to the front.

It was a bitterly cold winter. There were almost no trees in the regions of Tula and Oriol, just endless plains and steppes. Harsh winds made it even colder and temperatures regularly reached −40°C. Thick snow fell every night; but worst of all was the wind, driving them back, while the snow blew into their eyes so hard it almost took their breath away.

The division was composed of three ethnic groups: Russians, Lithuanians, and Jews, both men and women. Many volunteers, hearing the fate of their families under the Nazi occupation, joined the army to avenge their loved ones. The accounts of early encounters with the Germans are filled with tales of heroism, camaraderie, intolerable conditions, deprivation and hardship, unimaginable temperatures, a lack of military equipment, failed attacks followed by mass retreat, self-sacrifice, and countless fatalities.

One account by Meir Kark, who fought in this division, touched me deeply.

The Valley of Death

> *Oh, my friends, why are you silent*
> *If the silence is not?*
>
> Abba Kovner

Military orders were to split into units and to march along the wide highways during the day and to rest at night. We would stop in different villages, taking refuge in barns, usually sleeping on the floor, grabbing whatever we could find to eat.

The closer we got to the front, the more difficult our manoeuvres became. Soon, we could march only at night, and because the roads were strewn with shattered military vehicles, we could no longer use the road, and had to go cross-country, through the snow in our heavy boots.

For the last few days of the march, just before reaching the front, we walked day and night without stopping. The officers would drive us on, ordering us not to fall behind. We just dragged ourselves on with whatever strength we had left. It was a boring, difficult trek, and you could actually fall asleep while walking; a dig in the ribs from the rifle of the soldier behind would quickly wake you up.

The snow continued to fall heavily. Even if we had been able to reach the road, there was no way we could have used this route. Stuck in the deep snow, far behind the infantry, were all the motor vehicles, the mortars and the anti-aircraft batteries, as well as the units that were supposed to provide us with ammunition, food, and back-up. For days we had had nothing to eat but dry rusks.

During the one-and-a-half month-long march, we had advanced just a few hundred kilometres into the regions of Tula and Oriol, It was on February 20, 1943, as the sun was setting, that we emerged from a forest and were walking towards a shallow valley. In the distance we could see a vast settlement, and somehow it gave us hope; we thought we could rest there and, if luck was on our side, we might even find something to eat.

There was no time to look around, for suddenly we heard the noise of aircraft flying straight overhead, and our column immediately dispersed in all directions, taking shelter behind the burned out vehicles strewn over the field. Some even ran back into the forest we had just left. The explosions helped break up the snow and luckily no-one was hurt ... then.

We had barely gotten to our feet when the German planes flew over again, this time firing their machine guns directly at our column. Now the piercing screams of the wounded filled the air.

Undeterred, we grouped and continued our march, moving slowly, pushing ourselves to the very end. Eventually we reached a small settlement called Alexeievka, which had been completely destroyed. Trenches had been dug all around and there were strategic firing positions for artillery and other heavy equipment. Obviously, fierce battles had recently been fought here. Streets and yards were littered with corpses: dead Germans lay side by side with our comrades and horses. Tanks and vehicles stood motionless, totally destroyed, while the ground was strewn with pistols, rifles and ammunition. The whole place reeked; but worst of all was the stench of burnt flesh.

Soon we had to get going along the main highway, where we came across many wounded soldiers, the few survivors of the defeated Sixth Elite Division we had been sent to replace. Now that we had arrived, we learned that there was no one to replace. The former division no longer existed.

It was already well after midnight when we were awakened and lined up in the street. It was bitterly cold. Our teeth chattered as if we were stricken with malaria and we hopped from one foot to another to try to wake ourselves up. A thick white fog descended low over the ground and we could barely see a few metres in front of us. We moved along, in single file, in total silence. Now that we had left the settlement behind, we started to descend a hill and found ourselves in a field, with only one thing: snow, deep white snow as far as the eye could see.

After a few kilometres of marching like this, the officer announced that we had reached our final destination, and ordered us to dig ourselves in. There were no trenches here or any fences – just the vast expanse of fields covered in a thick white carpet of snow. An icy wind blew and pierced our clothing, right to the skin. To make matters worse, our canvas overcoats had become rock hard from the damp night fog and no longer served as a protective layer.

At dawn, we saw a hill about 3–400 metres away. Beyond it, we knew, were the Germans. We couldn't see what was happening there because, of course, everything was covered in snow; but, as we learned later, the Germans were well dug in and well prepared. They had built fences in front of their trenches and, as the snow covered the fences, they had poured water on them, which instantly turned to ice; and behind this ice-wall they had positioned their artillery, machine guns, and heavy mortars. From their superior position, they had a superb view all around, including, of course, the field where we lay.

It was very quiet that morning. It did not seem like a war. Even the wind had died down, and for once it was not snowing. Some of the soldiers had already settled in their positions in their ready-made trenches under the snow. We were preparing for breakfast and sent some people to the kitchen stationed far behind us. They returned with the kasha (a kind of porridge) frozen solid, but no matter. We did not even have time to finish when the order came to line up. We left our trenches and lined up in long rows moving forward like Russian soldiers in olden times. The orders were to attack the German lines.

Colonel Wolf Wilensky, later commander of the 249th Regiment of the 16th Division, wrote in his memoirs: 'the Commander of the Division General Balutishis-Zhemaitis and his Commissar, Yonas Matseyaunskas, displayed criminal ignorance in hiding from the headquarters at the front the exceptionally difficult situation in which the Division found itself: without support from the air, without artillery, tanks, anti-aircraft batteries, mine launchers, a medical corps or food supply. It was their duty to request a postponement of the attack at least by a few days – until the Division could summon up its full strength. The attack was catastrophic and left behind hundreds of dead soldiers, and many more wounded.'

At first the Germans did nothing. They wanted to draw us up on top of the white snow and wipe us out. After a while, the Germans greeted us with a hail of fire from every kind of weapon. We lay low and made a weak attempt to fire back, but we were shooting at an unknown target: we simply could not raise our heads to see them. The Germans, on the other hand, had a perfect view of us. We were like black ants on the white snow. As the firing subsided, all we heard were the groans of our wounded calling for help.

Suddenly German reconnaissance planes flew low overhead, circled a few times, did not attack, and disappeared. After a while, something happened that none of us expected at the time: the entire formation of German dive bombers appeared in the skies and opened fire. When they ran out of ammunition, they disappeared, only to be replaced immediately by a new formation. This bombardment continued for the whole day, assisted by batteries of mortars showering us with shells. We were powerless to respond; our anti-aircraft batteries were stuck in the snow way behind us, and there was no other assistance available.

The German shelling continued, stopping when they thought we were all dead since we didn't return fire.

It was a horrendous sight: the dead were scattered over the field, the wounded were wailing for help as they bled to death. The medics hadn't been able to reach them since the firing never stopped. The brave nurses could barely distinguish between the dead and the wounded.

It was only in the evening, when the planes stopped flying overhead, that we moved out of the trenches and decided to return to our unit. On our way back, we met many of the wounded soldiers, some just managing to walk alone, some being carried by friends; the medics ran towards the battlefield to rescue those who were severely wounded but still alive, and to collect the corpses.

The losses were colossal; there had been no cover whatsoever. As the planes flew overhead, they had sighted each and every one of us, and without any resistance, they just wiped us out, dropping bombs straight over us, firing machine guns precisely at their target, and even throwing hand grenades directly at us. There was no defence at all. All we could do was cover ourselves with our own bare hands.

The wounded lost enormous amounts of blood and some just froze in the arctic temperatures. They' talked of the pals they had fought with and, having spent so much time together, many of them having known each other from back home, they lamented the death of their fellow solders and friends. They grieved all the more because they had been powerless to help them.

Pranas Petronis, Major General Emeritus, formerly Commander of the 224th Artillery Regiment wrote: 'I reported to the Heads of the Division that the infantry, having marched for hundreds of kilometres in heavy snow and bitterly cold temperatures, tired and hungry, without food, ammunition or fuel, was in no way ready to take on the Germans and was certainly not in a position to attack. They ignored my warnings saying: "Do not worry, in a few days we will take up our positions, move forward and attack." When I reminded them of our limitations, seeing that our heavy artillery was stuck in deep snow kilometres away, and pointed out that the few weapons we had carried no more than 20 shells each, their response was: "Do not worry, the Germans will flee once three or five shells have been fired." There was no sense in discussing military issues with these people. It was a tragedy.'

And Pranas Petronis continues: 'On February 20, 1943, the division was ordered to take over a section of the front-line to replace those regiments who had suffered heavy losses inflicted by the enemy, and prepare to counter-attack. The other regiments in the area had also suffered great losses and one could not count on their assistance. Early next morning, the division took up its position on a snow-covered field, where the soil was frozen solid and therefore made it impossible to dig proper trenches. The temperature was $-30°C$. The enemy, seeing that the new field forces had arrived, opened heavy artillery fire. Mines and shells exploded over the heads of the soldiers, and many were killed or wounded.

'The same exercise was repeated on February 22 and 23. In addition to fire from the artillery, the enemy brought in its airforce. They came back again and again, with Messerschmitts and Heinkels. Those who survived, retreated.

'On February 24, we tried to attack once again, this time with what was left of our artillery covering our fire. Yet five batteries could not silence the German artillery and machinegun fire. We were short of shells. The heavy artillery which we had been promised never arrived.'

Officers of the General Staff of the Army who came to investigate the reasons for the failure and the horrendous losses, concluded that the 48th Army Command, to which the 16th Division belonged, was guilty of misusing the division of the front. At the same time, they highly commended their dedication and courage in attacking the enemy.

Soviet military historians, in their assessment of the battles of the 16th Division wrote that in spite of the fact that the attacks of February 1943 did not achieve the expected results, they still forced the enemy to use all its reserves to sustain their front-line position, which they finally decided to abandon on February 28. As a result, the front-line retreated to between 130 and 160 kilometres from Moscow.

The Division had certainly contributed greatly to this. The issue is that the historians and generals are there to assess and to write the annals of history, while the soldiers, sergeants and young officers are buried beneath the soil and the snow.

Among those killed that day was my older brother, Zvi. It was February 24, 1943, near the village of Alexeievka – known as the Valley of Death. He was not yet twenty.

Childhood re-visited

He shall return no more to his house,
Neither shall his place know him anymore

Job 10

Back in Rokishkis in 1994 with my younger son, the Lithuanian countryside no longer meant too much to me, though Ronny was very impressed with the beauty of the landscape. I suppose he could be more objective than I.

We went to the house where I had lived with my parents Abraham (Abrasha) and Dvora (Dora), my brothers, and our nanny. The Lithuanian driver knocked on the door and explained to the guy who opened the door that I had lived there more than fifty years ago and was eager to show my son where I had lived as a child. But he refused to let us in. Maybe it was just as well, for it would have been difficult to be transported back to those good old days of my youth, to the memory of my family, the happiness, the joy – a life so full of hope and expectation.

So we took photos of the outside and as we did, a lady came out of a neighbouring house and explained that seven families lived in that house and every one had paid his share and had permits from the authorities. She went to great lengths to tell us how everyone feared officialdom these days. I assured her that I had no claim to the house, but in the end we couldn't convince her that we meant no harm and had no intention of coming to live there. Who would ever dream of returning to a life in this graveyard?

We moved on to find the site of the family business. My father had dealt in all kinds of merchandise in large quantities; it was a wholesale enterprise with a huge warehouse, and now all that remained was a building site under construction. The business had been located on the main market square; now across the street from where it stood was a park, while some of the old buildings were still intact. But, after more than 50 years, most have disappeared. Were they afraid that surviving family members might claim these properties, and so it would be better to remove any traces of the past?

I looked around the square and remembered how we used to sit with friends discussing the world and dreaming about the future. I told Ronny who had lived where, that just across the square lived a girl I had loved very much when we were both 14 or 15 – and that she, too, had been killed with all the Jews of Rokishkis.

Then we tried to find my paternal grandparents' home. They had a lovely house with a pretty garden, and they kept a dog. My grandparents were a highly respected couple. Grandfather was well read, a dedicated Zionist – traditional, but not fanatic; he had been ordained as a Rabbi but had never practised, although he attended synagogue regularly. My grandmother was a small lady, very neat, very orderly, and highly disciplined; as children, if we were ever in trouble with our own parents, we would run to our grandparents who would comfort us and spoil us with sweets and ice cream. They were very German-oriented and often travelled to Berlin or other parts of Germany. They had had three children: the older son had died in the First World War in some epidemic while serving in the Russian Army as an officer and physician. His parents had never forgotten him; his photograph adorned every corner of the house and he was always mentioned with great reverence. His name was Zvi, known as Hirsch, as was my older brother, after whom my own son was later named. Then came my father, Abraham; and lastly there was a daughter, my aunt Fanya – known as Feigale (little bird) – who studied pharmacology in Berlin. There had always been a close link between Germany and Lithuania and the German influence remained strong. The second language taught in high-school was German. Eastern Lithuania was more Russian; but the German, hence Western, model prevailed. Fanya worked in Berlin-Charlottenburg and married a Polish-born violinist. My parents brought them into our home in 1939, arranged for their journey to the United States, and they left on the last boat from Sweden, before the outbreak of World War II.

Ronny and I looked for my grandparents' house, but did not find it. There are now high rise buildings where my grandparents' house once stood.

When we visited Kaunas some days later, I was shocked to see in the museum of the Ninth Fort photographs of the slaughter of the entire community, weeks after the Germans invaded Lithuania. It was a small, peaceful Jewish community, the salt of the earth. Today, without the Jews, the place is dead – it looks like a ghost town. They killed the Jews, and now they have a dead town. Now all that is left of the community are seven long mass graves with a plaque saying: 'Here on August 15 and 16, 1941, the Nazis and their local collaborators killed 3,207 Jews, men, women and children'.

This was one and a half months after the Germans entered Lithuania, but what really happened?

What follows is an account I found about the events which took place at Byorai.

Massacre at Byorai

Yea, when I cry and call for help, He shutteth out my prayer
Blessings 32

The persecutions started the first day after the Germans came to our little town of Rokishkis. Lists of communist youth members and other activists had been prepared in advance by the Lithuanian national organisations, and by the Nazi youth organisation – the Young Lithuanians. At the head of all these contemptible movements was a certain Pietrenas Jantzenas, who was in league with other local extremists.

Groups of these thugs moved in on identified addresses and arrested dozens of people, especially youngsters, whom they immediately took to the Gestapo. There they were all automatically accused of supporting and cooperating with the communists. People were also brought from the surrounding villages in the provinces and thrown in to the Gestapo cells, where they were interrogated, beaten, starved, and deprived of water. Their screams echoed throughout the entire town, day and night.

The first so-called 'Aktsia' or round-up, took place on July 27, 1941. 493 people were taken out of the village and shot near Lake Vižunka, by the main road close to the forest. This was a beloved beauty spot frequented by holiday makers for years, an area where the youth movements would meet, play games, and exercise.

The whole town was under siege. Those who had been shot were mainly Lithuanians and Jews who had cooperated with the Soviets. Real panic and fear broke out among the Jewish population. People were afraid to leave their houses, to go out into the streets, even for a loaf of bread.

The home of the doctors Gundelman was across from Gestapo headquarters. From their windows, they could see what was happening there. The Gundelmans heard the screams of these frightened souls while they were being interrogated, their long wailing cries piercing their ears like needles piercing the flesh. Imprisoned in their own home, they saw what was happening to the Jewish community of the town; and as they watched, they waited for the thugs to come for them. They were prepared to fight neither physically nor morally for their lives, and seeing no way out of this situation, they decided that their only choice was suicide. One night Dr Gundelman poisoned his wife, his two small children and himself.

The news of the death of the Gundelman family shocked and demoralised the community. Everyone became convinced that there was no escape from their tragic situation. Yet, these people had to exist, to eat, to drink and could not be left just to die of hunger, locked inside their homes.

Here the Germans took control of the situation and ordered all the Jews to assemble in the main synagogue, where they were told they would have to leave their homes and move to a camp, on a site formerly occupied by the local nobleman. The redbrick building which all the locals remembered, was used as a stable, and had recently caught fire. Only the walls remained. This is where the Germans decided to locate the Jews of Rokishkis.

Whatever they possessed was confiscated and distributed among the so-called needy people. Hundreds of Lithuanians leapt at the opportunity of grabbing any Jewish belongings and treasures they could – clothing, linen, beds, clocks, china, anything and everything. Jewish homes were given away to Lithuanians who flocked to the town from all over the country. The better Jewish homes were kept to accommodate the new leadership – either German or Lithuanian.

Meanwhile, the Jews were confined to those filthy stables, living, or barely existing, in unspeakably cramped conditions, lying on the floor, men and women together, the healthy together with the sick. The Germans and their Lithuanian collaborators did whatever they could to make their lives as unbearable and abominable as possible.

Some were more sadistic, forcing the women and children to remain in that same dirty, stagnant pond water for hours. I went to that pond with Ronny and I told him the story as I had heard it; I remembered how in winter during the 'good times', when the pond was frozen – in northern Lithuania the winters were long and cold – we children would skate on the pond till late in the evening, to the sound of music and laughter.

Although many Lithuanians behaved outrageously, there were a few, very few, who helped the Jews. They were prepared to exchange bread and potatoes for valuables; some would even just toss them the odd morsel of food.

Many Jews, who had tried to escape from Rokishkis and the surrounding towns – Rokishkis was close to the Latvian and Russian borders – were held back for days and nights by Soviet border police who refused to let them into the Soviet Union. Those families – and there were dozens – had no choice but to turn their bicycles, their horses and carts around, and return to the German-occupied villages.

Thus, back at the former stables, the numbers grew from day to day. At first, there were only a few hundred, but after people returned from the borders, and after the influx from round-ups in towns in the vicinity of Rokishkis, the number grew to more than 5,000.

The Germans surrounded the whole camp with barbed wire, and with no roof over their heads, they were exposed to the elements. During the day, it was hot, but at night there was always an icy wind, and when it rained there was nowhere to shelter. Some tried to escape, and were never heard of again. Soon the little food they had at the beginning ran out.

A few people formed a committee [Rabbi Zelig Orlovich, Attorney Trifskin, Kark, Resnikovich] to organise a system of obtaining food, to keep up morale. But in spite of the few provisions they managed to smuggle in – and the Germans blocked everything – people were still dying at a great rate.

Rumours of the slaughter of the Jews spread fast. At first nobody could believe that something so barbaric could happen in this day and age. Rumours came from reliable sources of Lithuanians who said quite openly that they had already participated in such slaughters, and that the day was not far off when all the Jews would be shot.

By the end of July, it was clear that almost 500 men had been shot – and the Germans and their collaborators made no effort to deny it – on the contrary, they wanted everybody to know about it. By then everyone in the camp guessed what would happen next and knew it was only a matter of time. People were so frightened, they didn't want to get up, to eat, drink, talk to each other, discuss the situation; they just lay on the ground, enveloped in fear, waiting for it to happen, and it happened very soon.

On August 10, the Germans summoned twenty of the strongest men, gave them spades, and told them they were being called to work. Then they marched them towards Byorai, where, two weeks earlier, the five hundred had been shot, and ordered them to start digging. They were to dig eight deep trenches, each about 30–40 metres long, and they knew exactly whom these pits were intended for. The Germans and their Lithuanian accomplices stood behind them, punching them and mocking them constantly as they toiled. They dug for a few days, working from sunrise to sunset, while their taskmasters pushed them to go faster and faster. Those who could not take it any longer were shot on the spot. When the trenches were ready, all those who remained were shot – the first victims for the graves they had dug themselves.

A few days later, on August 15, back at the camp, the Germans lined up 3,200 men; they were surrounded by SS officers and local police who did not even let them say goodbye to their families. They were marched away and those who were too weak were pushed along by the Lithuanian police. The very old who could not walk themselves, were loaded onto wagons.

Suddenly a terrible panic erupted in the camp; women wailed and screamed at the top of their voices and were soon joined by the children. The sound of this panic could be heard by the whole village. Many of the local inhabitants came to see this hellish scene; some out of curiosity, others out of sympathy, and some who actually enjoyed watching. The guards did not let the locals come too close, but they could see exactly what was happening. Even the German photo correspondents were there with their cameras to commit this catastrophe to posterity.

The column advanced, walking with their heads bowed and tears streaming down their faces; nobody said a word. All of them were prepared for the fate which awaited them at the end of this, their last march. Most did not even bother to pray to God for a miracle, knowing very well that no miracles were forthcoming; that they had been sentenced to extermination. But, there were a few of them who, until their very last step, did pray to God. They covered themselves in their tallit and prayed continuously, asking God why He had sold them out to these monsters.

The column continued to advance to the constant abusive shouts of the Lithuanian police. They moved towards Byorai, following in the footsteps of those 20 men who, only a few days earlier, had prepared the graves they were now approaching. They moved slowly, divided into groups each of about 500 people, a few hundred metres apart. The police drove them on with their rifle butts. Those who could no longer make it fell down and were shot on the spot.

It was four kilometres from the camp to the grave. First they had to pass through the village of Byorai where the locals lined the street watching this surreal scene. The women cried quietly to themselves as they recognised many poor souls stumbling past them. Children perched high up in the trees looked down in curiosity at this column of pathetic human beings trudging along the road to death.

Once past the village, they were ordered to turn right. There in front of them they saw the eight long trenches. They knew exactly what they were and what they were to expect.

They had been prepared all along. Or so they thought; but now, as they looked into the waiting graves they went out of their minds. Panic broke out and they started to scream and shout with whatever strength they had left. 'They're going to kill us, they're going to shoot us! Run! Run! Run for your lives.' They scattered, some towards the road, some towards the village, some towards the fields, some towards the forests, but to no avail. Their murderers had expected this and came from all sides, surrounding their victims and firing their machineguns at them. Some fell and were just wounded, so they crawled forward in a desperate attempt to escape, but again the shots rained down on them until the last fatal blow. Their killers dragged the dead and the wounded towards the trenches and dropped them into these graves like pieces of wood.

When the groups at the rear of the column, which was still some way behind, heard these tormented screams and the gunfire, they understood what was happening. Again panic broke out, and they too started to shout, 'They're killing us all.' Again they started to run in all directions to try to save themselves. Again, just as in the first column, they were instantly shot.

Not one person escaped.

The carnage continued for two days. No-one gave in willingly. They all resisted, but their murderers dragged them one by one, breaking their arms and legs until they had finished their crime.

Their last job was to fill in the graves, but when they left the scene, the earth on top of the trenches was still moving. They had buried some of their victims alive.

The screams of those sentenced to death and the endless sound of gunfire were heard back in the camp where the women and children and some of the men still remained. They couldn't see anything; but they heard it all. As soon as the Germans had finished with the men, they took the women. On August 25 they lined up the remaining inmates of the camp in the square: 112 men, 627 women and 421 children. They were taken to another place, not to where their menfolk had been slaughtered, but to a village called Obelai. It was a long trek; it was vital to stay together, no-one wanted to die on the road alone; all that mattered was to stay with their mothers, their sisters, the children.

Behind them were a few wagons on which they had loaded the old and the frail. *Ordnung muss sein.*

They reached the village of Obelai in the evening, but they went further. They were not allowed to stop there. On both sides of the road stood the local villagers; again some of them recognised their former neighbours, some even threw pieces of bread but the Lithuanian police would not even let them catch these meagre offerings. They beat the women with the butts of their rifles and lashed them with their whips. Past the village they were pushed towards a valley surrounded by gentle hills. Here, not far from the village of Antonoshu, lay their graves. They no longer resisted. They went to their deaths as though it was expected. They did not even try to escape, as their husbands, brothers and fathers had done.

These were my people.

Memories and Memorials

> *They shall grow not old, as we that are left grow old*
> *Age shall not weary them, nor the years condemn*
> *At the going down of the sun and in the morning*
> *We will remember them*
>
> Laurence Binyon

After we visited the site of Byorai, we stopped in Shirvintos, a town close to Wilkomir (in Yiddish) – Ukmerge – (in Lithuanian). This town had had one very long street, it was a fine Jewish stetl where my mother was born and where her parents continued to live when I was growing up. I spent many happy childhood months there, because at a certain stage I skipped a class. Rokishkis had a full gymnasium, eight school years, but in Shirvintos there was a pro-gymnasium of four years. For some reason I could not move into the higher class in Rokishkis, so I was sent to Shirvintos for six months, where I stayed with my adored maternal grandparents.

My grandfather, Yitzhak-Eliezer Baron, was a leading timber merchant. He would buy up forests and have the logs brought to his timber yard where they were cut up for different purposes. I can still see the local peasants and farmers in thick clothes coming to do business with grandfather, a tall imposing character with a small beard and a black capel-lusch hat, sporting a walking stick, very aristocratic and very much the leading light in the Jewish community. They had four children; the oldest had left home many years earlier to settle in America and eventually established a hotel in Chicago. The second son, Yehuda, also left for America, but died young of illness. Then came my mother, Dvora; and lastly, a fourth son, Mark, who left Lithuania for Rhodesia where he married and had four children. His widow still lives in Cape Town today as do two of the children and their children, while other members of the family have married and live in Johannesburg and the US.

With a heavy heart, we tried to find my grandparents' house in Shirvintos, which has become a delightful little town with a large artificial lake surrounded by new houses; a few old ones are left but I could not trace the house. I thought I could locate it, but we could not. Perhaps it has been destroyed. The street did not look anything like those days. All that's left are memories.

My maternal grandparents were killed along with all the Jews of

Wilkomir, and the other surrounding stetls, in a place called Pivonia which, in our day was a popular summer resort. It was an area of beautiful pine forests known as a particularly healthy spot. This is where they brought the Jews of Wilkomir to kill them in the summer of 1941, just as they had taken those from Rokishkis to Byorai and Obelai.

So Ronny and I went there too, to honour their memory. It took us a while to find the place, but when the driver asked a lady on the way if she knew the spot, she replied: 'Of course, I know, we all know where the Jews were killed. If you give me a ride, I'll show you where it is.' Here we saw the site where they were killed. A plaque reads: '10,239 Jews, men, women and children were shot here on this spot in 1941.' Here lay the same long mass graves, the same as in Byorai, only more of them, and wider, more Jews.

There was one particular place in Lithuania which I had originally wanted to return to and show Ronny, and that was Palanga, a resort on the Baltic sea where I had spent many happy summer holidays with my family as a child. Every year my parents would rent a house for the whole summer either in Palanga or in Nida, on the Baltic, in the vicinity of Memel, today Klaipeda. The atmosphere there was quite different from Rokishkis, probably because it had a strong German influence, almost everyone in the area spoke German. I remember that everything was very clean. The roads were paved, which they certainly were not in our hometown. We would spend the morning on the beach, then we would have lunch, change our clothes, jump onto our bicycles to go play ping-pong. Or we would go for a walk in the park where we would be made to sit down and listen to the orchestras playing light classical music: Rossini overtures, Strauss waltzes, and Souza marches. Father would join us only for the weekend, spending the rest of the week tending to business back in Rokishkis. And after two and a half months of bliss, we, too, would return to town, sun-tanned, rested, broken-hearted after summer romances, and feeling intensely lazy about going back to school.

It would have been a long journey from Rokishkis to Palanga and it was raining heavily that day, so we decided to go to Kaunas instead. I had not been to Kaunas since the second half of 1944.

Kaunas

I had not known Kaunas well, and apart from that short spell in 1944, our family had visited what was then the capital of Lithuania, only occasionally. I remember coming there for the 1938 European basketball championships with my older brother, Zvi, and a school friend, Mark Ettingof, who now lives in Moscow. I was curious to see Kaunas today and I wanted Ronny to see it. I was particularly interested in visiting the Ninth Fort where many Jews were imprisoned and then executed during the early 1940s.

The monument at the Ninth Fort is very impressive. It was put up by the Soviets after the war to commemorate not only the Jews who perished there, but all those who suffered under German persecution. It is built of granite – symbolising a fragmented world shattered by force – you can see in it faces longing for freedom, arms and hands looking for, grasping at, vengeance. The entire monument stands on a hill and looks down on open countryside, conveying the message that something of great significance happened here; that one world was forcibly ended and another had begun.

There is also a museum, and under the Soviet regime, it demonstrated the atrocities of the Nazi occupation of Lithuania. Since the country has now become independent, the exhibits focus mainly on the suffering of the Lithuanians during Soviet domination, showing how the Lithuanians were expelled to Siberia and beyond in 1941, how they lived, how they suffered, and how they died.

On the second floor there is an exhibition of the fate of the Jews in the early 1940s. The major emphasis was a group of Jews who were forced to disinter the corpses of their fellow Jews who had already been shot so that all traces could be burned; this group were kept chained like animals in the cells of this medieval fortress. The whole scenario is reminiscent of Alexander Dumas' novel, the Count of Monte Cristo, which for us was fairytale stuff, but here you see the starkness, the naked reality, in harsh black and white photographs. When one sees in those pictures as I did, the faces of real people, people whom one knew and loved, some of who, mercifully survived, some who tragically did not, one knows that this was not a fairytale, but a gruesome horror story of unprecedented proportions, cruelty and depravity.

One group of prisoners under sentence of death did manage to escape; miraculously they filed through the iron bars of their cells, and dug their way out; many were shot, but some escaped and today I have friends whose faces I saw there in the photographs.

Even though the place has been cleaned, it is dark, and wet and sad and it is inconceivable that people lived in those conditions. No wonder many went mad. Some were imprisoned in cells with iron stairs overhead; the noise of hundreds of people clattering up and down those steps literally drove them crazy and they did what they could to end their own lives.

I also discovered here that 900 Jews arrested in Drancy in France, were brought as prisoners to Kaunas as part of the German propaganda machine. The inmates were ordered to write to their families back home to create the illusion that they were still 'alive' and working in a foreign land, and would some day return home. Scratched in the walls of the fortress today we found an inscription that here, 900 Jewish prisoners from France ended their days, just as so many of the Hungarian Jews who were brought to Riga, and the Lithuanian Jews brought to Estonia, met their end.

In Kaunas, in that museum, my son Ronny saw all these images, and since he knows some of the survivors from the Ninth Fort, it made it all the more meaningful and all the more moving.

Shirvintos, Lithuania early 1920s: Mother at home with her parents and two brothers, Mark and Yehuda

Seated left: mother, Devorah Harmatz, née Baron; father Avraham Harmatz; his sister, Fanya, and standing: mother's brother, Mark Baron

The three Harmatz brothers, Rokishkis 1935

My younger brother
Efraim Harmatz 1927–1944

My mother: Devorah (née Baron) Harmatz, 1945

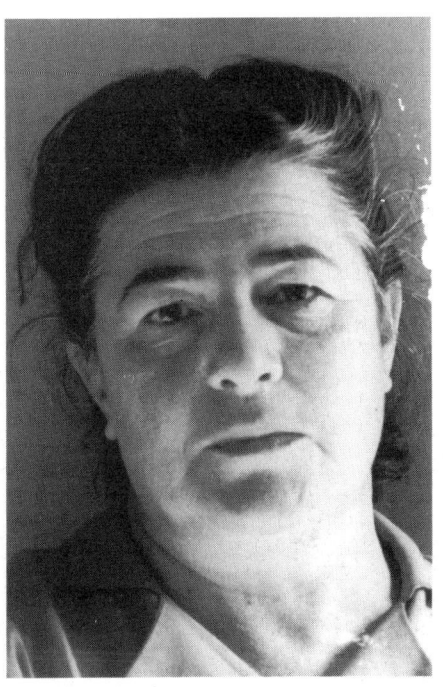

My older brother: Zvi Harmatz 1923–1943

Mother with her three sons, Palanga 1936

Father with the three of us, Palanga 1935

II

ESTONIA

Night train to Tallin – 1994

For reasons which will become apparent, I very much wanted to visit Estonia; so Ronny and I took the night train from St Petersburg to Tallin, capital of Estonia. The train was not full and the conductor, who spoke Russian, offered us two separate compartments, but we refused. We had heard too many stories about robbers so it seemed safer to travel together. The conductor asked if we wanted tea, but again I declined, recalling my train trip from Moscow to Leningrad five years earlier and the deplorable state of the toilets in all public facilities.

The conductor asked where we were from and Ronny replied: 'Israel. Why?' he added nervously. 'The stewardess in the buffet car is one of yours – why don't you go down there?' Still a little suspicious of any ulterior motives, it took him some time to convince me to go and talk to her, but, to pass the time, I did. She turned out to be a plump, lively young Jew in her mid-thirties who told me that she had heard a lot about Israel, and that several of her friends had already emigrated there.

'What's life really like in Israel?' she asked. 'Do you think I could find a job there? How much can you earn? Are things expensive?'

I thought to myself that travelling 'abroad' as she did on this train from Russia to the Baltic States and back probably provided her with plenty of opportunities to transport all kinds of goods back and forth and she seemed quite happy in her job. I wasn't at all sure how she would do in Israel.

Back in our compartment, Ronny was trying to sleep, but without much success. The train stopped and started, everything rattled, water leaking from the aforementioned 'conveniences' trickled along the floor, and if we tried to open the windows to get a little air, the compartment instantly filled with steam and smoke from the engine.

At one o'clock in the morning, a Russian soldier knocked and opened the door. This was the border police. 'Israelis?' Again the same question! 'Yes,' we answered. 'Have you got any shekels on you?' The question surprised us. What could these youngsters possibly know about shekels? By chance, Ronny did have some to hand. Suddenly another four or five shy young soldiers appeared on the scene.

'Any more for me?' said one. 'And me?' asked another. Ronny found a ten shekel coin which he gave them and soon they were all happy and on their way. The train continued rattling through the night, and at about two o'clock, it came to a halt at the border. There we were told by the conductor to disembark to obtain our Estonian visa. It was a dark night; the gloomy office was manned by sleepy soldiers (or perhaps police). At any rate, we paid what they asked – about $50 – and they gave us our 'all-in-one' transit visas to travel throughout the Baltic states – Estonia, Latvia and Lithuania.

We arrived in Tallin at five-thirty in the morning and were welcomed by Michael Beilinson, the principal of the Jewish school, a lively young man who was surprisingly friendly, considering it was Sunday morning and his one free day! He took us to the hotel which by Baltic standards then seemed quite reasonable. So we checked in, had a short rest and then Beilinson returned with Genadi Grumberg, head of the Jewish community. They took us to see the Jewish school, which is impressively active, although there is much room for improvement, with rooms desperately needing refurbishment, and equipment either missing or obsolete. I regretted visiting this place so late in my career, feeling that if I had come earlier, my organisation could have done much to help them.

Beilinson and Grumberg both knew that the main purpose of our trip to Tallin was to visit the site of the former concentration camp in Klooga. It was there that my younger brother, Ephraim, was murdered and incinerated by the Germans in September 1944.

Klooga

On June 13, 1994, Beilinson and Grumberg accompanied us in a minibus put at our disposal by the Tallin Jewish community, to Klooga, some 35 kilometres west of Tallin. As the bus hurtled along the well-built asphalt road, the scenery gradually changed from city suburbs to green fields, and soon we arrived at a small copse. A little further on, this cluster of trees, thinly spread at first, gradually became more and more lush until we found ourselves in a dense forest. In due course, the driver made a sharp left turn off the main road onto an unpaved path where, after a couple hundred metres, he came to a halt in a small clearing. We climbed out of the bus and saw before us a raised grass-covered mound of earth.

On the mound stood a small monument, a memorial to the Jewish people who were brought here, and later murdered by the Germans and their collaborators. We were told that when the monument was originally erected, two plaques had been mounted, one on each side, but that they had since been removed. Now on one side, scrawled in paint stood the words '*Am Israel Chai*' – 'The people of Israel live'.

Grumberg told us that the inscription on the original plaque had read: 'In memory of the Soviet citizens murdered by the Nazis'. There was no mention that they were Jews.

From that spot we walked some hundred paces further until we reached a large round pond. The stagnant water, full of algae and water reeds, was a sickly green, and a sinister deadly silence hung over the area, broken only by the twitter of birds and another, incredible sound. There were millions and millions of mosquitoes swarming and buzzing around us. They covered us, smothered us completely from head to foot – never, in all my travels have I experienced such a foul swamp.

Grumberg told us the grim story of the Klooga concentration camp.

He explained that here on this spot, immediately after the liberation on September 21, 1944, the Russians had found piles of timber, row upon row of 2 metre-long wooden logs stacked cross-wise on top of each other. Between the rows lay hundred of corpses – they lay there as they had fallen – shot by the Germans and their collaborators on September 18 and 19. Not wanting to leave any trace of their crimes, the killers shot their victims and set fire to the wooden stacks. The timber stacks found by the Russians when they reached Klooga indicate that these barbarians were interrupted and were forced to flee between the killing and the burning.

Jews caught trying to escape were shot immediately by the Germans and their Estonian collaborators and their bodies were simply thrown into the pond we had seen. For a long time after, the local peasants spoke of the fish in the pond suddenly dying because they were poisoned by the decomposing bodies.

Very few of the inmates of Klooga survived, said Grumberg, but those who did were able to recount what had happened.

Back in Israel, some months later I met with Benjamin Anolick, one of those few who survived. He had been taken from the ghetto of Vilna during the final days of the liquidation in September 1943, and sent to Estonia, like my brother. He was moved from one camp to another and in each one he was subjected to hard labour.

Benjamin told me the following story:

'When we were brought to Klooga, there were 2,500 prisoners: youngsters, elderly men and elderly women. The women and men were placed in two separate camps, each heavily surrounded by barbed wire. Klooga was the worst of all the camps I had been sent to. The living quarters were in huge dormitory blocks, with three-tier bunks. Food was scarce and lousy. The work was tough and strenuous.

'One day, in July 1944, our captors took us out of the camp for a "treat" – a picnic on the Baltic Sea – some two kilometres from Klooga. We were weak and covered from head to foot with lice. We touched the trees, the flowers, and soaked in the sun as if we had never seen such marvels. As we ran into the sea, and filled our lungs with the beautiful clean fresh air, we jumped the waves and swam in the clean water. It was a day for all of us to remember, to cherish forever. For a few moments I let my imagination loose and dreamt I had crossed the bay to Finland in a little boat I found on the sea shore – and sailed to freedom!'

'With a heavy heart we walked out of the water to return to the camp – to our cold, hard bunks, to mixing the concrete – the job I had been assigned to.'

My thoughts turned to what my brother Ephraim might have been thinking of then – if he was among the lucky ones taken to the sea that day. Did he think of the summer days we all enjoyed together when our whole family went to that very same shore on the Baltic Sea – albeit further south at the resort of Palanga? Did he remember the clean sand dunes, the chilly waters, the strolls on the wooden jetty that extended into the sea? Did he long for those days when all our friends went on bicycle rides up and down the streets of Palanga? Could he recall afternoons in the park with our mother listening to the concerts of light classical music played by the local military band?

Benjamin recalled how, at one of the many camps to which they were moved, the Germans would tantalise the prisoners by promising that whoever finished their quota of tree-felling first would get a cigarette. Everyone slaved like mad to get through their work, but more often than not, the German soldiers wouldn't come up with the promised fag. To cheat a Jew was a good deed.

On August 22, 1944, they were transferred to a camp called Agidi. Only two weeks later, while working outside the camp, a German envoy came to order them back to the camp immediately. The only word he uttered was: 'Evacuation'.

They learned afterwards that the head of all the camps in Estonia had arrived in Agidi and declared that the conditions were unacceptable: it was too cold, and since the prisoners had no warm clothing, they were to be transferred to a more convenient, warmer place.

A rumour spread that the Germans had prepared a ship to transfer them to yet another site. Anolick returned to the camp to try to find his father and brother, but his father had already been rounded up and transported with the first group. His brother had managed to wait for him. They were given proper food for the first time since they had arrived: each one received a loaf of bread, some sugar and jam. It appeared as though the Germans wanted to appease their victims, to ease their evacuation. Surrounded by guards, they were loaded onto trucks, one for women, one for men, and packed like sardines. There was much speculation during the journey: Where were they being taken? And why? Benjamin's mind was blank: he was quite simply paralysed with fear. At one point, the lorry carrying the women broke down; the truck driver stopped to help his colleague. It was late in the afternoon and the repair took until night, when they continued the journey until they reached a forest. A German guard approached their truck and shouted at the escorts: 'The job here has been finished. Continue on to Tallin!'

They were totally perplexed and had no idea what this meant. After the war, Benjamin's brother tried to find their father, and only then did he learn that it was at this station in the forest that the first transportation from Agidi had been annihilated. They had all been shot in the neck. Their father was one of those who died there on September 19, 1944.

Only two escaped: Ariel Shimovich, who was lightly wounded; and Rodbord, who, with a bullet lodged in the back of his neck, managed to roll off the burning woodstack and in the darkness of the night, escaped through the forest.

Benjamin recollects how he met Ariel Shimovich later at the camp in Klooga: 'He told us he had been brought there together with his son, and he described how the Germans had accomplished their wholesale liquidation process in that forest. They tied twelve people, one to another, and ordered them to mount the wooden pyre which had been prepared in advance. He was one of the twelve and as they lay on this pyre, the Germans shot them, one by one. Then they set fire to the pyre. When the shooting stopped, our friend, who was at that stage only wounded by the bullet, feigned death and waited for the right moment to escape. As night fell, the Germans went to fetch fuel to burn the corpses, and slowly Shimovich made his way, crawling on all fours, until eventually he reached the nearby forest. From there he saw the flames rising from the valley of death – the place from where he had just escaped.'

On September 20, the Germans dumped them in the prison at Tallin where they were kept overnight. They were all shocked to be told that they lodged in the wing for prisoners sentenced to death. Next morning their captors became nervous and greatly agitated. They knew what the inmates did not yet know: that the Red Army was close by.

The Germans were suddenly unsure about what to do. Once again they were loaded onto trucks and driven back to Klooga under heavy guard, surrounded on all sides by SS officers. As they approached the gates of Klooga, groups of prisoners, about 50 in each, some 2,500 in all, were gathered in the yard, all of them on their knees, their hands on their heads. Benjamin was amongst the last contingent, which was placed right by the fence. Then they brought in the women. They, too, were ordered to go down on their knees next to them. Those who had been there before informed the newly-arrived group that 300 had already been taken out of the camp. They actually saw them through the fence as they were being marched out, each carrying a huge log on his shoulder. They watched until they disappeared from sight. One tried to escape – but to no avail – he was immediately shot, stunned by the force of the bullets at such close range; they saw him stumble and finally collapse on the ground. German soldiers, armed with rifles, led one group after another outside the camp towards the edge of the forest. Hearing the automatic fire, it suddenly dawned on them what was happening: they were being annihilated – and they were next!

'Fear, terror, and panic broke out among our group. I looked at my brother who had always been the leader. He did not react. Suddenly I had to take the initiative. "Nissan," I said firmly, "we've got to run for it!" We slowly separated ourselves from the group, I was in front, my brother behind me and some ten or twenty more followed us. We took the first few paces very hesitantly and then ran full speed ahead – towards one of the prison blocks which were two-floor units. Dashing up to the second storey without looking back, we were convinced that the Germans were following right on our heels, and that any moment they would shoot or throw hand grenades at us. In a frenzy, my brother and I squeezed under one of the bunks and covered ourselves with a blanket and some pillows. From the floor below we heard a series of shots and then suddenly: silence. Silence reigned, but that very stillness broke our nerve. We were paralysed with fear. Hours passed, so slowly we could hardly stand it. Then cautiously, we gradually dared to creep out of hiding and edge towards the window. Only then did we notice that several more poor frightened souls had sought refuge under some of the other bunks. Through the windows, we also saw tongues of fire rising from the forest beyond the camp. More hours passed. Some of us crept out to look for food. Even rotten vegetables were welcome to quell our hunger at this stage. One of the others moved out to do a little reconnaissance work and reported that the yard was littered with corpses. We learned that the last group had not been taken out to the forest – they had just been shot on the spot.'

Benjamin continues:

'I edged my way out of the building and stumbled over the corpse of a mother holding a baby in her arms. One of the female inmates changed her prison uniform into civilian clothes which she found there, to go see what was happening outside. She came back screaming at the top of her voice: "The Germans have gone!"

'It was September 22.

'We arranged to stay in that same building. The Soviet military arrived by boat across the sea and on land. "Is it true that the Germans are no longer here? Is it true that we are free people?" Here they came, the solders of the Red Army. We touched them, we embraced them. It was still difficult to believe that someone in uniform could extend his hand, and take ours, and shake it and call us "Tovarisch" – "Comrade".

'The first thing we wanted them to do was to accompany us to the forests to see what had happened to the others.'

Hesitatingly, the Soviet soldiers walked into a burned out building; all they saw were the smouldering remains of the burnt out barracks and piles of burnt bones and corpses. These were the people Benjamin had seen carrying the logs on their shoulders – the logs that became their funeral pyres.

A few days later, Avraham Vatnik came and told them that only he and one other Jew named Yitzik Obyalevich had survived this catastrophe. The Germans, he said, had brought them into the barracks; they had shot his father dead, and then they shot him, but the bullet in his neck only wounded him. Then they had thrown him on the pile of wooden logs and piled more corpses on top of him; some were still alive, barely, but still alive and dying, slowly. Somehow he had managed to crawl out while the Germans went off to fetch petrol; they failed to notice him there and that's how he had survived: he had jumped through the window and although it was already dark, the Germans saw him running away and started to shoot. This time they missed and he escaped into the forest.

Now, together with their Red Army liberators, they continued to move through the forest. Before them they saw the remains of more and more bonfires, and in between the burnt corpses, massive burnt boulders. Each fire had been built up with large logs and in the middle a tall chimney had been created so air could get underneath to fuel the fires.

The Germans had forced their victims to lie down on the logs, their heads facing outwards, and then one by one, they shot them. When the first rows were dead, sometimes half-dead, they would put additional logs on and then on top of them more victims – building up to four layers of bodies. Then they poured on petrol and set it all alight. The fires were still smouldering – both logs and corpses. The pyres were completely burned through in the middle, but some were still intact on the outside.

Often they recognised some of their friends. All around their clothing was piled high; they had been forced to undress before being subjected to this torture. Eventually they came to yet another wooden pyre, built with the same chimney through the middle; they knew instantly that this one had been prepared for their group.

In the neighbouring cabbage patch lay several corpses of women who had obviously tried to escape. Each had failed and had been shot dead. No-one had escaped.

2,500 Jews were incinerated on those pyres, all of whom had been with them only two days earlier in the camp at Klooga.

'We did not cry as we faced the valley of death. Our tears had long since dried up but the soldiers of the Red Army cried like little babies at the sight to which they were now exposed,' said Benjamin.

3835 – My little brother

The voice of thy brother's blood crieth unto me from the ground
Genesis 4.10

There I stood, at the edge of that stagnant pond, almost fifty years to the day, remembering my little brother, two years younger than me. What happened to Ephraim? Was he one of those who tried to escape? Was he among the 2,500 murdered and burned like Benjamin Anolick's father?

Next to me stood my younger son, Ronel Ephraim, 33 years old, nephew of a potential uncle murdered 50 years ago, who bears his name, listening to the story. Ronny asked me when and how I was separated from Ephraim. It was painful for me to remember the circumstances of that terrible time, but I tried.

I started recalling early September 1943, back in the Vilna Ghetto, the last time I saw Ephraim, when he was caught by the Gestapo when the Ghetto was liquidated. It was only much later, when the war was over that I learned he had been taken to Estonia.

When I first joined the underground, my mother had implored me never, ever to implicate my younger brother in the movement.

'You have chosen your way and your fate, and may God bless you,' she said, 'but please don't involve Ephraim. Let me believe that one of my children has a chance to survive.'

So when Ephraim came to ask me how he could join the movement, I felt honour-bound to keep my promise to my mother. I gave him no assistance and in fact actively discouraged him. He was so young then – just 16.

Then I remembered September 23, 1943, when all members of the organisation still left in the ghetto, were told to assemble in a workshop; the day we descended into the bowels of the city, into those foul sewers which were to be our escape route from the ghetto to the partisans in the forests outside the city.

We had been told to come alone, that is, without any family members who were not in the organisation. Just before entering the sewer, I suddenly saw Danka Lubotsky, who had been captured earlier by the Gestapo, but had been released from prison, and had returned to the ghetto that day, since the Germans believed he would be rounded up with all the others when it was liquidated. Danka was a member of the organisation and a good friend. He came close to me and in a rather perplexed tone he asked me where Ephraim was. I told him that I thought Ephraim had already been taken. The liquidation of the ghetto had commenced on September 1 and by now was almost completed.

Then Danka dropped a bombshell. 'Listen, Julik, it's true Ephraim didn't really belong to the organisation – maybe you didn't know, but he did belong to the youngsters sub-group. We were just getting ready to recruit them into the underground and I was in charge of them.' I couldn't believe that Ephraim had found a way of joining the organisation. Danka, on the other hand, could not believe that Ephraim was not with me. It was too late.

It may be hard to understand, but no-one told anyone anything during those times. We were bound by strict rules of utter secrecy in the organisation which applied even to your own family. To understand this, you had to realise that life in the ghetto, after the various Aktsias (round-ups) when the Jews were taken out and exterminated, there were long lulls where one day was much like the next. This, too was a German scheme designed to suppress fear and panic. We clung to every fragment of hope and once again believed that there was reason to be optimistic.

This was just after the Battles of El Alamein and Stalingrad in the winter of 1942 and spring of 1943, the turning point of the war. There was such optimism that people in the ghetto even created a theatre, set up schools, formed a choir, and organised welfare programmes and social activities. As grim as it sounds, there was also more room in the ghetto since so many had already been taken for extermination.

It is, after all, human nature to struggle for survival and it may be difficult, even impossible, for those who were fortunate enough not to have lived such times to understand. Those who had not been taken away seemed to close their eyes to the fact that even their nearest and dearest had been taken for extermination. That they themselves had not been chosen to be slaughtered gave them the feeling that they were still of some importance to the Germans. Their jobs as munition workers or furriers providing clothing for the German soldiers on the front were vital. The Germans, who had clearly evaluated the basic instincts of people in such conditions, played on these 'quiet periods'.

We, in the underground, did not let the Germans fool us. We mistrusted them, we saw through them, we knew what they were doing to us, how they demoralised our people, how they created illusions in the ghetto and used them for their purposes.

We suspected that they knew of the existence of an underground organisation, or that one might yet be established; for this reason, they were keen to build up a situation of Jew against Jew. Therefore, the underground organisation was absolutely secret. We closed ourselves in to a greater and greater extent, turning inwards and not allowing ourselves to open up to anyone in the Jewish community, not even our own family, for fear of being compromised.

I stood there thinking that if Danka had not been arrested by the Gestapo and had been in the ghetto when the liquidation began, he might have informed the group of youngsters in his charge, including Ephraim, that they could retreat to the forests to join the partisans.

Nobody could guarantee lives, even in the forests; there, too, the battle was hard and bitterly fought. Danka himself was killed, along with his brother Imka; but if Ephraim had made it to the forests, he might have survived. His registration card as a victim of the massacre at Klooga bears the following data: born in 1927, brought to Klooga from Vilna, worked as a carpenter, and was part of the SK commando. I asked some of those who had escaped from Klooga what SK stood for and was told that it meant Straf Kommando, which translates as Punishment Unit. Was he just working for that unit or was he punished more than the others? What for?

What is left is his number – 3835.

He was murdered, aged only 17, between September 20 and 21, together with 2,500 others.

The next day, September 22, the Russian Army entered Klooga.

III

LATVIA

Riga 1994

The next stop on my nostalgic roots tour of the Baltics was Riga, capital of Latvia. From Tallin, with the assistance of the deputy-head of the Jewish community, Avi Dobrisch, we travelled along the coastal road, through beautiful rich pine forests, glimpsing the Baltic Sea, until we reached Riga.

The visit to Riga was timed to coincide with a meeting of the Memorial Foundation for Jewish Culture of whose executive I was a member. At a special ceremony held in the presence of the President of the State, heads of the community, and leaders of the Jewish organisations worldwide, a plaque was unveiled commemorating the site of the former Riga synagogue which had been burned down by the Germans and their local collaborators on July 4, 1941, with hundreds of Jews who had been driven into the building. The President of Latvia, Guntis Ulmanis, made a point of mentioning the suffering of the Jews under the German invasion, but he used linguistic acrobatics to combine these facts with the suffering of the Latvians under the Soviet regime, referring specifically to the expulsion of the Latvians to Siberia in 1941.

It is a well-known fact that the Baltic people, Lithuanians, Latvians and Estonians alike, accused the Jews in those countries of collaborating with the Soviets in their efforts to expel untrustworthy and undesirable elements of those societies just before the Germans attacked Russia in June 1941. What they fail to mention is that among those expelled by the Soviets to Siberia were also many thousands of Jews. Figures presented more recently by scholars show that the percentage of Lithuanian Jews persecuted and expelled by the Soviets was proportionately greater than the number of Lithuanians expelled, whether for social, economic or political reasons, bearing in mind the number of Jews who lived in Lithuania.

The fact is that many of those Jews and non-Jews expelled to Siberia and other remote places in the Soviet Union, in spite of difficult conditions and hard labour, *did survive* and return to Lithuania or Latvia, or wherever they came from.

If my family had stayed in Rokishkis, since my parents were members of the so-called bourgeoisie, we would almost certainly have been expelled; and there might have been a chance that some, if not all, of my family could have survived and returned like so many others.

Josef and Sanna Levin

Deep in the Siberian mine
Keep your patience proud
The bitter toil shall not be lost
The rebel thought unbowed

The heavy-hanging chains will fall
The walls will crumble at a word
And Freedom greet you in the light
And brothers give you back the sword
            Message to Siberia (Alexander Pushkin)

June 12, 1994: Two brothers, Ilya and Sasha Levin, have taken their seats in the reception hall at the residence of the President of the State of Israel in Jerusalem. It is late in the afternoon and they both admire Moshe Kastel's fine reliefs on the walls as they wait for the ceremony to begin. The setting sun pierces through the strong reds, yellows and blues of the stained-glass windows by the Israeli artist Rubin, while from the ceiling the lions of Naftali Bezem look benevolently down on them.

The two young men are there by personal invitation, clearly stating that only the named invitee will be admitted. Each of the brothers is the member of a team: one belongs to a group of scientists working in a high-tech industry, the other is a lieutenant-colonel in an Israeli airforce team; both are to be honoured at the impending ceremony for their outstanding contribution to the defence of Israel.

The project the two teams have been working on is of fundamental worldwide importance and is still top secret.

A slow, deep voice resounds through the room: 'The recipients of the Israeli Defence Prize who are assembled here today and who deserve the gratitude of the State of Israel, are only the tip of the iceberg, they are the first echelon of many hundreds and thousands who employed every brain cell they could for the benefit of the defence of the State. Their deeds cannot be revealed. Their names will not be published but they are entitled to our eternal thanks because they cannot even enjoy the public recognition of those whose defence they concern themselves with day and night.' These words of praise are spoken by the Prime Minister and Minister of Defence, Yitzhak Rabin at the award presentation for the sixteen nominees. It is the 37th year that the Defence Prize has been awarded at a ceremony attended by the President of the State, the Chief of Staff, the Director General of the Ministry of Defence and the military elite. Also present are close members of the family, usually the proud parents, of the recipients of this prestigious award.

* * *

The two brothers were born in Russia to Sanna and Josef Levin who, as children themselves and together with their parents, had been exiled from Lithuania to Siberia by the brutal Stalinist regime in June 1941, exactly 53 years earlier.

Their mother, Sanna was then 13 years old; the boys' father, Josef, was 17. Sanna's parents owned a factory, while Josef's mother (his father had died) ran a small trading company. As such, both their parents were identified as capitalists by the Soviet regime, and were expelled to Siberia with their whole family. They had all been prominent members of the Jewish community of a few thousand people in a small town in north-eastern Lithuania, called Rokishkis.

* * *

Jewish communities had existed in small towns and villages in Lithuania for more than 500 years, the Jews having been invited by the Lithuanian Dukes to help develop and expand the economy. The Lithuanian Jews adhered to tradition and in a way stood apart from other East-European social and cultural trends. They lived peacefully with their neighbours and were not specifically affected by the various pogroms as were communities in other parts of Tsarist Russia and the Ukraine. The worst conditions they had to endure were during World War I when the Jews were sent into Russia in 1915, but when the war was over, the majority returned and settled in the same villages where they continued their quiet and protected existence.

The generation born between the two wars was partly traditional, but the majority of youth was emancipated and drifted towards more modern lifestyles. On the whole, they were not content with just primary and religious schooling, but went on to high school and university; they were literate, highly educated, and influenced by western and Russian literature, arts and industrial development. As in so many other towns and villages, youngsters joined youth movements, many of them Zionist, as well as those embracing ideologies preaching freedom, social justice and other kinds of promises with little hope of being fulfilled.

The average Jewish family was hardworking; these were lower-middle-class folk who observed Shabbat and filled the synagogues on high holy days. There was a general spirit of philanthropy, a practice of helping the needy, and relations between Jews and non-Jews were reasonable, until Hitler's rise to power in 1933 when they began to deteriorate, as the Lithuanians kept one eye on Germany, mainly for fear of Bolshevism, and gradually became more and more nationalistic.

In June 1941, a week before the outbreak of war between Russia and Germany, the Soviets had expelled what they called 'unreliable elements' and exiled them deep into the wasteland of Russia. Among them were thousands of Jews, mainly business people, industrialists, and intelligentsia who were suspected of becoming an anti-Soviet threat since their businesses and industries had been nationalised or their careers cut short.

* * *

Sanna, who was thirteen years old at the time, remembers those tortuous years when they were sent into exile: 'They just sent us off – my father, my mother, my 14-year-old brother and me, along with my three uncles with their families, but we never saw the men because the cattle wagons they put us into were kept locked. Father was sent straight to a concentration camp where he was sentenced to ten years' imprisonment with hard labour. There was no trial – just three men in a room who called their victims in one at a time and pronounced sentence. "What for? What are we accused of?" we asked. The only answer we got was: "That's how it is now."

'From the very start, right there at the Rokishkis railway station, the men were separated from the women and children. Not only did they not want to have us close to the front line, but they also needed the men to carry out certain labour-intensive tasks. Since Stalin had come to power, the Soviet system was to use men for forced labour. Older boys, too, were taken with their fathers. "Why must you separate us?" I asked the Commissar. "It does not suit us to have you all together," came the non-committal answer. And again, when herded like cattle with six other families into the wagons, we asked where the men were being taken, came the retort: "We don't know."

'The journey took two months. Since war had broken out one week after our expedition began, we were constantly exposed to fierce bombing raids from the Germans. Every time there was an attack we would have to leave the wagons and take cover. The train would stop and start, stop and start. It wasn't until the very end of our journey, after eight and a half weeks, that we knew just how far the German troops had penetrated into Russia. As for food, at each railway station they would bring a huge bucket of soup and dish it out in meagre portions. That's all we got. For eight and a half weeks.

'After two months we reached our destination – a place 90 kilometres from Banaul in the Western region of Siberia. There we were put to work in the forests.'

* * *

Meanwhile Josef, aged 17, was with his mother and his three sisters in another remote area of the Siberian region. At first he worked as a labourer carrying materials on a construction site, which appeared to be some kind of top security plan. After four or five months they were all sent into the forests to cut down trees – even the girls. There was a general fuel shortage in the whole country, and since the lorries were steam-driven, wood was a vital source of energy. The trees were chopped, the logs dried, cut to size, bound with a rope, and eventually loaded onto wagons. Everything was done manually – there was, after all, no automation at that time. Josef worked very hard and was later appointed head of supplies, then he was made foreman in the forests and was sent to study timber engineering in a local college.

'The whole family lived together in a wooden hut for five years. Later we moved into a house belonging to a lady whose husband had been mobilised into the army, and there we lived in two small rooms. The salaries we received were unimportant,' said Josef, 'What was important was how to overcome the problem of food rationing, 400 grams of bread per day, a kilo of sugar per family per month.'

The fact they were given a plot of land to plant vegetables was of great help. 'We learned to make the best of what we had and would, for instance, use the top part of the potato, the seed, to replant it to generate more produce.'

They had also brought clothes from home, and from time to time, they would barter these for foods they were short of.

That is how Josef survived those difficult years.

* * *

Meanwhile, Sanna recalls that after a year or so, they learned that the men had been taken to a concentration cap near Krasnoyarsk, several hundred kilometres from where they were. She wrote to the camp and after about six months received confirmation that her father was there. Eventually she got news from him that his three brothers had died of hunger and disease, that they had had a very difficult time, and that he had been unable to do anything to save them. He wrote of his terrible living conditions and said that if he didn't get help, he doubted if he himself could survive. He explained that he was expected to do what amounted to hard labour and he did not know how much longer he could carry on.

Sanna and her mother's reaction was immediately to prepare packages of dried food, and Menia, Sanna's brother, took the parcels to the postal depot, a journey of 90 kilometres on foot. It took two days there and two days back – just to deliver the package to the post office where mail was sent once a month. It was two months before the parcel reached their father.

Sanna, now 16, received a letter one day from her father reporting that he was now half free – that is, he had to sleep in the camp at night, but was free to choose his job. Since he had exemplary handwriting, he had been accepted as a clerk in an office. She resolved to go to see her father immediately, which meant leaving her mother alone, because her brother, Menia, had volunteered for the army and was admitted to the military academy in Novosibirsk, and later in Moscow. (By 1944 he attained the status of a free citizen because he had completed his military service and additional extensive studies.)

Sanna left without a ticket, not knowing exactly where she was going, without documents or permits, which she would have needed because she was not allowed to leave their place of residence without permission. Little did she know what a heavy price she would pay later.

'I travelled from station to station,' she said, 'and at every station I would get out and wait for the next train so that, in case they were looking for me, they would not be able to follow me. Off and on I got, for two days, until eventually I reached a town next to Krasnoyarsk. Soon I found the camp where father was; it was surrounded by a double fence, but I found a passage between the two fences and started walking towards a building.

'"Stop! Get out of there," shouted the guard, "the whole area is mined – it could explode any minute."

'I crawled under the fence towards him. "Please," I said, "I am looking for my father, can you help me?"

'"So, who's your father?" he asked, suspiciously.

'"Yehuda Meller."

'He walked over to his cubicle, took out a sheaf of papers and started to leaf through them. He came to the end of the list and shook his head. "No-one here by that name," he said. "Oh, please," I implored him, "please have another look, I know he's here." And sure enough, he found Yehuda Meller on his list.

'"He's at work right now but he'll be back this evening," he replied. I could wait no longer. "Where's his office?" I asked the guard. Finally, just to get rid of me, I think, he directed me to father's bureau and off I went.

'It is hard to explain how I felt when I walked into that room. It was rather badly lit and at first, I looked right past the small stooped gentleman bent over his books, pen in hand, deep in concentration, and thought I must have entered the wrong room. After all, I had not seen him for more than four years, how was I expected to recognise him, and after everything that had happened to him? Then I looked again; he was thinner, and greyer than I had recollected, but when I called out "Papa, it's me, Sanna,", the smiling eyes were the same I remembered all those years ago. It was a moving moment, and neither of us knew what to say at first. We just held each other tight, not believing this was happening. After hours of explaining how I had found him, how my mother was, and Menia, my brother, and learning all about him, father decided not to let me return to Barnaul.

'"We must bring your mother here immediately. How did you arrange your departure?"

'I explained that I had left without a permit and gave him the details of my journey. "Your mother will have to do the same; I want us all to be together now." And so mama came and we all lived together in father's little home, until a few months later when the war came to an end and we were told that we were free to return to Lithuania. This we did in 1946 and Menia, my older brother, joined us a year later.'

* * *

Back in Vilna, the family found themselves in an unpleasant position as far as their legal status was concerned. Father's status was legal, as was Menia's, but Sanna and her mother had no legal status whatsoever, because they had left the camp without permission from the authorities and had no legitimate documentation. They tried all kinds of ways to obtain certificates, some proof of identification, but without success.

In 1947 the process of repatriation of the Jews to Poland began and the family started to look for a 'chatan', a husband, for Sanna, but this course of action, which many used just to be able to leave the country, also proved unsuccessful.

In 1949 Josef Levin – Sanna's future husband – returned to Vilna illegally. His mother and two sisters, Ida and Judit, stayed on in a place called Bisk, in Siberia.

Josef and Sanna became friends and fell in love. But all did not go so smoothly. Sanna studied at the university and was such a diligent student that she won a prize of a holiday in Palanga on the Baltic coast. And there, one day, out of the blue, the authorities came to arrest her. She was taken back to Vilna and thrown into Lukishki prison, the main jail of Vilna, where she also found her mother.

She was held there for almost a year without trial, but interrogated constantly. After eight months Sanna and her mother were released on bail, on condition that they did not leave Vilna until a verdict was reached. It was now March 1950, and that May, Sanna married Josef. She was sure that once she had changed her name, the matter of her status would be resolved. Nobody would follow her any longer and her problems would be over. But it was not to be.

In 1951 came the verdict. Since she had left Siberia without permission, the instructions were that she should be returned there. 'We certainly did not expect *that*,' said Sanna. 'In January 1952, they took father, mother, and Menia back to Siberia.'

'I was pregnant with our first child. At first they had compassion for me, but a month after Ilya was born, they came and took me back into prison in Vilna. What can I say? I thought I would go mad and all I wanted to do was to die, to commit suicide. I started to tie bits of rag together to make a rope. I had undoubtedly gone crazy. The guards didn't know what to do with me. They started to ask me what was wrong. "Look," I screamed – "I left my baby behind, – he's only one month old; they wouldn't let me take him; I don't know where he is, how he is, who is looking after him; maybe no-one. Maybe he's ill," I cried hysterically.

'The guards suggested I write a letter to friends and they would deliver it.

'"Oh sure," I said, "I know your tricks, I know what you'll do; you'll just hand my letter to the authorities and then I'd be in real trouble; they'd stick me into solitary confinement. I know all about that, thanks very much. They'd put me in a cell the size of a cupboard with no daylight where I can't even stand up. I'm not ready to end my life like that, like an animal in a cage."

'I don't know exactly what happened then but three days later I found myself in the prison hospital and I no longer cared what would happen to me. So I wrote the letter. I addressed it to my good friends, Liova and Gita Yakubovitch, whose house was close to the prison – I could actually see their roof from my cell. When the female guard finished her duty, she took my note and put it under the Yakubovitch's door. In that note I asked them to find my baby, feed him and bring him up. I did not believe I would ever get out of that hell hole.

'The Yakubovitches received the letter – signed simply "Sanna". They had been wondering what had happened to me. Even Josef didn't know where I was. They thought I had been taken back to Siberia. They assured me that my baby was being looked after, and they started to send me parcels in prison.

'Half a year later the authorities decided to send me back to Siberia. They took me from one place to another, and in each town they threw me into prison. This lasted for two months, until eventually I was returned to the place I had left, illegally. There, too, I was imprisoned.

'Meanwhile, Josef took my mother and Menia, and Menia's wife back to Siberia. Josef's mother took Ilya, who was by now almost a year old, and brought him to me in Altaisky Kray in Siberia. Then Josef asked his employers and the authorities to transfer him from Vilna to Krasnoyarsk, where he had been before, and I asked to be relocated to the same place. This took another six months but eventually they agreed – and there once again, they threw me into prison.'

It took what seemed forever, but once all the documentation was in order, the authorities released Sanna from prison although she was still obliged to report to the police every two weeks. She had two identity cards, one in her maiden name, Meller, under which she was prosecuted: and another in her married name, Levin, under which she managed to get a teaching post in a local school. Still she lived in constant fear that the authorities would find out one day and would come to arrest her once again.

In 1964, after years of writing to the authorities, quoting from the Soviet Constitution which states that children are not responsible for 'crimes' committed by their parents – letters which evidently went straight into the waste basket – Sanna was suddenly told when she went as usual to report, that she was now a free citizen.

For twenty-three years – since she had been arrested in 1941, she had been punished for whatever the authorities believed her parents were guilty of.

Today Sanna smiles to herself when she reads of prisoners in Israel complaining about conditions in jail – that they don't have enough access to TV or radio, or sufficient exercise facilities – if only they had known what bad conditions really are – not seeing any daylight for months on end, asking to use the loo just to get out of your cell for a few minutes.

Sanna and Josef and their, by now three children, finally returned to Vilna from Siberia in 1970 having collected references and recommendations to apply for exit visas for Israel.

* * *

Many years earlier, Josef's younger sisters, Ida and Judit, who had both married ex-Polish citizens from Vilna, had been able to join the second repatriation wave from Lithuania to Israel via Poland, which took place in 1957. They came to Poland with their husbands and their mother (Ida already had a baby daughter), but they were caught there because at a certain stage the Polish authorities had ceased to grant exit visas because of pressure from the Soviets. When the first repatriation from the Soviet Union started, many hundreds had left Poland for Israel and families left behind in the Soviet Union started getting letters from Tel Aviv. This is not what the Soviet authorities had in mind when they permitted them to return to Poland.

During this period, around 1959, Sanna and Josef who by now had their second son, came to visit their sisters and mother in Poland, managing somehow to obtain travel documents.

It so happened that a friend of theirs from their earliest days in Lithuania, was in a position to arrange for them to leave almost at once for Israel. Their departure was planned down to the last detail. Sanna would have to go with the two children on her passport via Zurich and Josef was to go via Berlin and later they would be united and travel en famille to Israel.

Before leaving Poland, they decided to call Sanna's parents back in Siberia to say goodbye. Her parents begged them not to leave, feeling that if Sanna and Josef departed, conditions were such that they themselves would never have a chance of getting out of the Soviet Union. And so, even though Menia urged his sister to take the opportunity of leaving, assuring her that he would take care of their parents, Sanna and Josef agreed not to go and returned to be reunited with her parents in Siberia.

Sanna said: 'Apart from the worry of leaving my parents behind, I felt, too, that there was always a risk. Since the plan was for us to leave Poland separately I thought I might not be reunited immediately with Josef and I was scared of what might happen to me alone with the children.'

* * *

After a few hitches, Sanna and Josef and the three children finally emigrated to Israel in 1972.

Josef never saw his mother again. Sanna's parents did eventually come to Israel and lived there for several years enjoying freedom and watching their young family grow.

Ilya, who was 20 years old, studied physics at the Technological Institute in Haifa, where, in spite of the language difficulty, he was an excellent student. He earned a bachelors and masters degree, and was then employed in a high-tech industry.

Sasha (Yitzhak), their second son, went to secondary school, served in the army, joined the airforce and graduated in computer studies. Today he is a colonel in the Israeli airforce. He was responsible for bringing down two Syrian aircraft, one of them a Russian Mig – a symbolic gesture to the Soviet regime for the 'courtesies' they had extended to his parents!

Their youngest, Mickey (Misha), went to high school, joined the army, served as an officer, then studied architecture and after graduating, worked for the army. One day he read in the newspapers that the government was looking for people fluent in Russian and English. He was accepted into the Foreign Office and sent to Kazakstan, where he was involved in a terrible car accident which he miraculously survived.

But this is a family of survivors. In Israel Sanna, who graduated in Vilna as a teacher, was hired to teach in a comprehensive school where she worked for 20 years, while Josef became the manager of a huge workshop in his own field as a timber engineer, and is still active. Sanna is now retired and keeps busy with her many grandchildren.

And so we return to June 12, 1994. As the proud parents of two prize-winning sons, Sanna and Josef sit absolutely still in the splendour of the President's Residence, listening to every word, every syllable which echoes around the room where this dignified ceremony is held. The opening words were preceded by a silence which you hear only at very special times, like the eve of Yom Kippur just before the Chazan begins to chant the holy prayer of Kol Nidrei. In the corner of each of Sanna's eyes huge teardrops start to well up which threaten at any moment to fall onto her festive new outfit. And the memories of the past years flash through Josef's mind just like a film in fast forward mode, from those early years of youth, when, he and Sanna, had to grow up much more quickly than the youth of today. Their pride in their sons is infinite; the boys themselves are indeed a credit to their parents, their heritage, and their country.

Mother: Kaiserwald – Stutthof

Back to Riga 1994 – and at another ceremony during my stay in Riga, a Jewish girl choir performed their version of the well-known song based on a poem by Gebirtig: *'Meyn Stetl Brennt'*, 'My Village is Burning'. They sang it in the original Yiddish and those of us who understood could sense that these girls did not understand the song they were singing, even if they did know the words.

The Israeli Ambassador, Tova Herzl, did not hesitate to remind the President of the bitter truth: that some of us may forgive, but none will ever forget, the events of fifty years ago.

The reason for putting Riga on the agenda of this trip was not just to attend the Memorial Foundation Meeting and visit the Dubnov Jewish school (named after the great Jewish historian), which ORT had been supporting for some years in partnership with the Doron Foundation. The main purpose of coming to Riga with my son was because my mother, who was rounded up by the Germans with all the others during the liquidation of the Vilna Ghetto in September of 1943, was brought to the Kaiserwald concentration camp in Riga.

Here, in June 1994, talking to the local inhabitants who survived the Holocaust in camps or in hiding, we learned the grim truth of Kaiserwald:

Five weeks before the Vilna Ghetto entered the last weeks of its existence, on July 21, 1943, Reichsführer SS Himmler gave the order to liquidate the ghettos in the East and transfer all able-bodied Jews to concentration camps. In accordance with this order, a camp was established at the Riga Mezaparks (i.e. Forest Park) known by the German-speaking Baltics as Kaiserwald. As in all other Nazi camps, the ration was a thin slice of *erzatzbread*; there were the same *appels* – roll calls, in the morning and in the evening, which often lasted for hours. Here people were forced to do 'exercises': to stand up, lie down, jump like frogs, crawl, squat – over and over again. Many perished during the 'night alarms', when the prisoners had to stand in front of their barracks and after a signal, kapo supervisors, armed with clubs would begin their outrageous sessions of violence. The rest were waiting for the prisoners behind the doors and under the windows. Often such 'alarms' were repeated – and the driving back and forth would go on for hours. Each time there were more victims.

Inside the camp the Jews were deprived of all their personal belongings including their civilian clothes with the yellow six-pointed Star of David. In Kaiserwald camp, at first the prisoners were dressed in threadbare rags marked with red and white oil paint. Everybody, including women, had their hair cropped and later the prisoners were dressed in striped clothing with their cap numbers printed on the jackets and on the pants above the knee.

In addition to the Jews rounded up in Latvia, 1,700 women and 80 men were brought to Kaiserwald from the Vilna Ghetto along with smaller groups from other camps in Lithuania, Poland and Northwest Russia. In the summer of 1944, the last train with prisoners arrived in Mezaparks from Osvientzim (Auschwitz), bringing about a thousand young Jewish women from Hungary. Thousands of prisoners passed through the main camp of Kaiserwald and its ten branches, the number regularly reduced by the constant 'selections' – murders of teenagers and elderly people. Each time, the workforce would have to be re-formed with the strongest men. They never returned to the camp. It was discovered later that those prisoners had been used to clear the mines on the front, while others were sent to dig up and burn corpses at the huge mass graves where they were almost always kept chained up while they fulfilled this task. Most were unable to survive for long and those who did were then killed on the spot.

In the summer of 1944, once the Red Army reached Latvian territory, the inmates of Kaiserwald were taken by sea to an even more terrible place: Stutthof concentration camp in Germany. The first group was shipped there on August 6, 1944, the last – during the first ten days of October, just days before the Red Army entered Riga on October 13. From the beginning of 1945 the Martyrs of Kaiserwald were driven from Stutthof to other camps on senseless 'death marches' and some prisoners were saved from inevitable death by the offensive actions carried out by the Allies in the East and West. Not more than a thousand of the Latvian Jews who were taken to Germany survived until the liberation.

Many years later I received a document signed by the Director of the Stutthof Museum, Mrs Jamina Grabowska-Chalka, confirming that my mother had arrived in Stutthof from Riga on August 9, 1944. The number allocated to her was 62074. There was no record of her final destination.

My mother, Dvora Harmatz, née Baron, had survived Kaiserwald and was taken to Stutthof. She was also one of those who took part in the Todesmarsch, and mercifully, survived that too.

I asked the head of the Riga Jewish community if we could go to Kaiserwald to see the remains of the camp. He looked at me blankly and said: 'I'm sorry, the area where Kaiserwald stood has been completely built over with houses. There is absolutely nothing left to indicate that the area was once the site of a camp. We are hoping that if the community survives and the authorities support us, some kind of memorial might one day be established.' When I told my son there was nothing for us to see at Kaiserwald, he was shocked.

* * *

Mother never talked about how she was taken from the Vilna Ghetto, about events at Kaiserwald, or about Stutthof. Most of the survivors refused to speak for years. Not that they couldn't remember, they probably didn't want to be reminded. They wanted to settle down, rebuild their lives, resume a 'normal' routine within normal societies; they were keen to integrate and intuitively felt that telling their stories of horror would create resentment. Only many years later, when these survivors felt integrated in society, when they had established their own families, when time had passed, did they feel inclined to talk about their experiences and pass it on to their children for posterity. Only then did they start to speak. By then Mother was no longer alive.

Those who were younger, however, like Musia Daiches and Irena Lusky, did tell their stories later – the stories Mother failed to tell.

My friend Irena, who was eighteen at the time, recalls the day the ghetto was liquidated – September 23, 1943:

'We were all taken to an open field just outside Vilna, called Rossa. There, the men were separated from the women and children; we were kept on our feet all night long, mothers searching for their children, children searching for their mothers. There was total chaos; we felt that we had been hurled from an abyss into an inferno – and then came the selection process, as we stood before the Germans, before the Lithuanians, and worst of all: the dogs.

'We were told to go either to the left or to the right. Mother was sent to the left, and my sister and I to the right. We did not follow our mother. We were too frightened, even though we did not really know then what "right" meant, we just thought it might give us a little longer to live. We merely left our mother … and went. Even though many have similar stories to tell, only each individual knows what a terrible thing it is to leave your own mother behind, knowing she was being sent to her death. For the Germans it meant merely moving a finger, either to the left or to the right.'

The 'lucky' ones were sent to the 'right' and were destined for transportation to do hard labour. Many years later Irena, after giving birth to two children, philosophises: 'Mother was probably satisfied and maybe even happy that we were given the chance to survive. For her, to see her children murdered in front of her eyes, without being able to do anything about it, would have been unbearable. Yet, we know today that we did not pass the test as her children.'

To this day, Irena cannot forgive herself.

* * *

Just outside Vilna, they were sealed in the barred cattle trucks and there they met the first horror: the Germans' accomplices, the Ukrainians, who pushed and shoved their way in, wild and drunk, immediately started raping the women. After one night or possibly two, half suffocated, half dead, beaten and in shock, not knowing where they were or what to expect, they reached Kaiserwald.

As the doors of the wagon opened, blinded by daylight after the darkness of the sealed trucks, they were greeted by orders in German to: 'Move! Run! Faster! Leave your belongings! Leave everything! Go! Run, faster, faster!' This was followed by a hail of batons raining down on their heads and backs; the beatings became harder with the shouts: 'Faster, don't take anything with you, just move.' 'If anyone is found with gold or money, they'll be shot on the spot!'

They soon learned that it was the custom, or rather the system, to frighten, to confuse, and to intimidate. The shouting and screaming combined with the whippings and beatings made them jump and run – as fast and as far as possible.

This was their welcome to Kaiserwald. Those who really 'distinguished' themselves above all were the *Blitz-mädchen*, professional sadists, who had most certainly passed special tests and were thoroughly accomplished in the art.

The day after their arrival in Kaiserwald, they were hungry. Some had already experienced hunger in the Ghetto, although most had not. That same day they were taken to be disinfected, *entlausung* as it was known. Herded into a large barrack, they were made to strip naked, and ordered to run to the showers and from there to a large hall, where the Germans were waiting. Young SS officers stalked around them, looked them up and down, 'evaluating' them. Suddenly they felt they were no longer women, no longer human beings.

Musia was just twenty years old. She recounts the following: 'After being disinfected, we returned to where we had left our clothes, but they were gone. On the table were piles and piles of other clothes. They did not let us choose garments according to size, they just threw them at us – quickly – one at a time, just as they came off the heap, and so I ended up with a long dress and a little girl's coat. Our hair had not yet been shaved but was wet from the petroleum they had poured on our heads for de-lousing; so we were cold and we shivered as we came back into the barrack. Then we all broke into laughter, which turned to weeping and sobbing mixed with giggling, all out of hysteria.

'One day they took us out of the camp and put us in rows of five, ordering us to stand there and just wait. For hours we waited. We did not know where they would take us; to the right, or to the left? We had no idea what would happen to us during this *appel* (rollcall). We were consumed with fear for our future.

'These *appels* were particularly dangerous for those of us who had our mothers with us, so we would watch them, hide them, and use all kinds of tricks and manoeuvres to protect them. When I say we, I mean a group who all worked together. Individually you didn't stand a chance. I prayed that we would manage to save them, telling myself we *would* succeed – I just convinced myself that we would.

'The result of this *appel* was better than expected. They transported us all to the AEG factory. For us, it was paradise – given the conditions during those years of occupation. We had a roof over our head, out of the torrential rain of Northern Europe at that time of year. There were toilets with showers and there was even hot water from time to time. We later remembered this as the best experience of our whole Holocaust, and it was this spell at AEG that helped us endure the whole of that period.

'This does not mean that life was easy. There was plenty of anguish and distress. We were packed together like sheep in a pen – 150 women in one room. The wooden bunks we slept on were three-deep. The worst position was the middle one and it was my fate to be given one of those. Every time I went to sleep it reminded me of the beds of Sodom (the biblical tale of those who had small beds having their legs cut off so they would fit, while those with longer ones being stretched out for the same purpose). There was only one position to adopt in those bunks: you just had to lie flat all the time. If you sat up – you'd get a sharp bang on the head from the rack above. I had to crawl in and out of this space and coming down I'd jump so as not to step on the person below. Going up and down was an exercise in acrobatics and when I finally reached my bunk, I felt as if I was lying in a drawer with no air to breathe.

'Later on they brought us paper mattresses, filled with sawdust, and even blankets. The downside was that we were soon covered with lice and bugs. This was a terrible shock for us. I remember the horror when one of these bugs got into my ear; before they eventually managed to get it out, I thought I would go crazy with the sensation of something crawling around inside. Someone "nicknamed" these bugs: raisins. The name stuck. From that day on I cannot see, eat or cook anything with raisins ever again.

'We were assigned to work on electric wiring; we worked twelve hours a day, from six in the morning till six at night with a half hour break for "lunch". Lunch meant soup, and was in itself an exercise. The eating hall was a ten-minute run from where we worked. Ten minutes there and ten minutes back left ten minutes to eat. The whole thing was a blitz operation: when we got there, the soup had already been dished out, so we tried to go for the ones at the end of the table, praying that the soup in those bowls was still halfway hot. Hot soup takes longer to swallow and as long as you had something to swallow you felt as though you were eating something. We longed for dry bread because that, too, took longer to chew. Fresh bread was not as good – because we would eat it too quickly. You could play around with dry crusts – keeping them in your mouth, savouring every crumb, so that the "feast" lasted longer.

'The two afflictions, lice and hunger, came upon us as if they were created together. When the God of Moses cast the ten plagues upon Pharaoh's people – even if the curses were justified – He never sent two plagues at once, He would let one pass and then send another – far more liberal than the Germans!'

* * *

The Germans also 'took care' of health. Many suffered from furunculosis, a terrible condition that was treated with a foul-smelling thick black ointment smeared on their afflicted bodies. You could hardly breathe with this smell pervading the air, but people looked after one another and helped apply the cream to their neighbour's painful open wounds.

Hunger, hunger, hunger; they all returned to it in their memoirs. It was at the very centre of everything. The daily piece of bread was never enough to sustain the older women; nor was it enough for the girls of 13 and 14. So very soon, they realised they had to initiate some scheme to help the needy ones as much as they could. A few women in the camp had a certain relationship with the Latvian department heads in the factory, from whom they got additional rations of daily bread.

They drew up a list of between 16 and 18 women out of the 150 who were desperate and particularly in need of special assistance: the elderly, the sick, and the young. A second, longer list included those who were able to get some form of additional supplies, and thus they established a true self-help organisation.

Every day 15 portions of bread were available from the women who were willing to donate their ration – not that they didn't need it, it was just that they could do without it. Each would give up a portion of bread once a week, and those in need, either the older women or the young girls, would receive an additional ration from the bread bank every day. This 'bank' saved many of the inmates.

* * *

Punishment was a natural course for the Germans and they applied it frequently and excessively in the camp. Everything that they decided was a crime *was* a crime and deserved punishment. Crimes large or small, trivial or serious, most punishments involved a beating, and the women were beaten for crimes they did not commit.

One of the most serious offences committed was menstruation. Most of the inmates were young, healthy women who, despite hunger, performed the work they were ordered to do. Like most healthy young women, however, the problem of menstruation visited them every month, and hygienic measures were, of course, not available. So, if while going to, or coming from work, or standing at the *appels,* or in any other situation, a German officer, or what were known as the *blitzmädel* (German female officers) saw any trace of blood on a leg or skirt, the offender was immediately beaten; there was no choice, since they had no means of avoiding the problem, no way to avoid committing the 'crime'.

Only after many months of suffering did this come to an end; the Germans put some potion into their soup, and instantly all the women lost their monthly 'period'. Although it alleviated the problem, it was a 'bonus' mixed with fear and sorrow. On the one hand, they were no longer beaten like dogs, and it removed an inconvenience for which they had no solution. Yet they all feared the possibility of not being able to bear children some day. After all, they still cherished the hope that they *would* survive, that the day of liberation, even if that day was far off, *would* one day arrive. In that sense, they were like religious Jews waiting for the Messiah. Had they not clung to that belief, many would probably have committed suicide; still they were petrified that those artificial means of stopping their natural monthly periods, would make them sterile.

Musia says proudly: 'Despite the attempts of our enemies and persecutors to ruin us, after our liberation from the camps, we *did* establish new lives for ourselves, and we *did* give birth to children – as many as we possibly could.'

* * *

One day they were evacuated to the Castle of Torun, in Schlesia, a journey that took four days and four nights. The wagons were so packed they had to sit on top of each other, face to knee. They were given nothing to drink, yet they were all soaked; the air was so dank and humid, they could barely breathe. In the middle of the wagon was a bucket for their needs, but it was so full that every time the wagon shook it slopped.

'After four days and nights, packed like sardines, the doors opened and again the familiar shouts: "*Heraus! heraus!* get out! move! run!." We didn't know where we were, or what to expect. Was it slave labour, worse than in AEG, or was it death? Their orders sliced us like knives. Our legs were swollen, our backs broken from the days of sitting doubled up, and we were frozen to the core, – still they made us run for kilometres to the castle. To this day, I don't know how I did it – but when we did arrive in the fortress square, and once again they called another *appel* – I broke down, collapsed and lost consciousness. That had never happened to me before. I, who had always been a healthy young woman, thought I was one of the strong ones.

'A brave young woman doctor, who dared approach the German officer to tell him that one of the girls had fainted, asked if she could give me water. The officer, being "generous", pointed to a receptacle in which rainwater, mixed with muddy sewage, had collected, and said I could drink that. I was so desperate with thirst that I did, and even that vile liquid made me feel a little better. Later I learned that the other women standing around, envied the fact that I had fainted so that I could at least have that to drink.

'We stayed at the castle for about half a year – 90 women sleeping on wooden planks on the floor in one room. We could sleep neither on our backs nor on our stomachs, we could only lie on our sides, and on one side only, for if one of us turned, all of us had to turn, like dominoes. If one woman pushed her neighbour in her sleep and occupied one of her planks, she would push the next, and so on. Night after night there were endless arguments which deprived us of even those few hours of poor sleep.

'Our work was tough, tiring and even dangerous. Our job was to check electric cables and their resistance to water, which often caused us electric shocks if we weren't careful.'

* * *

'From time to time exceptional events took place on Sundays – either in spring or summer. They would let us out of the camp for fresh air. To this day it is hard to understand what made the Germans pretend to behave vaguely like human beings on these occasions. Maybe they got prizes or promotions? Most of our time in the prison fortress was spent underground – seeing no daylight. We would go to work in the dark and return to camp in the dark. So here we were out in the fresh air, smelling the hay, the grass, the trees, the flowers. Girls who had lost young husbands or friends or babies were suddenly overwhelmed with nostalgia, longing for the love of near and dear ones, for freedom and happiness. All this brought back memories, and while it was meant to be a joyous event, it was really heartbreaking. I remember one of the *blitzmädels* who accompanied us with the soldiers to make sure we didn't get lost, walked into the nearby forest with one of the officers – how we envied her! This "treat" in the fresh air lasted only a few hours; too soon we returned to the familiar orders: "Forward! Walk! Run! Fast!" and we were swiftly brought back to the bitter misery and reality of our situation.

'The burden of work depressed us – physically, morally and spiritually, especially when we were moved to the barracks. We now no longer worked in electrical production in the factory, but with concrete on the railroads – carrying heavy loads from sunrise to sunset. For months. At night rain and snow and wind would penetrate our dormitories. Women who slept near the wall would wake up in the morning with their heads covered in snow, and remember, our heads were shaved and we were forbidden to cover them with scarves, specifically the white ones worn only in the factory, but under no circumstances in the barracks. Hunger, hard labour, lice, no sleep – it all disheartened us. We no longer yearned for our mothers, fathers, brothers and sisters; all we wanted was a little more warmth and a little more to eat. It seemed as though we were close to collapse, and we knew that was what the Germans wanted – to bring us to our knees. So we tried to fight back, but sometimes it was impossible.

'Meanwhile, the Front was getting closer – we knew the Russians were approaching. It was January 1945 and we had no idea what was going to happen. We were petrified that they would annihilate us before the Russian Army reached the camp and as they dragged us from one place to another, there were rumours that they would take us to an extermination camp. Our main fear was that they would take us to Stutthof.'

That is where my mother was taken.

Irena Lusky and Musia Daiches were the same age as I at the time, that is, in their late teens. My mother was a generation older; she had already lost her parents, and her husband; she knew nothing of her children, and lived constantly with the fear that they had perished, and occasionally with the hope that they had survived, maybe one or two, or perhaps even all three of them. Maybe that hope was what kept her alive through all these circles of hell.

Irena recalls seeing my mother at the railway station at Bromberg, a small Polish town where they had been taken in a death march from Torun. She told me that mother was also on that march, but not in the same group as Irena.

The Germans, fearing the arrival of the Russians, were desperate to exert every last ounce of sadism and cruelty on their sick, exhausted, emaciated, and broken captives, and so they marched them out of the camps, and for days they beat them along the way as they fell in the snow. This was happening everywhere as the allies defeated the German war machine: thousands were just left to die along the way. Eventually the Germans themselves were forced to flee as the Russians reached the town where Irena and her friends were now hiding.

* * *

Chaika Grossman, a fighter in the underground, wrote the following eulogy to women who endured the horrors of Kaiserwald and later Stutthof:

'I was never at Kaiserwald, I was elsewhere fighting the Germans; it seems to me from their accounts, that these women endured intolerable conditions: hunger, persecution, torn as they were from their families, thrown into hostile environments, bereft of their children and their husbands; they fought the Germans their way: clinging together, helping one another, each supporting the other, assisting, both physically and morally, the sick, the old, and the very young. Thanks to their selflessness many, who would not otherwise have survived, did so. This was real heroism – at least as profound, significant, and human as the function we, who fought in the forests and in the underground, performed. As one who did her share in the underground, I am filled with respect and admiration; the more such accounts we publish, the greater the chance that they will reach more young people as a testimony and maybe a lesson for the future.'

Irena and Shimon Lusky

I had known both Irena née Deul and Shimon Lusky individually from back in the 1940s in Lithuania and I have learned that sometimes you know people for years, but don't really know them. Last year when I visited Irena and Shimon Lusky in their home near my own, I discovered truths about these two fine people I had not previously known, and it has given me a further insight into what human beings are able to endure and how experiences the average person does not normally face can turn out for the good.

Two women arrived about the same time as I at the Lusky's home, and explained that they had come to present Irena with a certificate in honour of her work for Nitzana. The name was not familiar to me and when I questioned the nature of their charitable work, I learned that it was an organisation to help people with minimal brain disorders such as dyslexia, dysgraphia and hyperkinesis. Irena, it seemed, had been active for many years in this field, raising money through fashion shows, working in some of their many centres and raising public awareness of what is a very serious problem in many children today. I also learned that Irena had been working tirelessly for years with new immigrants from the Soviet Union, helping them integrate into their new environment. In particular, she had been active in a feminist movement to combat crimes against women and help Russian girls to cope with the problems of rape and prostitution.

Why was I so amazed at this revelation? I had known Irena, back in Lithuania, a girl from a privileged family. Yet, I knew little about what had happened to her since those grim days in the Vilna Ghetto. Learning that she was so immersed in charity, I wanted to know what made her tick; I knew she had been very sick for many years and was constantly under medical supervision. Physically she was weak, but I had always sensed an inner strength. She explained to me that people's need for her gave her a certain fortitude; and that during her captivity in Kaiserwald and Torun, she had been sustained by her friend Esther, and resolved that if she survived, she would somehow repay her indebtedness by helping others.

Born in Kaunas in Lithuania, Irena had moved with her family to Vilna in 1940. We attended the same Lithuanian high school there and were trapped when the war between the Soviet Union and Germany broke out in 1941; by September both of us were in the Vilna Ghetto.

Irena was a friend of Ada Gens, the daughter of the Head of the Judenrat in the ghetto, an interesting but controversial personality. In the ghetto, Irena's boyfriend was Gamek Sturman, who was connected to the underground movement and served in the ghetto police. But nothing helped anyone in those days, and like everyone else, when the ghetto was liquidated in September 1943, Irena was taken with my mother to Kaiserwald in Riga, and from there to Torun, again like my mother. Irena was then 19. Eventually, once the camps were liberated, together with friends, she made her way to Poland, and then, via Czechoslovakia, Hungary and Romania, she finally reached Palestine in 1946, where she settled in Kibbutz Beth Zera. There she fell in love with a young army officer, and they eventually moved to Tel Aviv.

Irena was eight months pregnant when the War of Independence broke out. On June 1, 1948, the Egyptian Airforce bombed the central bus station in Tel Aviv, and one of the crowd was Irena's husband, Michael, who was killed instantly. A month later she named her newborn daughter Michal. By 1950 Irena was struggling to support herself and her baby. One day, in desperation, she went to a store in Jaffa run by Shimon Lusky, an old acquaintance of hers, and asked him for a loan of 80 lira to pay the other couple in her small flat to move out. 'Give me a kiss,' joked Shimon, 'and you can have your 80 lira.' And so began a romance between two people who until then had known little but tragedy.

* * *

I had first met Shimon in my battalion in the forests outside Vilna; he was the younger brother of Chaim Lusky whom I had known from the underground movement inside the Vilna Ghetto. We had both served in the Jewish police force at the ghetto gates, where our task was to give cover to those who smuggled arms in. Chaim had been a good-looking, friendly character whose ghetto police cap did not sit happily on his head. He had been among the first to escape to the forests outside the city, and he was killed during the early days fighting in a partisan unit.

My profound sentiment for Chaim made me feel close to Shimon. He was an exemplary fighter, who participated in many bitter battles, and, like me, he survived those times. As soon as Vilna was liberated by the Red Army, Shimon started to make his way to Palestine, where he immediately joined the Haganah. Here I met Shimon once again when we found ourselves serving in the same military unit for a short time: following the November 29, 1947, United Nations resolution to declare Israel a state, the authorities mobilised volunteers to counter the attacks of the various Arab semi-military organisations on Jewish settlements, individuals, and transportation lines.

Defending a position south of Tel Aviv some time in April 1948, Shimon was heavily wounded and his leg was amputated. He tells with some amusement of how, when he was recovering in hospital, they finally brought him his military ID number, for only then had Israel been officially declared a State. By then he was ready to be discharged from the army and was afraid of being discharged from the hospital and having to rehabilitate himself. He recalled the Polish veterans of World War I sitting in the streets of Vilna, bedecked with all their military medals, begging for money. After all he had gone through, he did not intend to end up like that; so when the authorities offered him financial assistance, he used it to open a general store in Jaffa.

This is, of course, when Irena came into the picture.

Thus, after so much suffering, these two individuals created a new life and a new family. Soon after their marriage, they had a son and named him Chaim – 'to life', after Shimon's older brother.

* * *

Postscript

Irena's son, who was studying in France, sent a German boy to his parents' home and asked them to take care of him while he was staying in Israel. This young man had long harboured the desire to become a Jew and to convert to Judaism in Israel.

Once Irena had overcome the inclination merely to reject the son of a Nazi (as she saw him), and seeing that he was suffering from an injury to his leg, she summoned up all her humanitarian values and did whatever she could to assist him: first she got him to a doctor who healed his leg; then she sent him to an Ulpan where he would learn Hebrew; and then she helped him enter a Yeshiva so that he could fulfil his dream. The young man eventually joined the army and advanced to the rank of a tank commander.

Irena had taken care of him as her son had asked her, and one day the young man's parents came from Germany to visit their son, only to find him, cloaked in a tallit, wearing teffillin, and praying day and night. Somehow Irena derived a certain satisfaction that justice had been done. After all that had happened, she was proud that the entire Nazi machinery had not succeeded in killing off her own dignity, and had not robbed her of the humanitarian values her parents had instilled in her.

IV

VILNA

Vilna 1994

*How mourn a city
whose people are dead and whose dead are alive
in the heart*

Abba Kovner

Continuing our journey to our roots, Ronny and I drove into Vilna on Thursday, June 16, 1994, more than 53 years after I had first arrived there from Rokishkis with my family. This time, my old friend Shmulke Kaplinski was there to welcome us. Shmulke had been the commander of my battalion when we fought as partisans in the forests outside Vilna, and had also been a leading member of the FPO, – the *Veraynigte Partisaner Organisatsye* – in the Vilna Ghetto. An expert in drainage and sewage, he was responsible for leading us out of the ghetto through the sewers into the forests of Rudnitski when the ghetto was finally liquidated in September 1943. But that is another story which I shall come to later.

Here I was, this time with my son Ronny, who has heard stories of my early years ever since he was a little boy – far away in the village of Kfar Shmaryahu in his own independent state, surrounded by trees and flowers, in a sunny climate, protected by loving parents. There he frequently listened to anecdotes when old war-time friends came over to reflect on those ghastly times. I remembered one evening, when everyone had gone home, Ronny came to ask me: 'Father, where was our army then?'

Now we were together in the very place where these atrocities happened. Ronny is too sensitive to comprehend the circumstances we encountered, the situations we faced, the conditions of our life. But we had come – and we would see it all, together! I still find it incredible that I survived it all and was fortunate enough to create a family of my own.

Back in Vilna, the old ghetto looked so tiny that I wondered how it could possibly have contained tens of thousands of people living there for two years: 1941 to 1943. The area today is divided into two sections; one part has been rebuilt, where the main street, Rudnitska, leads down from Zavalna, passing by the church. Soon we came to number eight, the *Judenrat*, only then it was Rudnitska six. Why the numbers have been switched is not quite clear – perhaps some of the buildings were so badly ruined they had to be demolished and the numbers became muddled, or perhaps the authorities were worried that former owners of these properties might return to claim them, so they created this confusion deliberately.

All the buildings across the street have been torn down, and the area has been planted with trees and a small lawn. Sadly we found no trace of the building on Rudnitska, from which we descended into the sewers when we left Vilna after the final liquidation of the ghetto. Neither does Straschuna 6 exist where the headquarters of our underground movement was based, nor number 16, the building where my family lived during the ghetto years.

Other buildings have been reconstructed but very roughly. Those which have not been refurbished have become slums, with peeling paint, broken windows, and missing roof tiles. The Lidska prison is the one building on the corner of Oshmianska and Lidska, which is still there – a prison where I myself was once held.

One night in late April 1943 I was walking along the streets of the ghetto with Chaim Lazar and Mira Bernstein, a policewoman and a member of the underground. It was late at night and as we approached the ghetto gates we were suddenly confronted by Lev, commander of the ghetto gates. He asked why we were out so late and since he had always suspected me of something or other, he ordered me to report immediately to the prison officer. It was just a whim of his, yet I had no choice but to obey, and so I landed in jail.

What really upset me was that we were fast approaching May 1, 1943, an important date for us, especially in the ghetto underground. I knew that a meeting of our people had been planned for that night and I was desperate to be there.

Somehow I managed to communicate with Chaim Lazar who was on good terms with Lev, and I asked him to tell Lev that my mother was very sick and I was anxious to visit her. The plan worked, and I was released on the morning of May 1. That night I attended the festive meeting of the underground in Izka Matskewich's apartment. The Matskewiches were two large families who occupied a whole apartment, a rare phenomenon in the ghetto. We blacked out all the windows – obviously we had to conceal our presence since all the leaders of the underground movement were there: Wittenberg, Sheresnevsky, Chiena Borowska, and many other leading lights of our movement. Amazingly, despite the tension and the appalling conditions, the atmosphere was optimistic and hopeful.

There was a large ghetto and a smaller one. Today, a plan is mounted on the wall of a building where the main entrance to the ghetto stood; it declares: '30,000 Jews passed through these two ghettos. Most of them were later exterminated at Ponar'.

There I stood in June 1994 looking out towards what was then, in those ghetto years, the 'outside world' – with the church on the left, and the street leading to Stefanska crossing Zavalna. And I remembered ...

The Vilna Ghetto

I remembered a young man by the name of Kalinauskas, who had been at the same Lithuanian Gymnasium as I in Vilna – the Vytauto Didziojo High School. In June 1941, two days after the Germans invaded Lithuania – it was a Tuesday – at the age of sixteen and a half, I was in hiding. As a member of the Communist Youth Movement and, as a Jew, I was an obvious target for the Germans; Jews were not yet being rounded up in masses, but a Jew who was known to be a communist, was actively hunted by the Gestapo. Anyone in this category was immediately arrested and shot on the spot.

Kalinauskas, now collaborating as so many Lithuanians did immediately after the Germans invaded, came to my parents' home with two Gestapo officers to find me.

'I haven't seen him since last Sunday,' said my father to the 'guest'.

'That's not true,' he shouted 'he was seen carrying a gun at the railroad station on Monday night.'

This *was* correct. We had been given arms, carbines and other weapons, and told to keep a watch on strategic sites, so we could secure public buildings and factories and check the movement of trains and lorries, in case of sabotage. That's where they had seen me.

Kalinauskas and his fellow officers threatened my father, hit him in the face, grabbed a radio and his leather portfolio, and told him that if I returned he was to inform them immediately. So I remained in hiding in people's homes, often crouching in tiny spaces, under the stairs, or confined to the attic. One man in particular helped me a great deal during those days in hiding, a Pole, Francisek, the concierge of our building at Great Stefanska 17. (Much later, after the liquidation of the ghetto and during our escape from Vilna, I also sought his help.)

On September 6, two and a half months after the Germans had declared war and entered Lithuania on their march to Moscow, all the Jews in Vilna were herded into the ghetto – and there I was able to lose myself in those narrow, crowded streets. So they stopped looking for me or at least I hoped so. Conditions that were tragic for everybody else became my salvation.

In our family business in Rokishkis, we had had a bookkeeper, Miss Henie Slepp, who served us loyally. She was fond of our family and particularly liked us children; I remember her pinching and squeezing my cheeks as a child. How I hated her for it then – it really hurt. She had a brother living in Vilna. In 1940 father had only recently left Rokishkis for Vilna where, strange though it seems in retrospect given the situation, he had bought several factories, and Micha Slepp, Henie's brother, had been hired to manage one of them.

At that stage my mother, my two brothers and I were still living in Rokishkis. The family business had been nationalised by the Soviets. As youngsters we had all been greatly impressed with the Soviets; we loved their music, their dancing, their joie de vivre. We did not see the downside, did not realise how our parents suffered. Worse still, we held it against them, and even spurned them for being business people – for that was contrary to the ideals of communism. The Soviets did not tolerate businessmen; professionals and workers were acceptable: doctors or shoemakers were fine, but not merchants, landowners, or industrialists. That area belonged to the State. So there was a clash between the life experience of our elders and the naiveté, even stupidity, of youth, even though many of our own friends came from modest backgrounds. Many of us youngsters were dragged into the communist fold, either by our friends or out of conviction of what appeared to us as the right ideology to pursue. We were infatuated with the idealism – future dreams and promises of a New World.

To put matters in context, one must remember that in the eastern reaches of Lithuania, with Hitler's rise to power in Germany, particularly after Kristallnacht on November 9, 1938, and after the invasion of Poland in 1939, and even earlier in Czechoslovakia, had come the gradual trickle of·news that Jews were being discriminated against in those regions. What started as rumours soon became alarming information which rapidly became more and more dramatic as we learned about the Germans' active persecution of the Jews; that Jews were expelled from their homes and stripped of their property. We started to hear that they were being beaten up in the streets and sent to concentration camps.

Indeed there was already a Jewish movement in Lithuania which encouraged the boycotting of German goods because of the persecution of the Jews. As youngsters, we were much affected by such news, and so, of course, we believed, were our parents. Again this situation made us far more sympathetic towards the Russians who, even though they were nationalising our parents' businesses, were basically friendly chaps. In contrast to the Germans, the Russians seemed to us 'real' people we could communicate with.

Back to the Slepp family. Once inside the ghetto, in September 1941, I looked for Micha, who was far older than me and my brothers, but probably younger than my parents. He had certain useful connections and he managed to fix me up with a job at the railroad station in Vilna, in the signals department. I was one of a small group of people who were collected from the ghetto each day by a Pole wearing a railroader's uniform, escorted to the railway station and brought back after work in the evening. Most of this group were elderly Jews, many of them were sick, and yet they were expected to do manual labour. There were only three or four of us youngsters who did the work for everyone, including the hard, but important task of laying rails. This was my job. The routine of carrying those heavy iron rails on my shoulders, day in and day out, helped to build up my muscles, but it also created a stoop in my back which has remained with me to this day.

Our main concern at that stage was how to buy a few potatoes and smuggle food into the ghetto so our families would not starve. Among those working in the group were a few rich Jews who had money, gold, and valuables they used to bribe the foremen so they could stay on. Having a work certificate meant staying alive.

At that time, we did not know exactly what was happening to our fellow Jews. We just knew that people disappeared – and did not return. Later, of course, we learned the truth – that they were being taken to Ponar and shot. I had no money to buy my way out of a situation, but I was young and able-bodied and could make myself useful.

But by then, the Germans had made the decision to annihilate the Jews of Europe, and various tactics were devised to keep the victims from realising what the Nazi plan was and, at the same time, to use professional and young people as labour to support their military machinery. This reflected on the lives of the Jews inside the ghettos, and the ghetto council – the *Judenrat* – was used as a tool to 'deliver' quotas of Jews by separating the so-called 'productive' ones from the others. The plan was to provide working Jews with certificates, pink ones and yellow ones, and take them out for the day with their families – while the Gestapo would go into the ghetto and seize so many thousands of those left behind on the pretext that they were being taken to work elsewhere, while in fact, their fate was sealed, they were destined to be shot at Ponar. At the end of the day those who had been taken out would return to the ghetto and continue their daily existence.

Father

For a while, I was able to protect my family and we survived the first couple of *Aktsias* (round-ups), but soon my father, who did not manage to get his own work permit, couldn't take any more. He left the ghetto one night, and as far as we ever knew, he took his own life.

He had a Lithuanian friend, Mr Bichunas, who had been the local tax inspector back home. Many people used to come to my father for financial advice in Rokishkis – he had once been a member of the town council and did what he could to help those in need. He would approach this tax inspector, Bichunas, and request tax exemption or assistance, whatever was appropriate, on behalf of needy Jews. Bichunas was later transferred from Rokishkis to Vilna. He was fond of the Jews, especially my father, and the friendship between them remained. In fact, when the Soviets nationalised the business and father moved to Vilna, we decided to send our Bechstein piano to Bichunas for safekeeping.

The night my father left the room where we lived with three other families, he said he was going to Bichunas; when he did not return, I crept out of the ghetto at night, and went to see Bichunas. I asked him if he had seen my father, and he said that he had been there earlier but had left. 'I have no idea where he went,' said Bichunas, 'but he left this piece of paper.'

On that fragment of paper, the triangular section torn off the back of an envelope, was written: 'My dear ones: we are living through very difficult times; I can find no way to endure this kind of existence. I am sorry – I am withdrawing from this life. Be well.'

If my father did commit suicide and was not caught by the Germans, was it a sign of strength or weakness? My father had always been a man of honour, who worked hard all his life and was successful. I believe he had accumulated a great deal of money which gave him a sense of security and independence. The fact that he moved to Vilna when it was returned to Lithuania by the Soviets and hastened to buy three factories proved either that he was not intelligent enough to see what was going to happen, or that he was so self-confident he believed that this was the right time for a new beginning, since factories were going cheap.

It is all hypothetical and one can only surmise what went through his mind. My mother was extremely pro-Zionist, while father was a *Volkist*, believing that Jews must co-exist wherever they are and should not look beyond. Once he was asked by a friend why he was not leaving for

South Africa, America, or Palestine like so many others, and he answered: 'Why should I leave? I've got America, South Africa, and Palestine right on my doorstep, here in Lithuania. I can do no better anywhere else.'

After the German invasion, however, he found himself in the ghetto knowing almost no-one because he had only recently arrived in Vilna. Lacking a trade to suit the Germans so he could obtain a work permit to keep his family alive, he was suddenly dependent on my ability to find work, a mere boy of sixteen and a half. All that must have hit him very hard and, who knows, he must have accused himself for bringing this upon his family, while the gold and dollars were buried somewhere under ground back in Rokishkis – all that was left of the business he had built up, and which had then been nationalised by the Soviets, now the Germans.

My father's disappearance frequently preoccupied me and I questioned whether it was correct of him to run away from the situation as he did. Should he not have stayed with his family to protect them? Shouldn't he have at least tried to find a solution instead of abandoning his wife, and two young sons and leaving them to their own fate?

Yet, how dare I accuse him? Why should I not rather look to those who forced him to take this course of action, those who were the real perpetrators of our tragedy and that of so many others, thousands, hundreds of thousands, millions? It is the Germans who stand guilty. Not only their leaders, whom everybody points a finger at, accusing them of being the only criminals; it is the entire nation that is culpable, the whole nation who not only raised their arms in salute, but shouted Heil Hitler at the top of their voices with heart and soul in devotion to their beloved Führer. As we watch documentary films of this period, we see how the people, the masses, welcomed the Nazi leadership with open arms. They were *all* only too ready to fall into their roles as criminals, murderers, collaborators, perpetrators of the vilest crimes history has ever known.

Why then should I cast blame on my father?

FPO – Veraynigte Partisaner Organisatzye

'It is better to die on your feet than to live on your knees'
Dolores Ibarruri – La Pasionaria

One day, as I was leaving the ghetto to go to work, I suddenly saw Kalinauskas, who had come to our house with the Gestapo to arrest me. He was standing at the gates of the ghetto; somebody, I suspect, had informed him of my whereabouts. At that stage I concluded that I was taking a great risk leaving the ghetto every day. He would have had me arrested and shot, just like that. So I tried to get some job inside the ghetto.

It was 1942 and I had by then already joined the underground Partisan Movement.

It was quite a complicated exercise to join the ghetto underground movement – the Veraynigte Partisaner Organisatzye, the FPO as it was known. The FPO was an all-party organisation, requiring each movement to recommend its own people as candidates for membership. I had belonged to the Communist Youth Movement (Comsomol) for the past half year while I was in the Lithuanian Gymnasium, but I knew none of the Vilna people in the ghetto. After all, I had had no contact with Jews except for a handful of Jewish students at school who themselves came to Vilna from Lithuania at the same time as me (the city had belonged to Poland between 1922 and 1940). We were all in the final graduation year of what was the only Lithuanian Gymnasium in Vilna. Inside the ghetto, I came across Chaim Lazar and Grisha Weinstein, who both came from Ponivesh, Lithuania. Somehow I sensed that Chaim had to be connected with some kind of underground movement. Chaim was a Revisionist (the right-wing Zionist movement), while I was on the extreme left and, at first, this seemed to me to be something of a drawback. Still, we frequently discussed an uprising, and since he did, in fact, belong to the FPO and since he saw how eager I was to join, Chaim Lazar eventually agreed to introduce me to the Communist Party inside the ghetto. The contact was made through Sonia Madeisker, one of the heroes of our movement. Sonia later became my divisional commander.

They accepted me into the Comsomol inside the ghetto and soon assigned me to an underground cell within the organisation and later in the FPO where I became a member of a five-person cell. That was the basis of the organisation's structure. Each cell had its own head. I soon became an active member of the organisation within the ghetto and went through military training in the cellars of deserted buildings, learning to use grenades, pistols and other weapons. Chaim Lazar, who had served in the Lithuanian Army, was also in charge of one of the five-person cells, and became my military instructor.

The head of the *Judenrat* was Jacob Gens, a former Lithuanian army officer. I was quite well acquainted with his daughter, Ada, who was one of the few people I knew from the Gymnasium. We had, in fact, come to Vilna at more or less the same time and graduated together from school. As former fellow students, and friends, we would meet from time to time in the ghetto. Ada lived outside the ghetto with her mother who was not Jewish, but since she was closer to her father she would visit him quite frequently.

Without telling her too much, I said that I was in some trouble and wondered if her father could help me get a job inside the ghetto. There were all kinds of jobs within the ghetto and if I could stay inside, I would not have to leave and risk my life, and not only my life, but also that of my mother and my younger brother who depended on me and my work permit. Ada talked to her father, Gens, who suggested that, even though I was young and did not appear to be the greatest hero, I could join the ghetto police. Now I had a new problem: How would my friends in the underground react? It was a decision with serious consequences.

I went to the FPO headquarters where they explained that as a clandestine organisation based on small groups of five, even though I might not know more than the five or one or two other groups of five, there were, in fact, several members of the underground within the ghetto police, something I had not been aware of at that stage. If I joined the ghetto police, it would be important to secure a post at the gates of the ghetto if possible, since that was the channel for smuggling arms. FPO members who worked in arms factories were smuggling in weapons and ammunition under cover, and it was vital to staff these points of entry with our people. I could not be sure I would be stationed at the ghetto gates, but I assured them I would do my best to be assigned to such a post.

Sure enough, after a while, that's exactly where they put me. As time passed, we felt that the ghetto would not survive, and it became very important to have more of our people within the police. It was then that I was appointed group commander, in charge of all the police within the FPO. I was told that I could appoint people of my choice and at my discretion, those I believed could be trusted.

Curfews were imposed more and more frequently, restricting movement within the ghetto, and since communication between members of the FPO headquarters and its members was vital, it became even more important to increase the numbers of uniformed policemen. We did our best to select reliable people and my group gradually grew to twelve.

Then came the day, July 16, 1943, when everything changed; the day they arrested our leader, Itzik Wittenberg, the head of the FPO, on the night of July 15 when Gens summoned him for discussion to his quarters, where the Gestapo and the Lithuanian police led him away.

Wittenberg was the head of our underground movement but, as a communist leader, he was also a member of the Central Committee of the Lithuanian Communist Party, which had its own underground movement outside the ghetto, led by a group of three, including Wittenberg, a Lithuanian, and a Pole. The Gestapo caught the Pole and tortured him until he exposed the Lithuanian. They caught the Lithuanian, tortured him and he disclosed Wittenberg. That's how Wittenberg came to be arrested.

Whenever anyone from the FPO was summoned to Gens, we would mobilise our people. As Wittenberg was led down Rudnitska Street, the main street leading from Gens's office towards the ghetto gates, a small group of our FPO members jumped at the Gestapo, grabbed Wittenberg and took him into hiding.

Gens immediately announced that if we did not release Wittenberg, the ghetto would be liquidated within a week, and not a single Jew would remain alive. At the time, there were only a few thousand Jews left, exceptionally tough Jews, known as the 'Starke' – the physically strong ones. They joined the campaign led by the ghetto police to find Wittenberg. They went into the streets, they caught eight of our people, including me, and took us hostage. They beat us and took us to Rudnitska six, the headquarters of the *Judenrat* – the ghetto administration, where there were two courtyards with a flight of steps to the right of the first courtyard. They put the eight of us on these steps and there, Dessler, the chief of police and his second in command, Bernstein, beat us mercilessly with their truncheons.

They had caught me when one of our finest men, Baruch Goldstein, was attacked by a gang of the Starke. Baruch was a member and a division commander of the FPO and he worked in a *Beutelager* – a German camp where arms were assembled, our main source of weapons. They were smuggled in by all kinds of ploys at times when we knew that the gates were busy. On such occasions, as members of the FPO ghetto police, we would make sure we created enough commotion and confusion to divert attention. Whenever I saw Baruch coming towards the gates from afar, I knew he would signal that he was carrying something important, and that was my sign to act.

On July 16, as I was patrolling the streets to see what was happening and to report as usual, I suddenly saw Baruch lying on the ground at one of the Oshmianska crossroads in the ghetto, his head smashed with an axe. As I looked at him lying there on the ground bleeding, I saw his revolver and a box of bullets slowly slipping out of his pocket; we in the underground movement were mobilised and already armed by then. Naturally as members of that illegal group, and given my function, we were expected never to act in such a way as to reveal our identity; but seeing Baruch lying there, bleeding profusely, I rushed to his side. As I tried to lift his head from the ground, those who were hunting us yelled: 'He's one of theirs – grab him.'

That's how I was caught. Even in my police uniform, they took me. Both of us, Baruch, bleeding from his wounds and me, bleeding later, for they dragged us by the ankles, our heads bumping along the cobbled streets, to that courtyard.

The FPO leaders met with Wittenberg and much has been said, written, and performed in plays, about what happened; but essentially we know that Wittenberg surrendered himself. He would, of course, have been shot, and we hoped he would have first taken the cyanide capsule he had with him. The eight of us were released immediately. No-one knows exactly who made the decision that he would give himself up, but if that decision had not been made, clearly the Jews would have started killing each other well before the Germans came to liquidate the ghetto, so highly charged was the atmosphere. The FPO faced an awkward situation: there were no Germans inside the ghetto. The only targets would have been the Jews, who regarded the underground as troublemakers endangering the very existence of the ghetto and their lives.

As a policeman I was, of course, court martialled – hauled before the Jewish court in the ghetto, accused of wrongful behaviour during these events, and dismissed from the ghetto police. This did not suit me in the least. I needed my uniform and I hung on to it; none of the real police officers dared touch me; and I kept it until the very last day when the ghetto was finally liquidated, in late September, when I left the ghetto for the forests with the last group of FPO members through the sewers.

To convey those days to Ronny was impossible. How could I make him understand the realities of life in the ghetto 'then'. Today children are playing in the streets, the trees are swaying in the wind – elderly people are sitting in the sun, a car passes by, – how could he understand this other world? I left Vilna disappointed, empty-hearted; there was no nostalgia, there was a blank. I could hardly believe that we lived through all that suffering. Looking around the streets I could see in my mind's eye the sadness, the despair in people's eyes those days, the fear of the German oppressor, the terror they felt at being pursued by the enemy; I could barely believe myself that it had happened. It is impossible to transport oneself back to those days where terror reigned and fear eclipsed every single day of our lives. And yet happen it certainly did. Fifty or so years ago.

Escape through the sewers

> *'And who made him so beautiful?*
> *My mother*
> *You ingrate! And you left your mother there'*
>
> Abba Kovner

We left Vilna on September 23, 1943, the last day of the liquidation of the ghetto. We were told to assemble in a workshop at Rudnitska 11. To this day I am not quite sure if, when we were told to assemble in that room, we were also told that we would be leaving Vilna. All I know is that we were told to meet there and according to instructions, I took the group under my charge. The orders from headquarters were that only members of the organisation, and no family members, were to meet there. It was only then that I learned we were about to escape, although I did not yet know how.

The passage out was through the sewers in a plan master-minded by Shmulke Kaplinski. I was one of the last to descend into the sewers with Rushka Korchak, and Abba Kovner behind me. We had entered the sewers in the oldest part of Vilna, where they were extremely narrow. The diameter of the pipes was barely the width of our bodies, so we had to crawl on our knees, and in some areas even to slither along on our stomachs. It was a very rainy day, the stench was unbearable. Often those in front would pass out, asphyxiated by the gases rising from the water, and blocking the route.

The problem of those who had fainted was solved by those in advance who dragged them to where streets above crossed, and where the pipes were high enough to stand up in. Since the air was marginally better here, they would soon recover and we could continue. Eventually we reached an opening on Ignatovskia Street, where two members of the communist underground movement outside the ghetto at the end of the tunnel pulled us out.

From there we were told to walk in pairs – it was night and still raining. The idea was to follow the couple in front, keeping them constantly in sight. We knew we were leaving the city, but were told that if we got lost, we were to go immediately to Kailis, a block outside the ghetto where Jewish furriers were concentrated in specialist workshops. For the Germans, furriers were among the most important element in the workforce, providing the soldiers, particularly those serving on the front, with fur coats, a top priority, and thus the Jewish furriers were kept outside the ghetto. We were told that if we had to go to Kailis, we would be assisted by one of the Jewish policemen there, another member of the underground, Tolia Telerant.

I was walking with Matla Stuhl; in front of us were Abrasha Chwoinik and Asia Bick. Jankel Kaplan and Wittenberg's son were in front of them. Chwoinik and Kaplan were members of the Staff of our organisation. Keeping a distance between ourselves, we kept them within our sight. Suddenly we saw the four of them being arrested by the Germans. We learned later that all four were hanged. At that moment I had to think fast. We had no-one to follow, I was not familiar in the least with the back streets of Vilna, and it was night. So I decided to take Matla to Stefanska 17, the house where my family had lived before we moved into the ghetto. We found our way there and knocked on the door of the concierge, Francisek, whom I remembered as a helpful guy. He opened the gates, I begged him to let us in and promised to leave at 5 o'clock in the morning when it was still dark. He ushered us in, and swiftly pushed the two of us into a cupboard under the stairs, covering us with old sheets and blankets. I remember thinking that while I had managed not to suffocate down in the sewers, I could easily do so in this tiny hole. At 5 o'clock in the morning we asked him to direct us to Kailis.

As promised, our man was there to receive us and the next day they took us to a nearby building, the Gebietscommissariat, the main administration building of the German occupation forces, where they shoved all twelve or fourteen of us who had made our way there, into the attic. The concierge of that building was a member of the underground communist party, who took a tremendous risk in hiding us there. It was certainly a good cover, but it was tricky. He told us that hardly anyone ever went into that attic and that we would be safe there for a while. We were told not to lock the door, but if someone did happen to walk in, we would have to throw a hand grenade. We lay there for several days and several nights, with the concierge bringing us food and water. Every few hours we took turns standing behind the unlocked door, a grenade in hand, pistols at our side, in case a German discovered us, even by mistake. In that case, it would have been the end of all of us; but, again, luckily, we emerged from this situation more or less intact.

While we were still waiting in Kailis, Vitka Kempner, later Abba Kovner's wife, who acted as liaison with headquarters, came to tell me that Abba had appointed me commander of the group. It was a strange scenario to be a commander of a group stuck in an attic of the German Gebietscommissariat. It could easily have been my last appointment.

A few days later we were collected by our people and marched through the night into the Rudnitski forests where we began yet another chapter of our chequered lives.

The Rudnitski Forests

During our 1994 trip, while in Vilna, I called Oleg Dolgunov whose name I had been given by an acquaintance in Moscow, Yitzhak Rize, and he was kind enough to put his car at our disposal, an old Volga with a young Lithuanian driver, Jonas. We picked up our friend Shmulke and drove toward the forests of Rudnitski, some 45 kilometres south of Vilna. This had once been a huge densely-grown forest of pine trees, almost impenetrable in parts, where our partisan bases were located; now we found the forest divided by asphalt roads – something unthinkable fifty years ago – some of them were just dirt tracks where we could now actually ride in the car to where the bases were situated.

Fifty years ago the base consisted of a series of bunkers dug into the ground. The area was marshy, sand-covered hills with swamps on all sides. To cross these marshes and get back to the main base we often had to build a special route of stepping stones, or mini 'bridges', or damn up the water to make a path. The bunkers themselves were constructed of young trees, cut down, covered with sand and grass so they could not be detected from the air. The only way to spot the camp from above was by the smoke rising steadily from the makeshift chimneys: one column of smoke came from the cooking fire, and the other from ovens constructed of large empty metal barrels with a chimney stack pushed through the roof used to heat the bunkers. That was a hard but vital task because winters in Lithuania are bitter; there was, of course, no electricity, so for lighting we would heat long thin pieces of wood in the fires until the embers glowed to provide us with a little light. When they died down, we would heat up some more and the only additional source of lighting was among the smokers – for their cigarettes, too, would glow in the dark.

Apart from providing low-level lighting, these cigarettes also smelled repulsive; they were made from various potent leaves obtained from the local peasants; the leaves would be crushed and then rolled into newspaper – Pravda was known to be the best smoke. Their degree of strength varied: some preferred 'light' tobacco and some liked it strong – these were few and far between, because the lightest variety was itself incredibly strong. At one stage during our spell in the forests, Moscow parachuted in arms and explosives, and several packs of cigarettes. This was my first introduction to Camel cigarettes, but when we heavy smokers tried them, we threw them out immediately since they had absolutely no taste at all compared to our local blend.

It was autumn when we first arrived in the Rudnitski forests, it rained heavily, and we were helpless. At first we built a hut – a real *succah* – with an open roof we covered with pine tree branches. It took no more than an hour for the rain to pour in and there we were, lying in water, praying that the next day would be sunny so we could dry ourselves, and our new home. We had escaped with nothing but the clothes on our back, so within a very short time we were faced with problems of hygiene. Something had to be done.

In general terms, two very different challenges faced us: one was to attack the Germans, wherever they were: in their bases, stationed at specific posts, en route from one location to another. The second, and by far the more dangerous, was to provide an on-going supply of sustenance for our people. This meant regular expeditions to the local villages to obtain food, a dangerous mission and one we faced throughout our entire period in the forests, and as time wore on, it became more and more of a problem.

The offensives against the Germans, blowing up trains, telegraph poles and railway tracks, burning down bridges, anything to cause maximum interruption to the German communication lines, were usually carried out at night. These were militarily planned campaigns, and although they were often dangerous; there was always the possibility of retreat and repeating or varying the strategy later or the next day. Going into the local villages to get food, however, was another matter. We came in like bandits and, after all, we were robbing the local peasants of their livelihood, first a sack of flour, then a pig or a cow or a horse. In the early days, we were able to befriend the locals and persuade them to give us food voluntarily, but soon we would need another sack of flour and more cows, and more chickens. In addition, the number of partisans inhabiting the forests grew, as more and more people fled from the ghettos into the forests and as the Red Army moved westwards, Russian soldiers who had been imprisoned by the Germans and had escaped, tried to join the partisans. If they were not able to prove to the Russian Army after the liberation that they had joined the partisans to fight the Germans, they would – at best – have been sent to Siberia. These people begged us to let them join our partisan group – the Armenians, Kirghesians, Tartars, and Kalmuks; Lithuanians, Dutchmen, Italians, all were desperate to join the partisans, and they all needed food.

As a result of this 'invasion' of the forests, the villages close to our base soon ran out of food; everyone was after the same source of supplies. Gradually the villagers, with whom we had at first tried to negotiate, became our enemies. We explained our needs to them and we did our best not to take too much of their livestock and their crops, but there was just so much they could provide, and finally we ended up not taking just one cow but by leaving just one cow. We would arrive in the village and load up wagons, or in winter, sledges pulled by horses – which we'd also taken from them, and which we often did not return. After all, their very existence depended on their livestock. Sometimes we would even take a farmer or two with us just so they could return the horse and cart we had used to their village. This also made them less likely to alert the German police that we had been in their village and taken their goods.

Extraordinarily, we suffered more casualties from our expeditions to find food than we did blowing up trains, bridges, railway lines, and telegraph poles in our fight against the Germans. These raids were always carried out at night, but expeditions to the villages for food took hours – and usually ran into daylight hours. A fully laden wagon train – which inevitably moved very slowly along the dirt roads – took hours and hours to reach base, and it was not uncommon to come across peasants who rushed to denounce us to the Germans who waited to ambush the wagon on the way back to camp. Once a train was blown up, it was done. Perhaps in another few days there would be further instructions to bomb a local bridge. That too would be done, but we needed food every single day.

I remember one episode when we managed to get hold of some pigs. We salted them thoroughly and then, planning ahead for winter, we buried them and left them there. When we dug them up in spring there was practically nothing left on the carcasses – they were just rotten through and through. We had done something wrong – either we hadn't salted the meat properly or we hadn't buried it properly – whatever it was it meant that all we had to sustain us were the rotten remains of those pigs.

In our first weeks in the forests we had no idea of how to feed ourselves. We would get hold of a sack of flour from the local village, mix it with water, and wound up with a tasteless, floury concoction that was more paste than food, its only flavour the taste of burnt charcoal splinters that had flown off the fire where we heated this delicacy. This is what we had to eat – three times a day! When we had something more solid to eat we didn't mind using our fingers – we weren't too fussy about plates – but when it came to soup, we had to devise some kind of vessel, which we made from aluminium cans. Then there was the question of serving everyone. Those who ate slowly – either out of habit or to make the food last longer – were served last so that the fast eaters could be quickly satisfied. And if they were lucky, there was even a second helping.

Within the battalion, there was a fairly strict hierarchy of three ranks: at the top was the Commander, the Commissar and the Head of the special department, who took orders from the high command of the Brigade; then there was a middle rank consisting mainly of ex-military personnel; and there were the lower ranks – group-commanders, regular soldiers and the administrative staff. There was also a medical unit: a doctor, and a nurse.

Tevya Rubin

The Sergeant Major of my battalion was Tevya Rubin, who had been a stevedore in Vilna before the war. He was not an educated man, but he was blessed with natural common sense and immense physical strength, and was one of the finest human beings I ever met in those days.

Tevya didn't just give orders and wait for them to be carried out, but would more often than not accompany his troops on assignments himself, and on one of these missions, his reaction to the situation probably saved my life.

We would be ordered to blow up a certain train, or bridge, and in winter this meant trudging through deep snow often for 40 kilometres, laden with arms, pistols, grenades, and seven or eight kilograms of dynamite. Normally we took turns carrying the dynamite, but Tevya almost always volunteered to carry it the whole way. Then we would have to cross a river and someone would have to go ahead to see if the village on the other side was safe to approach. Tevya was always the first to volunteer, checked everything out, and then we followed. Crossing even the narrowest river in winter in Lithuania with temperatures of minus 30 meant that our clothes instantly froze to our body and we would stand on the other side of the river with frozen sheets of what felt like tin clinging to our shivering bodies.

Blowing up trains and railway tracks was dangerous and over the months – by trial and often fatal error – we learned which techniques to employ. First we would hide a mine between the rails, lay down the detonator, and attach a thread which we would take back some 50 – 80 metres into the bushes behind us. Pulling the cord at the right moment triggered the detonator. The most strategic position for blowing up a train was a curved section of the railroad where the land sloped away. There we could trigger the detonator just at the right time so the engine would be detached from the carriages, roll down the hill and be destroyed. Sometimes it worked, often we failed. It was vital to destroy the engine, since they were irreplaceable while the wagons were expendable.

I remember the particular incident when Tevya saved my life. On that occasion, I was assigned to pull the cord to detonate the explosion in an attempt to blow up a military train; the surrounding terrain was covered in thick bushes. The fibre we used this time had been taken from cord we had cut off from parachutes dropped from Moscow with all kinds of supplies. This cord was thin and we tied it together four-ply for the required strength. You always had to leave plenty of slack in the rope, but I had probably left too much. As the train approached I pulled the cord towards me as fast as I could and triggered the explosion. The next task was to run from the site to an assembly point for all those taking part in the exercise. The trains were guarded by armed German soldiers and they would often move in to attack us.

But, because the rope was tied together, some of the knots got caught in the bushes and in my haste, I became totally entangled in several metres of rope and could not move. Suddenly out of the bushes I heard a voice calling softly: 'Juluk, Juluk.'

It was Tevya – the sergeant major! When he saw that I was not at the meeting point, he came back to look for me. He took out a knife, cut me free and we ran away together.

Life in the forests was tough and everyone had to find his own way to survive. Often people would decide to 'get sick', say they were not well enough to go out either on a military operation or to fetch food from neighbouring villages. They would rush to the camp doctor and it was up to Tevya to control insurrection within the battalion. He had to maintain discipline, respect and order, and he had his own principles and standards. If someone said they had a cold or were too ill to do their job, he asked them if they had a temperature. If it was under 38, he would say there was nothing to discuss – it was work as usual. If it was 38 or over, he would send them to the doctor and obey the doctor's decision.

Tevya himself was strong – he was never sick – he had the constitution of an ox. He could smoke the strongest of the strong tobaccos – the kind of stuff others wouldn't touch – he and I were the only ones who would smoke unsmokable tobacco leaves. I never understood how I could stand it, but I liked it strong.

Tevya's other great love was alcohol. Alcohol was a problem in the forests. We could get it from the local village peasants, each house had its own recipe they were reluctant to give up, but they were all lethal. Called Samagon – which means 'home brewed' – you never knew exactly what had gone into it, neither the level of alcohol it contained nor the amount of poison. Just smelling it made you reel. One day someone brought two huge casks of Samagon to the base; they were massive old petrol cans covered in straw that I kept in my bunker – as an officer I had my own private bunker. I, personally, couldn't touch the stuff although it was important to drink alcohol from time to time because it kept you warm and killed off bugs, but this brew was undrinkable. Tevya, however, loved it. We had no glasses, only aluminium quarts.

Occasionally, Tevya would stop off at my bunker during his patrols, report on events and I would offer him a tankard of Samagon. 'No, no, no,' he would protest, 'I'm on duty, I cannot drink.' He didn't need too much persuasion, however, and I would pour him a litre of Samagon. He would lift the tankard to his lips and take just a sip at a time just as later, when life became a little more sophisticated, we would sip a good French cognac. Then he'd take another sip savouring the mug between his lips like the mouth of a lover. Finally he would throw back his head and finish off the litre, wipe his mouth and say: 'Ahh! that was good, that was really good.' So I would offer him another and he would protest. Then he would give in and say 'OK, give me a half.' So I'd give him a half – he would drink it exactly as he'd drunk the first, and then he'd ask for the other half.

By this time anyone else would have been staggering, but Tevya would just wander off slowly to his bunker, lie down, and sleep for about half an hour. Then he would wake up, fresh as a daisy.

He was a fascinating character: one side of his nature was warmhearted and understanding; yet on the other hand, he was a strict disciplinarian. Although he was a simple man, he had his own principles, his own standards, his own morals. He and his sort knew how to distinguish between right and wrong in the conditions under which we lived. Their code of behaviour was certainly more appropriate in the forests than that of those with a high school or university background.

Tevya Rubin lost his wife and all his family during the war. He remarried and he and his new wife eventually settled in Israel where they had a son. Tevya took up his old trade in haulage, transporting heavy goods all over the country. One day, on my way to work in Tel Aviv during the 1960s, I suddenly saw him in the street; I recognised him immediately by his characteristic bearing. He saw me, too, and seemed rather embarrassed, unsure of whether to approach me. As I walked towards him he greeted me and said, in that distinctive tone: 'Juluk, Juluk, can I talk to you, is it all right to speak to you?'

'Sure,' I said, 'come up to my office.'

'No, no, I can't possibly do that,' – just like all those years ago he pretended not to be able to drink the Samagon. So up he came and he told me that his son was 14 and that he wanted him to go to an ORT school in Cholon and would I be able to arrange it? (ORT being the educational network in Israel which I headed in those days). I was happy to do this for him. His son studied auto-mechanics and when he was 18, he joined the army. Tevya came to me again to ask if I could arrange for his son to go into a specific unit in the army so he could continue in his chosen field of study. Again I did whatever I could to help him.

I would meet Tevya from time to time in the street and enquire after his well-being. As he got older, I would ask him about his health and how he was managing all this heavy physical work. 'Look,' he said, 'I don't know about my health – all I know is as far as lifting a table, or carrying a refrigerator is concerned, I can still manage the third floor, but when it comes to a piano these days, there I do have problems!'

Then his son got married. He invited me to the wedding and seemed delighted I had come. I could see that he was sick. He told me exactly where I should stand, placing me at the side of the Chupah, facing him directly. Throughout the service he frequently looked at me, somehow deep in thought, and when the Rabbi who performed the wedding ceremony handed him the cup of wine and asked him to drink from it, he took it to his lips, but he did not drink. Clearly he was not allowed at that stage to touch alcohol. He just took the cup to his lips and looked, long and hard, at me. And I remembered the Samagon. And I knew he remembered. And then the cup was passed on to the bride and the groom. He died soon afterwards.

* * *

So I visited the forests with Ronny and my old friend Shmulke Kaplinski. Shmulke is married to Chiena Borowska, one of the leading activists in Vilna, before and during the ghetto years, and then in the underground movement. After he led us out of Vilna through the sewers, Shmulke became a commander of the battalion, 'To Victory', and Chiena was the commissar. They remained in Vilna after the liberation where they still live with their daughter, Ruta (born just after we returned to Vilna from the forests in 1944), her husband and son.

We looked for the site of our brigade's base in the forest, which had been established as a historical monument and was originally well-tended. There had also been a museum with photographs, and a large monument with an inscription by the local citizens stated that it had been established in memory of the partisan movement who fought against the German occupation 1941–44. But we found no museum: it had been burned down, either by Lithuanian nationalists or by local peasants; the plaque on the monument had been torn off and was hanging on by a thread. The signs on each of the bunkers had either been removed or were bent. In short, the whole site was neglected. Clearly, the Lithuanians today are not thrilled by the idea of Soviet partisans; they had their own partisans, the nationalists, who were keen to get rid of ours.

Still, Ronny seemed impressed by what he saw. He began to understand what it meant to be a partisan, to live in the forests, and he asked pertinent questions. It was, of course, a lot easier to answer his questions here and now, than to live it all then.

Ponar – Motl Zeidel

From the Rudnitski forests we went to Ponar, where the Jews from Vilna and surrounding districts were executed by Einsatz commandos – special units of Latvians, Lithuanians, Estonians and Ukrainians, under the orders of the Gestapo. Even these murderers could not execute thousands of Jews without first drinking themselves into a stupor.

Several memorials had been put up by Jewish, Christian and other ethnic groups, but it was mainly Jews who were massacred at Ponar. Today it looks very peaceful, the trees are tall, the area is covered in lush green grass, but suddenly your eyes focus on the vast ditches used for the slaughter. One is a round ditch where prisoners were kept chained, who had to dig up the corpses, then burn them after the German high command decided that all traces of their atrocities were to be covered up. When their work was done, these prisoners, too, were shot, and more were brought.

Between seventy and seventy-five thousand Jews were annihilated in Ponar. Among the handful who escaped, was Motl Zeidel.

I had not seen Motl for about fifty years. In May 1996 I asked my good friend, Menasche Gavissar, who came from the same home town, Svenzian, as Motl, to accompany me to his flat in Petach Tikva, where I asked him to tell us about Ponar.

Svenzian was outside Vilna, a part of Lithuania captured by the Poles between the two World Wars. It had a wonderful Jewish youth, most belonged to Zionist movements, and some to communist and Bundist groups. The whole village was surrounded by lush green countryside full of lakes and forests. When the Germans reached the town, the Jews easily escaped into the countryside, and from there into the forests. Motl's family then managed to reach the Vilna Ghetto, where they lived until his sister and parents were taken by the Germans when the ghetto was liquidated.

Motl himself is angry to this day that, since he wasn't a member of the underground, the leaders did not let him join us in our escape through the sewers into the forests. He still harbours that grudge, but then my own younger brother wasn't accepted either.

During the liquidation, Motl managed to find a hiding place where some 50 people hid for about 50 days, until eventually they feared they would die of starvation when their food ran out. A few Christians who had hidden Jews were caught and tortured, and revealed their former hiding places. That is what happened to Motl. The Gestapo arrested them and Motl was imprisoned with about 140 people shoved together like sardines. He was a 16-year-old apprentice carpenter, so he was often taken into the prison yard to chop firewood.

One day the Germans took the women and children on one of their regular *Aktsia* (round-ups). No-one ever saw them again. Meanwhile, the men were selected to disinter the corpses in Ponar and burn them.

The sign on the camp gate at Ponar read: 'Entry Strictly Forbidden, Mortally Dangerous Mines'. Barbed wire formed two walls, and as they discovered later, there were mines in the space between. Ponar was impenetrable.

First, they were all placed in iron shackles, tied just below their knees with the chain hanging down to the ground, but they were permitted to tie half of the chain to their belt so it did not prevent them from walking, or more important, working. The *Sturmführer* – a dandy in white suede gloves and shiny black boots, reeking of cologne – warned them in no uncertain terms, that if they tried to remove the shackles, or made any attempt to escape, they would be hung from the tree, or shot on the spot.

It was immediately made clear to them that their task was to burn the tens of thousands of corpses in several enormous pits – 24 metres in diameter and four metres deep. There were two ladders going down into the pit, a clean one (for the Germans who continually urged their captives to work faster and faster) and the other for the workers.

The first pit Motl worked in contained some 22,000 bodies which had not even been treated with chloride. His task was to dig up the corpses and then pile them onto a 'pyramid' – a funeral pyre constructed very precisely: over a small hearth, seven-metre-long logs were stacked criss-cross with a chimney in the middle. The corpses were placed on these logs after begin carefully counted. When the logs and spruce branches were stacked on the first layer of corpses, black fuel was poured over them and then a second layer was piled on, and then a third, until the pyramid was four metres high. It was considered ready when it contained three and a half thousand corpses. Then it was ignited.

As Motl recounted these details to me he said: 'I see this view in front of my eyes every single day and I begin to wonder whether I really lived through this hell or whether it was a nightmare.

'Everyone has had terrible experiences but this is something that you cannot even imagine in your wildest dream. They pushed us and drove us on; often we just could not carry on; we were broken people.

'The *Sturmführer* told us all that it was the Russians who had killed these people, but then the Germans referred to the corpses as 'figures' or as '*shmuttes*' – rags. It was all quite clear to us.

'When we worked in the pits removing the corpses, those on top were still recognisable as bodies,' he continued, 'but as we reached the bottom of the pile, the corpses were disintegrating – there was barely anything left. Often we recognised people by the tools at their side. Naked corpses lay like herrings in a net; there was a system of removing them with a hook since the bodies fell apart and the Germans wanted whole bodies – intact, so to speak; we were even forced to look into their mouths for gold teeth, and if we did not do all these terrible things, we were beaten mercilessly.

'The chains on our legs were so heavy, we could hardly drag ourselves, let alone shift these mountains of bodies. We had to shovel the corpses onto the pyramids and as soon as one was full and burning, another group would prepare the next, so there was a constant and steady stream of destruction. The stench of the burning flesh was so overpowering it would make us nauseous and dizzy. Each pyramid burned for four to five days and what was left? A small pile of ashes that was once the Jewish people.

'When we returned to our barracks after our work for the day was done, we washed our hands in a special chemical and then we got a piece of bread and some tea. During the day they gave us a cup of broth – *ballanda*. There were eighty of us in all – seventy-six men and four women.

'It was not long before we started to think of an escape plan. At least one or two of us would survive and could relate what happened in that hell-hole.

'So we started digging a tunnel from the store room in our – so-called – living-quarters. There was a kitchen and a store-room and in that store-room they kept bread and the two ladders, one for the Germans and one for the prisoners. We had found various tools amongst the corpses and that is what we used to dig. Sometimes we dug just with spoons. Or, our bare hands.

'After a heavy working day, and constantly chained, it was tough. First, we excavated down to a depth of two metres. One would shovel and one pushed away the earth. We knew we were digging through a hill and exactly where we would come out at the other end. The ground was sandy and that made it easier. Of course, we had to reinforce the tunnel as we went and this we did with pieces of wood we had chopped for firewood.'

'One day the Germans called an *appel* – a roll-call. Five of us were working in the tunnel. We had electricity in there (extended from the store-room light) and they could signal to the five, who quickly joined the *appel* and everything was fine.'

Everyone worked on the tunnel except for the elderly who found it difficult to breathe down there. Motl admits he was obsessed with the operation and wanted to work on it all the time. Others told him to let go occasionally and not to be so crazy – but he did not want to give up. His determination was not in vain, for eventually, when it came to the escape and to selecting the order to leave, Motl was fifth in line, since they were ranked by the work they had put in. Out of 80, he, at least, had a chance of getting through.

'Meanwhile, work in the pits went on, and when we finished the first one, 22,000 corpses had been dug up and burned; then we moved on to the second: 12,000 more corpses. From time to time we found documents with the bodies which were by now unrecognisable as human beings, and one day one of us came across the documents of his own wife and children. To say that his reaction was heartbreaking, or devastating, does not even begin to convey how he felt.

'Finally the tunnel was ready. It had taken about three months to dig and it measured 70 centimetres high, 60 centimetres wide, and about 32 metres long. Even though we could see daylight at the other end, it was not so simple. It was decided to start the escape on the night of April 15, 1944. We knew that the whole area beyond the tunnel was mined, and that at the end of that stretch were two rows of barbed wire and two more rows of mines, in addition to the barbed wire surrounding the whole of Ponar.'

They entered the tunnel crawling on all fours and in absolute silence, removing their chains before crawling towards the fence. At the perimeter fence the guards realised that there had been an escape and machine gun fire and mortars rained down on them. Twenty-five of the eighty who crawled through that tunnel got through. Of the twenty-five, eleven escaped. The others were caught and would, of course, have been shot.

'We had scissors to cut the barbed wire, and some of us just jumped over it. Then we came to a railroad track, and zigzagged our way through it in case there were mines. Surviving that, we ran all night until we reached a few houses in a little village.'

There they hid during the day, and as they lay in the manure of the local farmers' barns until night fell once again, they allowed themselves to think for the first time that they had been lucky to escape and survive, so far. Then they walked to the next village of Sorok Tatar, one of several villages surrounding the forest where the partisan brigade, *For Victory*, was based.

Of the eleven who escaped, nine were Jews, and two were Russians; five of them then met a reconnaissance unit from this partisan's group in the forest, who invited them to join the ambush they were carrying out. In spite of their condition, they were only too pleased to join – after all, they had escaped and were free. The all-clear signal of two shots was fired and then they were brought back to the partisan base, where they were segregated until they recovered. They were soon ready for action once again.

In the nearby village of Kanyuchi, where the locals collaborated with the Germans – these newly-recruited partisans, furious at what they had seen at Ponar, burned down all the houses and killed every single one of the inhabitants, shouting as they shot each one: 'That's for my mother, and that's for my father, and that's for my sister,' and so on.

The partisan's brigade, *For Victory*, which Motl and his fellow escapees had reached, was, of course, my brigade and that's where I first met Motl. What I remember most clearly to this day is the smell on their bodies – the unforgettable stench of burning flesh – the smell of death that never left them.

Back in the Vilna Ghetto, Motl had worked with my younger brother Ephraim in the carpentry workshops. He told me that Ephraim was a wonderful boy and they became close friends. Ephraim taught Motl to use a circular saw, for Ephraim was evidently an expert. 'He handled it as tenderly as a violinist plays his violin,' Motl told me. 'And he introduced me to your mother – what a fine lady.'

* * *

I was at Ponar, too, right after one of the executions that produced those corpses Motl saw. It was April 1943 when, as part of the local ghetto police and as a member of the FPO, I was on patrol at the ghetto gates. A few days before a group of 20 to 30 Jewish ghetto police had been taken to Oshmiana, a town near Vilna, to help the Germans round up all the Jews. They announced that they were taking them to Kaunas, but instead these poor souls were taken directly to Ponar and shot. The Jewish police were sent back to the ghetto and next day the same 20 or 30 were to return to Ponar to clean up. When they were loaded onto a lorry by the ghetto gates, and counted, one was missing. The head of the ghetto gate police, Lev, who had a grudge against me, pointed at me and said: 'You go with them!' I had to climb onto the lorry, and all I could think of on that journey was that no-one ever returned alive from Ponar.

What I saw when we reached Ponar was something I, like Motl Zeidel, will never forget.

There were three huge ditches, full of corpses. Dozens of additional corpses lay spread-eagled around them, helpless souls shot trying to escape. Our group was assigned to clean up all these remains and throw them into the ditch. When we finished, we were returned to the ghetto, and I went straight to my friend, Chaim Lazar, who had introduced me to the underground movement, and there I cried for hours. I could not speak until morning, when I told him what I had seen.

* * *

And now, 51 years later, here I was with my younger son, Ronny; he, too, saw the cloudless sky, the trees, the rich, green grass, and the monuments; it was difficult for me in such a moment, to express what we saw there together and compare it with what happened then. It is true that we saw the same blue sky – the same, or perhaps new, younger pine trees, it all seemed like a paradise. Then as I looked down, thank God I no longer saw that terrible hell hole, but I knew, I knew what had been there before, that beneath the green grass lay the remains of hundreds and thousands of good Jewish people, killed in cold blood just because they were Jews.

Sonia

In the underground was a group of girls who didn't look Jewish who served as liaisons between the headquarters of the partisan brigade in the forests, and the Jews in the HKP and Kailis blocks. Their goal was to get them out of these blocks and bring them to the forests.

Zelda (Treger, later Nissanelevich) and Vitka were in this group and on the day that Motl and the other few escaped from Ponar, they happened to be on their way back from Vilna to the forests. As they passed by Ponar, they heard gunfire, and knew immediately that something was up. Only when they returned to base did they learn of the escape and all the details.

Earlier that day, Zelda had gone into town to meet with Sonia Madeisker, an important member of the underground movement in the ghetto and of the Communist Party, who had stayed in town to serve the underground in Vilna, after the ghetto was liquidated. It was always difficult to meet with Sonia since she had to change her residence often; the Gestapo restricted her movements and she was constantly under surveillance. A few days earlier, Vitka and Zelda had met with her to discuss the possibility of rescuing the Jews from the HKP block and bringing them into the forests. They had fixed a second meeting on Saturday morning and the plan was for Sonia and her colleague Karol to wind up their activities in town, at least for the time being, and move into the forests.

Earlier that morning, Zelda had gone to see Sonia in her apartment. When she saw bullet holes in the building and signs of forced entry, she went to the back of the house hoping to learn more about what had happened and where to find her. As she approached, it was clear that something tragic had happened. At the corner of the street she saw a man dressed in civilian clothes, following her, obviously a German agent. Since he had probably been watching to see if Zelda would go into the yard, with the intention of arresting other members of the underground, Zelda went to a different exit and ran to tell the others what had happened.

Later they learned that the Gestapo agents had been following Karol when he went to Sonia's apartment. They broke in, and Sonia rushed down to the cellar, where she evidently tried to commit suicide by shooting into her mouth. She failed, but was severely wounded. Both were arrested and taken to Gestapo headquarters, and that was the last we heard.

Sonia was a wonderful person. She was my commander in the underground in the ghetto, and we all loved and respected her. Her dedication and love of people, her strength and the example she set, her hard work and sacrifice were extraordinary.

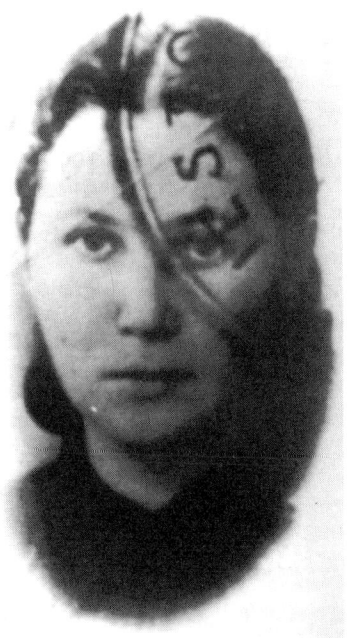

Sonia Madeisker

Motl Zeidl on leave during the War of Independence, with a neighbour's children

Vilna Liberated

Never say that there is only death for you
Though leaden skies may be concealing days of blue
Because the hour that we have hungered for is near
Beneath our tread the earth shall tremble: we are here
   Hirsch Glick, Hymn of the FPO, later the Song of all Jewish Partisans

In the summer of 1944, the Red Army had managed to push the Germans west more rapidly than we expected. On July 1, we received orders from the high command of the Brigade to start moving north from our base 45 kilometres south of Vilna. Meanwhile the Red Army was approaching Vilna from the east. The Russian armies facing the Germans on the Lithuanian front were led by Marshal Tcherniachovsky. Earlier, the Polish underground, the Armia Kraijova, which we referred to as the 'whites', had received orders from the Polish government in exile in London to try to enter Vilna so that the city would be liberated by Poles and not by Soviets; but at that stage the German garrison was still strong and they retaliated. The Poles lost hundreds of fighters and retreated to the villages. It was at this point that our brigade was ordered to take Vilna in co-ordination with the Red Army coming from the east.

We reached the outskirts of the city at the railway station thinking it was going to be simple, but the German bombardment was intense, and there were many casualties. The beautiful voice of the army spokesman, Levitan, announced on Radio Moscow, as every evening in those days, that Vilna had been taken. But we were a long from that!

The Red Army surrounded Vilna and moved towards Kaunas. We thought the airforce would bomb the German 'nests', but Tcherniachovsky declared: 'I am not going to bomb my own city; I won't destroy a single house.' Three days later, he had to shell the positions the Germans were defending with artillery, after reconnaissance conducted by the army and ourselves pinpointed the German strongholds. The next day thousands of Germans emerged waving white flags and were taken prisoner.

Most of us found nothing and nobody left in Vilna. Some individuals, or small groups of friends from the forests entered empty apartments and started to re-build a life. We were free, but morale was low. Memories were painful, the war had ruined everything, and our families were no more. The only thing to do was to try to find work to ensure some kind of existence. I started looking for a job in July 1944 and eventually found myself in the office of a military unit, headed by one Colonel Sabaitis in Kaunas. He was of Lithuanian origin, but was, in fact, a Russian colonel who dealt with ordnance.

At that time, many of us were mobilised into the Soviet army, since we were of military age and eligible for service. It was, after all, still wartime; yet the entire civil, military, and social fabric had to be restructured; everything was in ruins, there was no proper management, and they had to start all over again to re-establish a Soviet Lithuania with Lithuanians in key positions. There were, however, relatively few people left whom they could rely upon because so many had cooperated with the Germans and fled as soon as they were defeated; but there was a group who had held higher positions in partisan units and the Central Committee of the Party took them under its wing and used them to fill posts in the newly-structured government. When the authorities came across someone like me, who spoke Lithuanian, Russian, German, and some Polish, who had commanded a partisan battalion, they welcomed us with open arms, as people who could be trusted.

That's how I came to be in the office of Colonel Sabaitis in Kaunas, where I worked for a short time. He was in charge of office administration, partly civilian, partly military, and as his assistant he assigned me all kinds of tasks. There was plenty to do. The front had just passed, and we had to keep up with supplies.

Colonel Sabaitis always wrote instructions in red ink. One day I questioned the accuracy of what he had written since I did not feel his order complied with the regulations. He called me into his office. 'Sit down young man,' he said. I don't know exactly how old this colonel was, but at that time, he seemed like my grandfather. So I sat down. 'Young man,' he continued, 'when you walk down the street and you come across a row of telegraph poles in your way, what do you do? Do you climb over them or do you weave your way around them? You walk around them, right? Well it's the same way with regulations. If you don't work your way around them, you'll bang your head against them every time. Regulations are like telegraph poles – they're made for walking around. That's how life is – remember that.'

What I really wanted to do at that time was to return to Vilna, so I set about finding a way back. I called the headquarters of the ex-partisan movement, and spoke with a certain Philipavichus, the Lithuanian secretary general. He told me that heads of special departments at various ministries were needed and he instructed me to see the head of the Fifth department of the NKVD, in Vilna. I didn't know who he was or what the Fifth department was, but I trusted Philipavichus not to send me on a wild goose chase. So off I went, and there I was questioned. They checked up on where I came from, and who had sent me and eventually I was invited into an office where a middle-aged officer with piercing eyes and a wry smile asked me to sit down.

'I would like you to head the special department of one of the ministries,' he said and presented me with a choice of three. One was the Ministry of Industry, one the High Authority for Commerce, and one the High Authority of Building Materials. The High Authorities were smaller than the Ministries but had the same status. I was looking for the least important one after the ravages of the past few years, and seeking a Jewish name on the lists, I found a Mr Brunnas in charge of the High Authority for Building Materials, so that's the one I chose because it seemed the least demanding of the three.

At the age of 19, I took on this senior posting in the 'Spetz' department of a Higher Authority with great responsibility. My duties were the general supervision of manpower including negotiations with the Ministry of Defence for releasing our people from military service, which actually meant deferment for three to six months.

We were in a good bargaining position because, with everything in ruins, the roads, the factories, the bridges, all the buildings, that whole country was a sea of destruction, we needed engineers, technicians, etc. The army understood, of course, that for arms to be delivered to the front – the war was still very much in evidence – bridges and roads had to be repaired. To rebuild everything including the railway was a huge task – and it had to be done quickly. The army, however, needed their soldiers too – so it was a delicate balance.

There was another element to the job and this was the special mail. There was a system of delivering secret mail – what today would probably be called the diplomatic pouch. Certain channels existed between people in high places, who were trustworthy and reliable. There were strict rules about who could send such mail, and who could receive such documents and anyone entitled to this privilege was in a very strong position. They were automatically partners, witnesses to everything that was happening – mainly to other people. There were special regulations on how this mail was to be handled, closed, opened, who was entitled to carry it. Even here there were a few categories of secrecy. It was only many years later that I learned how instrumental this mail/phone system was in connecting a privileged group of people to build and keep the regime intact.

One day, through the special mail, I received a paper signed by Stalin, who was then head of the armed forces, stating that we could postpone military service to the 'end of the war'. This was the first mention of any end to that terrible war.

One day I had a call from the head of the Nationale Kommissariat for the Interior, the NKVD – as the Security Organisation was known before the so-called KGB was created. This senior official – a general, no less – asked me with some urgency to come to his office.

I was a little nervous at this stage because some of my friends, who belonged to various Zionist movements at that time, had decided to leave Russia. Having shared the experiences of the ghetto and the forests with me, they felt they could trust their old comrade, and they discussed their intentions openly. They felt their future in Lithuania was bleak – some had family and friends in Palestine and other places – and they were looking for possibilities of leaving the country. They asked me for assistance with travel documents. Since the war was still going on, civilian mobility was limited, no-one could move freely since military police were stationed at every crossing. If their personal papers had not been in order, they would have been instantly arrested. And who knows where they might have landed? So I provided them with documents to ease their movements and that was why I felt so apprehensive when I was summoned by the head of the NKVD.

Our meeting was fixed, and with mixed feelings, I set off with my Polish driver, Henrik, in an American jeep. 'Henrik,' I said to him in the car, 'I'm meeting the head of the NKVD this morning; if I'm not back in half-an-hour, go back to the Head Office and sound the alarm.'

I entered the building, a grand and beautiful edifice in the centre of Vilna; officials on the ground floor seemed to be expecting me and I was sent up to the appointed room. I knocked on the door, the general bade me enter, and greeted me effusively; for a few moments, we spoke about the situation on the front, about my work, about his office, and then he got down to business.

At that time, our Authority was dealing with all kinds of factories handling building materials: glass factories, brick factories, timber, cement, in short, anything to do with construction. These factories were spread all over the country and the management, the production, the general control and guidance were carried out by our engineers, who were constantly on the move and had to be armed. All kinds of undesirable characters were at large; German deserters, local bandits, and the like, and they would regularly attack people transporting important materials in strategic locations. There were also many Lithuanians who opposed the regime who had cooperated with the Germans, so our people had to carry arms to protect themselves against such situations, and to carry weapons they needed a permit from the NKVD.

On the general's desk sat a huge pile of files; 'Young man,' he said, 'I have here somewhere your request for arms, but I must tell you that your file is quite far down that pile. However, to help solve your difficulty, I have a proposal. You've got your dilemmas and I've got mine. My problem today is that here in the Ministry of the Interior, we have a huge number of people in jail. My prisons are overcrowded, conditions are bad; there are no windows, the glass has been blown out, doors are missing, we've been so badly shelled that these premises are totally exposed to the elements; and with winter approaching, this is a problem that must be resolved. Some of my prisoners are skilled workmen and can help to reconstruct these detention centres, but we just don't have the materials. So, let us be friends. You'll help me with the materials, and I'll help you with your permits. You have in your office my request for materials and I have here your requisition for the permits.'

Suddenly my file looked as though it would very soon surface to the top of the pile. Thus the deal was done. The general got his materials and I got my permits for arms for my staff.

What a system!? But a system it was.

Time to leave

> *Someone who is free can*
> *Get up and leave*
> *And someone who is free cannot*
> *Get up and leave.*
>
> Abba Kovner

I had been living with several friends from the partisans: Lena Zass, my girlfriend; Lena's mother; Chasia and her boyfriend; Dina and her friend Aron, and his brother. We shared an apartment and pooled our salaries from our different jobs, while Lena's mother ran the household. Food was scarce and heavily rationed. Someone I had known in Rokishkis, who had fought with the Lithuanian Brigade of the Soviet army, came back to Vilna and was in charge of food supplies to the military. He was ready to share and seeing that we lacked provisions, he did what he could to help.

What eventually persuaded me to leave Russia was probably a combination of two things. Lena told me that she, too, had decided to leave Vilna. She was one of Abba Kovner's group, the Zionist organisation, Hashomer Hazaïr. At the time Abba was collecting documents, and recovering and collating archive material for the Jewish Museum of Vilna where he worked with the writers and poets: Sutzkever and Katcherginsky. These were the last remnants of the cultural elite of Vilna.

One day, Vitka Kempner (later Kovner) came to thank me for helping their friends and asked how I would feel when Lena left Vilna with her mother. Then Abba tackled me: 'What kind of future do you think you will face here? All our friends have left and those who haven't yet are going very soon. You've got no family – more's the pity, why on earth do you want to stay?'

He came again and again, and slowly planted a doubt in my mind. Even so, my position was important, and if I left, I felt that I would betray not only the system and ideology but all those who had placed their trust in me.

Abba and Vitka continued to 'harass' me with the idea of leaving, and gradually the seed Abba had sown grew into a more positive notion, along with the fact that Lena was preparing to leave; until eventually, either in a moment of weakness, or perhaps strength, I gave in. For years afterwards I felt bad about it. It was not that I regretted the

Utopian ideology combined with the rotten implementation of all those idealistic theories, it was the people I felt I was betraying. And this sentiment haunted me especially later, in different circles, where people were surprised to see me, and asked what I was doing there. So, because of my communist past, I became a stranger in the Zionist world, and I felt I did not belong anywhere. Slowly things started to change and the warmth of old friends as well as the new ones I was lucky enough to make, gave me a new sense of purpose and belonging. When I later met my mother, who had survived the concentration camps, understanding her tragedy and seeing how happy she was that I had not stayed in the Soviet Union, helped ease my doubts and frustrations at leaving.

I left Vilna on January 17, 1945.

However, because of my position, I had to go to great lengths to make my departure look credible. I contacted Benik Levine, whom I had previously provided with travel papers. He had been a partisan with us in the forests, and was leaving before me, so I asked him to send me a cable when he reached Hungary or Romania saying that there were rumours that my mother was alive. In fact, I was convinced that she could not possibly have survived the concentration camp.

Benik Levine sent that cable, which was seen by my Minister. I had spoken with him about the possibility of going to that area to deal with affairs there and asked if he would agree to let me go on his behalf. We knew that there was a consignment of building materials delayed in the area of Kishenev on the Russian/Romanian border. Although the boss hesitated, when he read the cable, he gave his approval. Somehow that made my leaving the country more credible. I gave the Minister the keys of the safe where secret documents were kept, and I left.

In fact, the cable *was* fiction. I did not really know at that time whether my mother was alive or not. She was in fact still in the concentration camp at Stutthof. Later, I did find her alive in Bucharest. More precisely, she found me. I reached Bucharest on February 14, 1945, after an odyssey.

V

FROM VILNA TO PALESTINE

Heading south

I left Vilna with Lena Zass and Sanka Nissanelewicz. We travelled south via Lida, Kovel, and on to Lvov (Lemberg) where we were met by Zelda, Sanka's girlfriend who had gone on a mission ahead of us. It was a difficult journey even though I was travelling with official documents as Head of the Special Department of the Ministry, armed with my personal pistol. I wore civilian clothes, a heavy overcoat, leather boots, and a warm hat. Lithuania had been liberated half a year previously and with the Russian front advancing westwards, all railway stations were teeming with Russian troops. We travelled from station to station, mostly in cargo trains. Railroad traffic was heavy at that time and travel permits were required, and the military police checked everyone. Whenever Sanka saw a police officer approaching, he would face me, salute, click his heels, and shout: 'Comrade Nachalnik' ('Commander' – in Russian). Sanka was clad in the black leather overcoat of a Commissar and when they saw him saluting me like this, the military police hardly ever bothered to question either of us. In any case, we all had the official documents I had prepared, along with papers with our titles from the Partisan Administration testifying that we had fought with the partisans.

The plan was to go to Czernowitz and cross the Romanian border from there. As it happened, we could not get to Czernowitz because there had been an incident on the border and people had been arrested, so we decided to change direction and go back to Lvov, and from there to Lublin, Poland, where the new Polish government had started to re-establish itself. The battle for the liberation of Warsaw was still continuing.

Here I took leave of my past, dropped my identity documents, and left my little Mauser pistol that had accompanied me for all those years, meant to provide the means to commit suicide if you were captured.

From Lvov, we travelled via Pshemischl, a town on the border between the Soviet Union and Poland, where there was an amusing but potentially tricky incident. Our new documents were in the name of the Weinstein family. Sanka was the head of the family, I was his brother; Zelda (his girlfriend) was his wife, and Lena was his sister – we were all Weinsteins. Weinstein family. Sleeping accommodation of course was on the floor of the freight wagon as usual; the train was crossing the border at night, and since we knew that Sanka slept very soundly and it was impossible to wake him up, just before the Russian border police came to check the papers, I gave him a hard kick in the backside and said loudly 'Mr Weinstein, the police are here; they want to see your papers.' All Sanka did was roll over onto the other side and say sleepily 'Leave me alone – I'm not Weinstein.' Another kick, harder this time, and still he said 'Who's Weinstein?' In a fit of desperation as the police neared our wagon, I kicked him where it really hurt. That finally worked.

We arrived safely in Lublin, which had become a meeting point for the Jews who had survived the war, either in the underground movements in the ghettos, or with the partisans in the forests, or both. Some came back from Soviet Asia, mainly Polish or Eastern European youngsters who had escaped when war broke out, and joined the Red Army or others who had just survived as best they could in Asian Russia, either in Siberia or the southern republics of Kazakhstan and Kierghiesia. Moving back to the West, they had reached Lublin more or less at the same time as the first two groups. All were activists of various Zionist youth movements – they were not all that young, but they were rich in experience. Thus we all gathered on the fifth floor of Vishinskiego 58, where we lived in a kind of commune for about a month, and some even longer, two or three in a bed, eating from a common kitchen where food was scarce.

But we had spiritual nourishment. We shared our experiences; night and day, we told our extraordinary stories, each more dramatic, more moving, more incredible than the next. This was a unique group of people, intellectually, with a wonderful background of Jewish tales, culture, heritage, jokes and anecdotes. One learned more in those few weeks, than years and years studying at a university. This was the university of life.

Zvi Horovitz, for example, recited U.L. Perez's 'Bonsche Schweig'. Zvi was a tall slim character with long arms, long legs, long fingers, and piercing black eyes. Then there was the story Ben Meiri told when we all expressed our opinions about one thing or another and each thought he was right. This was the story of the cat who gave birth to four kittens. While the mother cat went in search of food for her young, the kittens, who had been born blind, suddenly gained their sight and the first thing their eyes focused on was a street lamp with four colours: The world is green, said one kitten; no it's red, said the next; it's yellow said the third; it's definitely blue said the last. They argued furiously, each declaring that the world was the colour she saw. Eventually three kittens died in the fight and only one remained when the mother came back with food. She asked where the other three were, and when she heard what had happened, she declared: 'What a mistake you made my little one. The world is neither red, nor green, nor yellow, nor blue. If you want, it can be all colours of the rainbow, it is just that each of us sees it his own way.'

All these people had spent their lives in Russia, they talked about the customs and habits of their different communities, about exile in Siberia, Soviet prison camps, disappointment with the communist regime; they told stories accompanied with bitter smiles about their expectations of the socialist movements, they had sincerely believed that those ideals should be implemented in Russia; about hunger, the tens of thousands imprisoned, the fighting and executions of masses of former communist leaders; about forced labour; about thousands freezing to death in Siberia. Those who came out of the forests spoke of fears, battles against the Germans, about friends who had been lost, about their families who had been exterminated. Each had his own story to tell and there were also lighter moments, when we told funny stories.

After we had shared our past experiences the group started to discuss where we should go from this point on. We knew relatively little about how many refugees there were altogether in Europe, where they were located, or how many more were yet to be liberated. We wondered whether our task was to find all remnants of all the communities that had been uprooted and then decide where and how to relocate them. Or should plans be made now to move south, to Palestine? How could what seemed (and then proved to be) like vast numbers of displaced persons be absorbed in Palestine when the British Mandate Authorities imposed an annual quota of 15,000 immigrants? And how many survived the concentration camps we were just starting to hear about? And the war was still going on. We talked, too, about the possibility of seeking vengeance on the German oppressors.

The stories and reports of the living skeletons who had barely survived were horrifying. Nothing was omitted from these discussions, and yet we were really operating in the dark.

Nevertheless I and two boys and two girls – Adam, David Blaustein and his wife, and Lena – were chosen to forge a channel from Poland to Romania, where we knew that representatives of the Jewish Authorities in Palestine had arrived – the aim being to direct Jews to Palestine. This was pioneering for what later became the mainstream of the Bricha ('flight') movement which branched out all over Europe. At its inception, the *schlichim* from Palestine were not yet on the scene. At the end of the war – in mid-1945 – the vast majority of Jews were concentrated in the American-occupied zones of Germany and Austria as well as in Italy, but our illegal movement continued to operate throughout the continent, through every possible port in Europe, whether in Bulgaria, Yugoslavia, Italy or France.

Ze'ev Rabinovich, known as Welvel, was the youngest one of us, a mere 16 years old, a dedicated and sensitive young man. He had been a partisan in the forests of Wolin, Eastern Poland, and he and a friend – both children during the war – were assigned the task of emptying live shells of gunpowder which were then used to blow up trains and bridges. This was probably the most dangerous job of all, and apart from experts, only young kids with their small nimble fingers could handle it. Welvel had been sent from Lublin to Bucharest to meet the Israeli *schlichim* and returned with information and money. Armed with the information he brought, the five of us left Lublin after tattooing numbers on our forearms.

For the first time we encountered people who had been liberated from the camps and had numbers tattooed on their arms. The tattooed number was, in fact, all these people had to prove that they had been incarcerated in the camps. We learned that, since they had no documents, they would go to the Russian police and show them their numbers; the Russians accepted this as identification and promptly provided them with a permit to return to their countries of origin. Among these camp survivors, we came across some Greeks who were returning south which was also our direction, and we decided to join them. None of us, of course, spoke the language, so we decided to speak Hebrew instead – after all, in those days, it was all Greek to them!

Mordechai Rosman – who was later the spiritual leader on the famous ship, *The Exodus*, was responsible for tattooing the number into my arm, in a very primitive way, using a needle and blue dye – not to mention the blood infection I ended up with. This 'cover' enabled us to cross borders without too many problems as we moved from Poland through Czechoslovakia, and Hungary into Romania. The journey was an arduous one, as we travelled either on foot, or by train, or scaling mountains, and we forged a route, appointing reliable people to cover future border-crossings for tens of thousands who eventually followed.

We encountered several awkward and embarrassing situations en route, one of which was rather amusing in a curious way. In Uschgorod, in Carpatho-Russe, we came across a feeding station for refugees and, since we were all hungry, we decided to enter. There we met survivors from the concentration camps and we somehow looked rather suspicious to them.

'Who are you?' they asked. 'Where do you come from?'

'We've been freed from Mauthausen – and now we're on our way home to Saloniki.'

'Oh yes?', they jeered, 'can you prove it?'

We rolled up our sleeves and showed them our 'numbers'. They took one look and suddenly exclaimed: 'You're spies! The whole lot of you.'

What happened was that, when we tattooed the numbers on our forearms, we had made the figures face the wrong way. The numbers were supposed to face outwards, while we, in our ignorance, had made them read inwards. We beat a hasty retreat from there as soon as we could.

Finally we reached Bucharest on February 14, 1945.

Bucharest

Huge groups of people were streaming into Bucharest every night, arriving by foot, horseback, car, or train, crossing the border stations – all of which were secured by our own people, or people we had appointed and compensated in various ways.

About two months later, some of the newcomers mentioned there were rumours in Poland that my mother was alive. It preoccupied me greatly because I heard it over and over again, but I did not dare believe it. Someone had probably made a mistake and it was now being spread.

Friends from the original group who were still in Lublin organising the exodus, gradually started moving to Bucharest. They arrived at the building at Maria Rosetti street where I was living and one evening, the door opened and in came my old pal Sanka, with Zelda, his girlfriend (later his wife), behind him. I embraced them both heartily – overjoyed that they had reached Bucharest from Lublin. We had been through a lot together and we were very close friends.

'Don't hug *us*, look who's right behind us.' And there she was! My dear mother, dressed in rags, in boots much too large for her. Everyone in that room, all fighters hardened by years of battle, combat, and the struggle for survival, had tears streaming down their faces. It was a rare occurrence in those times for someone to find their mother alive – and everyone in that room that evening cried, either with the emotion of the moment or with the thoughts and memories of their own mothers, or because of both.

So those rumours during the last few weeks were not empty rumours. Here she was in front of my eyes. We embraced each other and wept. Yet I knew what mother was thinking even though we were overcome with happiness, because I had the very same thoughts. Our hearts were with the other members of our family we would never see again – for we knew for sure that they were no longer alive. Mother knew more than I about the fate of Ephraim who had met his end in Estonia, and I knew more about Zvi who fell fighting in the army in Russia. We did not then know any details, but we did know the basic facts.

The last time I had seen my mother was during the final days of liquidation of the Vilna Ghetto. When we entered the sewers in retreat to the forests with the last of the underground members, we were forbidden to take family members. That meant not taking my mother or my younger brother, and that also meant they would be going to their death, while I was going somewhere, certainly not promising, but unknown. Parting from your mother and leaving her to her fate has elements of betrayal. Though I was not the only one to leave dear ones behind, this is not a collective issue; it is individual and personal and lonely. I was alone with my sentiments, my thoughts; alone with my conscience; and when we did meet again, I did not know at first whether I could withstand the pain of my conscience. That, too, is very individual.

And then mother said quietly: 'Couldn't Ephraim have lived?' She had of course forgotten what happened at the end of July 1943, when the head of the underground movement had surrendered to the Gestapo, the ghetto population demanding it after the Germans threatened to liquidate the ghetto if he did not give himself up. When I was caught as a hostage with the other seven members and beaten, and my identity was exposed, she had implored me not to bring Ephraim into the underground, hoping that the ghetto might allow some chance to survive the German occupation. She did not remember this and I did not want to remind her. I took it as a quiet reproach, and I did not mind bearing it along with my other transgressions.

I learned how mother had found her way to me. After Stutthof concentration camp was liberated by the Russian army, she managed to reach Warsaw, where she met Nusia Lubotsky. The Lubotskys had lived in the same room as our family in the Vilna Ghetto and later Nusia fought with me in the Rudnitski forests in the same partisan battalion. She, of course, knew my mother and she knew, too, that I had survived and was working with the Bricha movement. From that moment on, mother was connected with our people in Poland, who led her to our reunion in Bucharest.

Remnants of our people

Poland at that time, in late spring/early summer of 1945, was overflowing with Jews who had been liberated from the concentration camps, and repatriates from Russia and Eastern Europe uprooted from their homes, all searching for what was left of their families, all broken spirits, disillusioned and discouraged by the years of war, homeless and abandoned, not daring to return to their homes; or if they did, finding nothing but ghosts and cemeteries.

Clinging to small vestiges of hope that they might find somebody alive, a certain panic erupted as Jews drifted south by the thousands, realising that the only solution was a Jewish State. Some believed this out of conviction, while others thought that their countries' leaders had let them down, failed to protect them, even abandoned them, and maybe even wanted to get rid of them. After all, pogroms were still in vogue in places like Kielce. Here, a young Polish Christian child disappeared, and rumours were spread that the Jews had slaughtered the child because it was Pesach (Passover), and his blood used for baking matzos. This is the notorious blood libel story which was so often used against Jews as an excuse for pogroms. Forty-two Jews were slaughtered at Kielce, and many more severely wounded.

This flight to Romania, the southernmost state in Europe bordering the Mediterranean, meant that they all hoped that at this point, they were on their way to Palestine. Vast numbers of people congregated there and the Romanian authorities would have been happy to get rid of them. The problem now was not leaving the country, but getting a permit to enter a country that was not prepared to accept refugees. Under the British mandate, Palestine enjoyed a quota of 15,000 immigrants and, given the number of displaced persons in post-Holocaust Europe, that quota was quickly filled. The Haganah, Etzel and Lechi – terrorists, as the British called them – all launched attacks against the British, which gradually became more frequent and more extreme. Illegal immigrant boats constantly attempted to reach the shores of Palestine, and each time the British authorities reacted with defiance.

In Bucharest, we began setting up an infrastructure and planning a course of action. After the Holocaust, the survivors obviously could not return to their former lives. They were fed up with the political games that split the Jewish people into so many fragments. Although the *shlichim* from Palestine who were active in the newly liberated Europe brought along the political splits prevailing in Palestine, those in Europe tended to be united and came to Palestine as a united movement, and in the summer of 1945, led by such people as Abba Kovner and Lidowsky that movement assumed the name Hativa – meaning 'Unity'.

But our group was also divided, caught between our devotion to the unity of the remnant survivors, a utopian ideal, and our tacit objective of not leaving Europe before an accounting for the crimes committed by the German people against the Jews.

Abba Kovner, who arrived in Bucharest after us, told me that they had decided in Lublin to mobilise a select group of volunteers to remain in Europe, and if possible and necessary, go back to Germany to seek out Germans, the perpetrators of all the injustices we had witnessed and were now learning more and more about every day. A plan for a vengeance operation had been crystallised. This was the nucleus of the future Avengers. Abba, Vitka, Pasha Reichman (today – Avidov), Dorka, his wife, and I went to Northern Italy to meet with the Palestine Jewish Brigade. (Chaim Lazar and his wife, who were not part of the vengeance group also accompanied us.) We went by train from Bucharest on yet another arduous journey, via Hungary and Austria, travelling in overcrowded trains which were stopped frequently by Russian soldiers who grabbed whatever they could; they would push passengers off the roof, throw them out of the windows, and steal their suitcases; they were drunk, aggressive and angry. We reached Austria, and passed through Graz, crossing the border between the Russian and British occupied sectors. We walked two at a time, I went with Abba. The Russian soldiers demanded our watches – Russians always wanted watches. We had to hand them over. Once the Russian soldiers were far behind us, Abba turned and spat at them. Although I was Abba's close friend and we were ideologically close, too, I remember feeling shocked, even offended, that he had reacted that way towards Russian soldiers.

The Jewish Brigade – a historic meeting

If we believe a thing to be bad, and we have a right to prevent it, it is our duty to try to prevent it and to damn the consequences
                                                            Alfred Lord Milner

Finally, we reached Ponteba, high in the mountains above Tarvisio on the border of triangle formed by Italy, Austria and Yugoslavia, where the Palestinian Jewish Brigade were stationed.

The creation of the Palestinian Jewish Brigade was the result of a long struggle by the Jews in Palestine to have a military force of their own, a symbol of Jewish participation in the battle against Germany. The struggle was led by Moshe Sharet, head of the political department of the Jewish Agency, later Minister of Foreign Affairs, then Prime Minister of Israel. The Brigade was manned by army officers headed by a British Jew, Brigadier General Benjamin. But the Brigade was composed of volunteers, many of whom were politically-minded soldiers of all ranks, including high ranking officers of the Haganah, the defence organisation of the Jewish Agency. Their aim had been multi-faceted: first to fight the Germans, but also to assist Jews in Europe who had escaped German persecution and in the long-run to create a structure for future mass immigration to Palestine. Part of their function was entirely genuine, while the other side could have been interpreted as not entirely *bona fide* from the British point-of-view.

In our discussions with the leadership of the Brigade, priorities were inevitably different. For us, who regrettably had first-hand experience of German oppression, the aspect of vengeance was urgent and we felt passionately that this was our prime task. We believed that, whatever happened after the war, the most important task was to show the world the atrocities inflicted on the Jewish people, that the unprecedented scale of these crimes had to be avenged at all costs, and that it was the Jews who should carry out that vengeance. If they didn't, no-one would. In those early days we believed that that was the only reason we had survived.

We did not overlook the importance of immigration to Palestine, nor did we deny the importance of the creation of the Jewish State. After all, we had started the Bricha even when war was still on and no envoys had yet come from Palestine. Yet we knew our commitment towards the memory of those who had perished could not be understood by those who did not personally witness and live through those times. We were torn between two strong emotions: the memory of the past and building the future.

The Palestinian envoys, the Haganah, and the Jewish Brigade wanted the illegal emigration to continue, and we decided that we could provide some services, but the Brigade and the Haganah were clearly able to take over that function, while vengeance naturally fell to our lot. We chose to go back underground and try to fulfil what we thought was our duty.

Individually, some of the leaders of the Brigade were on our side emotionally; but many others were determined to follow the policy of the Jewish Agency, mainly Ben-Gurion, namely, the rescue of Jewish refugees, the acceleration and increase of immigration to strengthen the Jewish presence in Palestine. The goal of hastening the birth of a Jewish State came first and foremost; everything else; they believed, would follow.

Nevertheless we were welcomed eagerly and emotionally in Ponteba. It was an historical meeting of the remnants of the partisans and ghetto fighters with the armed force created by the Jewish community in Eretz Israel. Suddenly, after those terrible and solitary years, we felt as if we belonged. Those who did support our plans helped in every way: with communications, transportation, information, directions. We stayed there a few months, travelling to Austria and Germany (which were occupied by the four allied powers – the USA, the Soviet Union, Britain, and France) in groups of two or three, over the mountains, on foot, by car, into villages, and small towns – using all manner of documents; we wore British uniforms, although if anyone had spoken to us in English, we would have been stuck for words. The objective of these reconnaissance missions was to investigate concentrations of SS officers in the prisoners-of-war camps, to see what was happening, to discover the political inclinations of the super-powers. It was there that we really learned about the Nazi concentration camps, for in the forests, or even after the liberation, although we knew about conditions in the ghettos, we knew little about the camps. Only when they were liberated by the Russians, the British, and the Americans in April/May 1945, did we learn the terrible truth.

Then we split into groups, each acting on its own; our targets were sites near concentration camps or which symbolised the Nazi regime including Berlin, Weimar, Hamburg and Nuremberg. While headquarters was in Munich, the whole operation was conducted from Paris.

I was appointed to lead the Nuremberg group. Nuremberg was the city of the 'Reichsparteitage' (the Nazi rallies addressed by Adolf Hitler). It was the city identified with the racially discriminatory laws introduced by Alfred Rosenberg – 'the mastermind of the Laws of Nuremberg'. He was sentenced to death and hanged in 1946 as one of the prime-movers of the Nazi-state.

The Reckoning

'... Burning for burning, wound for wound, stripe for stripe'
Exodus 21.23

We finally left Ponteba in Northern Italy on September 7, 1945, and crossed the border into Villach in Austria the same night. There were all kinds of borders – the national borders and the allied borders – from the British Zone to the French Zone, and from there to the American, and then from Austria into Germany.

At one of the borders I lost the diary I had kept – it was neither the first time nor the last that I had lost something valuable – but it was a pity because I described the atmosphere at the time and it was probably quite interesting.

I set off with Manik for Nuremberg. We boarded a train and eventually got there; it had been bombed to the ground. We looked for a hotel and by pure chance came across the Jewish community, where we obtained vouchers for food and a permit to stay overnight. The next day we moved to Fürth, a small town next to Nuremberg, which was almost untouched by the bombing. After obtaining a permit to stay there, we found a room and moved in. On Saturday morning we decided to go to the synagogue; we stood in the street amazed at the American Jewish soldiers who came to the synagogue – by car! Smoking! Not that we East European Jewish boys were that religious, but we were not used to people driving to synagogue and we could certainly not understand them smoking there. As we walked into the courtyard of the synagogue, we realised that it was not so much a synagogue, as a market where people could trade – for the locals had nothing.

Manik and I set up 'home' in one room and gradually became less nervous, as we found our bearings. But at night it was hard to sleep. We knew why we had been sent to Nuremberg, but how were we to start the project? We chatted for hours throughout the night about how to fulfil our mission.

Manik was an efficient and high-spirited young man, able to get out of any intricate situation. I never knew how he did, but we communicated and worked together very well. It was only years later that he told me about his experiences.

Manik's tale: a leap from the train

I was born in 1926 in Poland, in a town close to the German border, where the majority of the population was Jewish. The area had been under German rule until 1918 and so many people spoke German. Our home was a traditional one and my parents were landowning business people. Both my sisters and an older brother were active in a Zionist youth movement, and I was about to join the same organisation but my other brother was seven years younger than I and still playing in the yard.

When the war was declared on Friday, September 1, 1939, I was thirteen years old. The Polish army retreated neatly, but very quickly, and a stifling silence filled the air. Three days later, the German army marched in and our land was immediately annexed by the Third Reich. A week later, the Great Synagogue was burned down and so were the surrounding densely populated Jewish quarters.

At the same time, they started their scourge. Bread was rationed, Jews were no longer permitted into the streets without a yellow J (for *Jude*) sewn onto their clothing, there were curfews at nightfall, there was a separate car for Jews on the trains, and Jewish-owned shops were closed.

Men went to work in large companies. Those who were important to the German economy had a better chance of survival and so the community leadership encouraged young people to go to work in labour camps inside Germany. This situation continued throughout 1940–41 until the middle of 1942.

The Poles had hated the Germans for many generations. We joined the Poles in hoping for a speedy German defeat, but the Poles also fervently desired to rid Poland of the Jews. This was seen in their quiet acquiescence to the Germans' attitude towards the Jews. The Jews, therefore, could find no escape or any refuge in this vast country, and thus they were trapped.

By now, I was 15 or 16 years. Occasionally, I would remove the 'J' from my sleeve and walk freely around the streets, which was, of course, strictly forbidden. Even so, I was frightened because the Poles could smell a Jew from a distance. One day, I tinted my hair blond and started travelling around on trains; somehow this gave me a false sense of security – I felt convinced that no-one could identify me.

In the autumn of 1942, Jews were arrested and taken to a certain place, which we later came to know as Auschwitz. Bit by bit, the Jewish population dwindled.

By the end of 1942 the Germans had selected an area for the ghetto at the far end of a poor neighbourhood, and the transfer of the Jewish population into their new quarters was carried out in an orderly way, over a period of a few weeks. The Germans were in no hurry at this stage.

Around this time, the Germans caught my father doing business with a Pole, and they ordered him to report to the police next morning. It was clear that he would never return, and so our entire family decided to go into hiding immediately. We knew from similar cases that the Germans would force the Jewish people to seek us out. We split up and hid in different places, and my older brother kept in touch with all of us, adopting different disguises each time: usually he came dressed as a woman, bringing us news of what was happening outside.

I then became terribly ill and with a deadly typhus! One day, I fainted in a narrow street, and luckily the people around who witnessed my collapse realised that I was in grave danger, and notified some of my friends. Four of them appeared with an empty coffin, put me inside it, and carried me into the mortuary of the Jewish hospital, which was still operating. From there, I was transferred to one of the hospital departments so I could not be identified by the Jewish police. The head of the hospital knew exactly what was going on and thanks to an aunt of mine, who was working as a nurse there, and a few dedicated doctors (who probably also knew my identity), I was nursed back to health, and survived what would have been a fatal illness.

Physically weak, I returned to the ghetto, where all the Jews had been moved. The town was now *Judenrein* and Poles were not allowed into the ghetto. We had fewer potatoes than ever and gradually hunger started to bite.

The Jewish leadership collapsed – it no longer functioned in any meaningful way and the end was clearly in sight. Even so, there was no sense of panic. It was as if everyone quietly and unquestioningly accepted the situation, and even the Jewish police stopped looking for or showing interest in us.

So we came out of hiding. It was the beginning of summer 1943 – a time of total disintegration. In spite of all this, we were happy that the whole family was now together. My heart aches when I think of our mother, who lived for every day she could shower us with her warmth.

We all knew that the ghetto was facing its end, our being together was like lovers before parting.

And yet, there were many Jews who left every morning for work and came back in the evening to their families. There were rumours that the Jews in Hungary were still living in their own homes: it looked as if there was no immediate danger there and that Hungary was a safe place to be.

The route from Poland to Hungary was through Czechoslovakia. Without telling anyone, I decided to try to make it there. With my blond and blue-eyed friend, Schmulik Grunner, who carried false aryan papers, we went to the railway station (carefully concealing the J on our clothing), and bought tickets for a town on the Czech border. We sat in the train with Polish men and women talking about this and that and they did not suspect us for a minute. We felt safe. Inside, meanwhile, my heart was breaking. Here we were on this beautiful summer day, watching the rolling countryside outside, as if on an outing, while my family was back in the ghetto. The scenery changed, and all I could think of was my mother, my brother, my father, my sisters.

When we arrived in Ziviecz, we decided to go away from the border, towards the mountains. The idea was to find out what was happening there. We pretended to be students on holiday, sleeping and eating with the local peasants, and helping on the farm in payment. We were good-looking boys and in the evening, I remember, the girls asked us to come out dancing with them. Yet we children of Moses could not risk embarking on such adventures!

From the local farmers, we learned where the border was, and next morning we made our way there. Veering off the main path, we eventually reached a clearing in the forest, with a sign reading: 'This is the border'.

We lay down, and watched for any kind of activity. At a certain moment, we got up, and ran! Suddenly, we were in Czechoslovakia. After half an hour, we returned to Poland, and to our Polish farmers, pleased with ourselves for achieving this feat. We could easily have gone through Czechoslovakia, and on to Hungary, or we could have found regular work with our local farmer friends.

But that night, we decided to return to the ghetto.

I do not remember why exactly. I think we were mainly homesick and wanted to tell everyone that we had found a way out. I simply couldn't leave my family alone. After being away for more than two weeks, we reached the ghetto late at night on July 31, 1943, and my mother never asked us a thing.

The situation there had not changed and I went to sleep with a friend that night, planning to tell the family and our friends the next day about the path to the border we had found. But next morning, the noise of engines, screams and shouting woke us. My friend's house was at the far end of the ghetto bordering wheat fields that were just ripe for harvesting. We realised immediately that the ghetto was surrounded by Germans, and so, pursued by automatic fire, we ran straight into the wheatfields to hide. My friend was badly wounded and I dragged him back into his house, where he died in my arms.

At eight o'clock the next morning, loudspeakers ordered all Jews in the ghetto to assemble in the central square. Everybody was to take only personal belongings.

I could not reach my parents because the SS were ordering everyone about and we were not allowed to leave our columns. There were hundreds of people, including my brother, who had become one of the leaders of the underground movement.

Once the Germans had rounded up a certain number of Jews, we were taken off to the railway station and herded onto cattle trucks. To the screams of the women and children, the train pulled out of the station. We understood that the destination was Auschwitz, some 60 or 70 kilometres from our town – a journey of two hours or so. Someone must have tampered with the little window in the upper part of the wagon, because the Germans, fearing an escape, opened fire and bombarded the opening with shots. Many were instantly killed, others were wounded, including me. I was caught in my right ribs, though I was lucky that the bullet did not penetrate deeply. On the floor next to me was the wife of the head of the Jewish ghetto police. A bullet, or perhaps several, had passed through both her legs and as she lay dying a peaceful smiled passed across her face.

The train jolted to stop. We had arrived in Auschwitz. The doors were opened, and the SS shoved us out with their rifle butts, shouting orders. Everything had to be done quickly. We carried out the corpse of our neighbour and laid her on the platform. In front of us, people in striped clothing came rushing towards us. We understood that these were the prisoners. They were doing their jobs, running. All the time running. Everyone was running. They emptied the wagons of bodies, helped the wounded to get out, and put their belongings into carts.

These prisoners, Jews, and the rows of barracks were a sign for us, confirmation, that life did exist here.

The SS officer arrived with an entourage and stood in the middle of the platform. SS soldiers were positioned between us and the officer, creating a narrow passage for only one person. Other SS men started to push us towards the officer – one at a time. With one finger he would direct each of us, either to right or to the left.

We did not know then, but we know now, that this was Mengele.

Soon, two groups were created. On one side, the elderly, women over 30, and children; on the other, younger men and women who looked strong and healthy. I remember how the officer looked at me. I remember the look in his eyes as I walked towards him. It was my good fortune that he did not smell my wound, and he directed me towards the younger group.

When the selection was over, they marched us away. We never saw the others again. I realised with a heavy heart, that my mother, with my little brother and maybe also my father, when they arrived the next day, would also be directed to that group. In the meantime, we were taken into a huge hall where we were instructed to strip. Was this the end?

My brother managed to hide his pistol under the floorboards. Inside the great hall we could see many of the earlier prisoners dressed in striped clothing running about doing everything. Some shaved our heads, some distributed clothing and the task of yet others was to tattoo our arms with a number. This was our new identity card.

When it was dark, we were taken to a huge transit camp, where we were placed in barracks close to the crematorium. We could not actually see it from our barracks but at night fire would light up the entire sky and cast shadows everywhere. Kazetnik called Auschwitz 'a different planet', and that's exactly what it was. A village of camps for men and a separate one for women, with no communication between the two, and a separate camp for the gypsies, who lived together with their families. They were all surrounded by an electrified fence, with armed guards in towers every few metres. There was no way out of this place.

My brother was four years older than I and a very close relationship developed between us. We were the only survivors of our family and I became my brother's follower. He was full of resourcefulness, and never stopped thinking of escape in spite of the fact that this was wild fantasy.

From time to time, people were taken out of our transit camp and sent to labour camps. One day, my brother and I were selected for one of these camps. We were shoved onto lorries, some 500 people or so, and taken to a new site. We were delighted, since nothing could have been worse than Auschwitz-Birkenau. In contrast to Auschwitz, these dozen or so barracks had probably been built before the war, for human purposes. They had separate rooms and windows. Yes, windows!

Through the windows we could see villages, fields, all covered in snow, and occasionally someone on a bicycle, or a horse drawn cart would trundle by, or people on foot from the village would pass by just ten metres away. And there were women. We had not seen women for a long time and such sights returned us to life. I could once again sense the smell of soil, the smell of life, but still the barbed wire, and soldiers of the SS separated me from it. I forced myself to forget about the guards around us and every such thought was a source of strength. Here in this camp I did believe in, and started to crave, an opportunity of escape.

There were about 500 of us. A third were put to work in a coal mine, another third were sent to the construction site of a new mine linked to the old one, and the rest worked on erecting buildings which we were told were for us! The German head of the entire project probably saw in us a vital workforce and this was evident from the larger food rations we received.

The head of the camp, a low-grade SS officer, cared very much about what was happening inside the camp. He had been a political prisoner, a former aryan communist, an anti-Nazi, by the name of Ludwig Wörl. The rumour was that he had been in charge of a huge concentration camp and on several occasions did what he could to save many Jews from the various selections. One day they caught him at it and he was immediately demoted to manage a smaller camp. It was our good fortune that it was in this camp that we landed up. Wörl was a man in his forties, heavily built, with lots of hair, large, blue, warm, piercing eyes. He was the one who organised the prisoners, appointing people to different tasks, and he would say: 'Let's get through this together. At a critical moment, we'll fight.'

Ludwig Wörl was recognised by the State of Israel as a Righteous Gentile for having saved the lives of Jews inside the camps in which he was active.

The days passed by and as they did so, I started to believe that perhaps it was after all possible to escape. But where to?

We were waiting for the Soviet Front to come nearer and that finally happened in January 1945. The Soviet armies broke through the German Front from Warsaw westwards, some 400 kilometres from our camp, and we could sense the nervousness among the SS.

On the afternoon of January 16, we were called to an *appel*. The camp commandant announced that we were to leave the compound in a few hours, that the bread store was open and that everyone could take as many loaves as he could carry. As soon as night fell, we were marched out in one long column, surrounded by SS soldiers and dogs.

This was the beginning of one of those death marches which went on all over Nazi Europe until the end of the war on May 8, 1945. Only very few survived the ordeal.

We were made to march through the night in a westerly direction, to distance ourselves from the Soviets. In the morning, we continued, worn out. Snow would stick to the wooden soles of our shoes which made walking very strenuous. Many who had taken quantities of bread started to throw them down, since they could no longer bear the additional burden of carrying the bread, and we were forbidden to stop marching. Those who could no longer make it were shot. Next evening, we reached a huge camp; and we knew that we were close to the town of Glaiwitz. It was there that many thousands of prisoners from all the other camps were being rounded together. Absolute chaos reigned that night. Glaiwitz is 70 kilometres from the town where I was born.

My brother, our friend Weinberg and I decided not to continue.

Next morning, as the SS took the prisoners to the train stationed outside the camp, we managed to find a large storehouse of some 5,000 square metres or so, filled from floor to ceiling with potatoes. We dived into the potatoes. As we listened to the shouting coming from the camp, the sounds gradually faded, and eventually it fell silent. We understood that everyone had left and the camp was now empty. We waited until night fell. Our plan was somehow to get out of the camp next day, and move eastwards in the direction of the Front.

To our great surprise, that evening, after a few hours, we started once again to hear voices coming from the camp, and to our even greater surprise, we heard them calling for Weinberg, my brother and myself. It turned out to be friends of ours who had known of our plans, and they told us that they had been loaded onto the train but the train had not been given permission to leave and so they had all returned to the camp.

Next morning, they pushed us all into a cargo train with open wagons which was normally used for transporting coal. There were so many of us in these wagons that we had to stand, for hours we could not move at all. When night fell, the rain started to roll. There were SS soldiers armed with machine guns in every third wagon, standing higher than everyone else, so that they could watch over all the prisoners. The three of us had already decided that we would jump from the train when it was dark, so when we got into the truck, we positioned ourselves close to the side, as far away as possible from the guard.

The plan was that at a certain moment we would lean over the edge, place our feet on the buffers between our truck and the next, and from there, jump. It was going to be a problem, because the buffers were constantly moving and the buffers being in the middle of the wagons, meant it was going to require a huge leap off the train.

At five minutes after midnight, we passed a railway station with an illuminated clock, and decided this was it. The prisoners were sleeping standing up, and we hoped the SS guards were doing the same. In the distance, we saw a forest parallel with the rail-line and we agreed that that's where the three of us would meet.

Weinberg moved over the side of the wagon first, disappeared between the wagons, and jumped. Two minutes later, I embraced my brother and he jumped. And then it was my turn.

I manoeuvred myself over the side of the wagon and stood on the buffers which were moving as if in the midst of an earthquake. I waited for a second, and was ready to jump when, to my delight, I spotted a little ledge the size of a cigarette box with a handle next to it. I leant down, as near as I could to catch the handle, put my foot on the ledge and then I jumped as far as I could, landing with my full weight in a ditch full of snow. The leap was not all that successful – lack of experience! – and I was suddenly aware of a sensation of heat, as blood streamed from my nose. I lay in the ditch until the whole length of the train passed me by and inwardly waved goodbye to my friends. Then I ran towards the forest. I was free! There the three of us met, embraced once another but – we were still on German territory.

We stayed in the forest for about two weeks, not without great tension, witnessing how the Front passed us by as the Germans retreated in confusion. Then we met the Soviet tanks charging into Germany with the Russian soldiers lying on the tanks as if stuck to them like leeches.

From there we made our way on foot to our home town which was already in the hands of the Soviet liberators and Polish communists. We were full of pride that we had survived as we witnessed the defeat of the Third Reich. And yet, our town was devoid of Jews. We looked into the homes where we had left our dear ones, while the cold eyes of strangers looked down on us from the windows – surprised that we were alive. Every house held a memory for each of us. From the same windows, only a year and a half ago, Jewish eyes had been looking down. The Poles were worried that we would force them to vacate our apartments, but no such thoughts ever crossed our minds.

One of our people went to Krakow to see if there were any Jews there, and when he returned he informed us that a core of Jewish leadership had been established in Lublin, and that this body had resolved that all Jews would leave Poland for ever.

The Jews who had survived had started to move towards Romania and from there, to the land of Israel. We decided to join them.

We reached Bucharest in March 1945, where we were placed in a multi-storey house on the Vittorolui Street, which served as a kibbutz, in preparation for Palestine. The majority of people there were partisans and ghetto fighters.

It was still wartime, but Bucharest at this time was a hectic city, full of life, restaurants, cinemas. The streets were full of people. Here in spring, peace and tranquillity prevailed; there was no longer a threat of persecution and I was on my way to a new life in the land of Israel.

And yet, here I started to feel uncomfortable with myself.

The tranquillity and the thought of my future life – a normal one, which I felt would have awaited me in Israel – disturbed me.

I felt as though I was having to jump from one important stage of my life to another without filling the gap.

Maybe, I thought, my sisters are still alive, and maybe they are still on a death-march, and here am I, ready to depart overseas. The Nazi regime is collapsing and I won't be here to witness its defeat. Am I ready to forget and disconnect myself from all this and start a new life? I would wake at night full of despair, bathed in sweat. I decided that I was in the wrong place: I should be in Germany and not in Bucharest.

I did not share my thoughts with my friends, but tried to get used to the idea that I would have to separate myself from them: they were, after all, almost like my family. Once I had decided not to continue with the others to Palestine, I was liberated from all the tension with which I had been consumed. I began to enjoy movies, spring time, walking in the streets, and to appreciate my new found freedom. A week or two weeks would make no difference.

During this period, Abba Kovner crossed my path. Was it a coincidence? We talked for a while, and then I remember sitting in a room, probably a day or so after our chance meeting, when he told me about a group of people being organised for a certain purpose: he asked me to join him.

I did not for a moment hesitate to attach myself to this group.

My reckoning with the Germans, and maybe with myself, was opened anew.

Only one and a half months had passed between the time Manik had jumped from the train and my first meeting him.

Crime and Punishment

Back now to Fürth. First we had to settle all the practical and legal problems of local registration and establish the right to stay in Germany, then we had to rent more 'appropriate' rooms for all the people we planned to bring in later; finally we started to look into which 'sites' should be targeted and how these should be tackled.

'Appropriate' rooms meant 'secure' rooms, at the end of a corridor, or preferably with a separate entrance, but certainly something with an outside window – nothing too internal. We needed to find buildings with landlords who were well disposed towards us, preferably older people – that is, those who had not been recently directly involved in the war. We wanted no discussions, no questions. Parents were waiting for their sons to come home from the Front, women were expecting their husbands, children their fathers. Everything was political in those days: the Germans could not accept that they had lost the war – after all, they had been the conquerors – the victors – for the last ten years. Were their 'heroes' still alive, imprisoned, and if so – where were they? Were they in those SS camps?

With so much destruction everywhere, rooms to let were at a premium. To find them, you had to go to the *Haus Amt* where they had a list of locations to choose from; but before you could obtain such a list, as foreigners, you had to provide proof of status. Our papers indicated that we were foreigners in transit, waiting for a visa to emigrate, and so we were legal.

Manik and I were the first to establish ourselves in Fürth. Since the locals were short of provisions, and to keep them sweet, we would supplement their rations by giving them alcohol, cigarettes, chocolate, all the luxuries they could not afford. This was no problem for us since we had the means to obtain goods of all kinds from the American military canteens. From time to time our landlords and landladies became suspicious about this, but since we were posing as foreigners, they assumed we had our own channels.

We were posing as Poles who had been brought to work for the Germans during the war years and were now waiting either to return home or to go to the United States or Canada. Chatting with our landlady, we could sense her deep-rooted anti-Semitism – she of course had no idea that we were Jewish, probably did not even think any Jews survived. I pretended to be the son of a high class aristocratic Polish family. I had to explain it that way because the handwritten identity document given to me in Italy bore a Jewish-Russian family name. The first name was Chaim and the CH were written close together making it look like an M, so I said it was MAIM. When she asked me, suspiciously, where the name Chaim came from, I corrected her by saying it was Maim – the well-known Polish aristocratic knight. I never knew whether she accepted this explanation, but it sounded good.

Occasionally, to pass the time, I would go to a football match, where the Germans stood around smoking the most disgusting tobacco. The stench from these 'weeds' was so unbearable that I found myself chucking American cigarettes in the air for the locals to smoke, just so I wouldn't have to inhale the ghastly stink of their cigarettes. How quickly the 'good life' can spoil you: the tobacco I smoked in the Forests of Rudnitski was much worse.

For the first four or five months in Fürth, our preparations were focused on Project A: the infiltration of toxins into the city water supply. The first task was to place an expert inside the water filtration company. For this we needed a good-looking, German-speaking person, who understood engineering. For this mission, I chose a young man from Krakow, where most of the young people spoke a good German. He was tall and handsome, with a smiling face and curly blond hair – a real Aryan-looking type. Above all, he was an accomplished engineer and with our assistance, obtained a job at the water filtration centre of Nuremberg. We had researched the employment system and knew exactly what was required and as a result, the technicalities and formalities were promptly completed. His name was Willek (otherwise known as Ze'ev), but we called him the 'water man'.

As with Manik, it was only many years later that I learned about his family background.

Willek was born in 1922, to a poor family in Krakow; his father and older brother had been bootmakers, while his grandfather before them had been a rabbi. Willek went to a Polish primary school and then learned heating and plumbing at a vocational school. Highly intelligent, he was also dyslexic, although he did not know it, but above all, according to his widow today, he painted exquisitely.

In the ghetto of Krakow, Willek had been incarcerated at nights, but during the day, he had been made to work in the prison garage. There he and his mates collected all kinds of spare parts of old cars and eventually managed to assemble a radio set on which they listened eagerly to the BBC to learn what was going on in the outside world. By 1944/45, they were able to track the advance of the Soviet army. As they did so, they sensed the nervousness of their German captors, and since they knew exactly what fate awaited them, decided to escape at the first possible opportunity. One day, the prisoners were called to an *appel* during which, by sheer chance, there was a bomb alert. As the wardens ran to the shelters for cover, they left everyone to their own fate. This was Willek's chance of escape, and he and his friends very quickly found a place to hide: a local greenhouse, which not only gave them shelter, but provided them with vegetables, water and heat!

Willek's parents were killed by the Germans as was his brother, sister-in-law and their child. Willek himself eventually reached Bucharest together with other survivors of the Krakow underground movement.

Many years later Willek married Lucia, a survivor of Auschwitz, whose mother perished in Bergen-Belsen, her father in Mauthausen and her brother in Lvov.

When Willek came to join my group, we had to find room for him and Mira, who acted as liaison officer for the whole group. Mira was responsible for organising all our supplies and it was she who 'disciplined' us. One day, I picked up Mira to accompany me to a meeting in Munich; she had been a close friend of ours in the underground in the ghetto, and later in the forests. The train station was quite a way and we had to carry our luggage, so even before we reached the station we were tired. Transportation was difficult in those days, nothing ran on time – not the so-called efficient Germany. We boarded a freight train that stopped often and took several hours to reach Augsburg. There we changed to a passenger train, where our fellow passengers were Germans, men and women, the men having recently returned from the war. Two of them had been released from an SS camp. They were telling one another how their units had fought the Soviets; you could see how brave they thought they were, how honourable they felt when they told their stories of blocking the Soviet advance at the Front.

The German women were smoking American cigarettes, eating American chocolate, and complaining how hard their lives were. At home they had been baking cookies but here they complained that they did not have enough food. The Germans here were getting food rations: we had been dying of hunger under Nazi occupation. The Germans here were taking their children out in little prams, they had milk to feed them and still they complained that the level of fat in the milk was not high enough. They, on the other hand, grabbed our children and babies by the legs or by the hair and threw them against telephone poles and into the furnaces.

Willek worked in the water filtration plant for many months, examining everything there was to know: how everything functioned, all the strategic points; we knew exactly how we would have to cut off the supply to the American residential areas to avoid a disaster there; we studied and memorised the blueprints of the entire network; we learned all the gauges of the various pipes, all the connections, exactly how they could be cut off; where they could be blown; where the alternative supply systems were located. We sat for days and nights studying and planning all the details.

Headquarters in Paris was informed of the precise quantity of water that passed through the filters, so that they could judge exactly what amount and strength of 'material' would be required to obtain the desired effect. Everything was in place waiting for permission to proceed.

Then we received orders to freeze Project A – albeit temporarily. It was a harsh blow after months of preparation and anticipation. There were other important factors we were unaware of that had influenced this decision. Even so, it seemed a good idea to let Ze'ev stay on at the water company.

Life then actually got boring. We were just waiting for orders to act, and when they did not come, we didn't know what to do with ourselves.

So I started to look for a library, and I found a good one with plenty of German books. German had been my second language at school and I was quite fluent, Latin and Gothic letters, and all. After so many years, I felt I was back at school and I started to re-read and enjoy literature. Here I came across Dante's *Divine Comedy* – reminding me how we had studied it at high school with a wonderful teacher, by the name of Tarvydas. I'll never forget him – although I was disillusioned when I heard he had collaborated with the Germans. I knew every circle in hell by heart. In school – there had been a girl, Dvora Joffe, whom everyone knew was my special girl. That teacher gave us some homework one day: to write about Dante's love for Beatrice. In class next day – he asked Dvora and me to stand up and read how we saw the love between Beatrice and Dante. Dvora, her sister Shula and their parents were all shot in July–August 1941 when the Germans and their Lithuanian collaborators murdered the Jews of my home town of Rokishkis.

Although I had lost one of my diaries, I did manage to retain a small notebook with a few comments which are still legible. This is what I wrote at the beginning of October 1945:

'It is now the beginning of October 1945 and I am reading Shakespeare. My landlady just came in to tell me that there are rumours that the relationship between the Americans and Soviets is deteriorating and I have the impression that the Germans are keen to see a war between the Americans and Russians break out. They are so keen to wipe out the Russians and to side with the Americans that another war would do them nicely.

'How they hate the Asians: the red ones, the yellow ones. They don't fit into their Western civilisation. The landlady goes on and on about the fact that leaflets are being distributed in Berlin saying – "bring back Hitler and we'll have bread". Not only are they short of bread – but it seems they also miss Hitler! Not five months after the fall of the Third Reich – they're already looking for the Fourth. They need militarism – they need aggression – they need new victims and the blood of millions more.

'Sitting reading Shakespeare last night, I was disturbed by youths singing German military songs in the streets. I was next to the window and heard how they gave orders – how they spoke – they still haven't forgotten the old habit – and they probably never will.

'Oh the pride and joy in the faces of all who participated in those huge parades and spectacles here in Nuremberg's stadium, waving their flags, brandishing the swastika – how they raised their arms with dedication and love for their Führer; it was real – not just show. He promised he would wipe out the Jews; he said it, they accepted it, and they helped however they could in his mission.

If only the Jews had listened.

* * *

Soon after Project A was frozen, we put Project B into action. The plan here was to contaminate thousands of loaves of bread supplied to a camp housing tens of thousands of SS personnel. Located on the outskirts of Nuremberg, it was known as Stalag 13.

From my notebook:

'January 1st 1946: A young lady, by the name of Dobka, was selected as one of our liaison girls to form part of our group, and to find out where the bread for that camp was baked.'

After doing her research very thoroughly Dobka produced a full report on the bakery, its precise location and the name of its manager.

The vital player in this project, however, was Arye. He was to be our baker. We managed to get an appointment with the manager of the bakery and tried to convince him to hire Arye as a worker in his enterprise. The story we 'sold' to the manager was that Arye had an uncle in Canada who owned a huge bakery. The uncle was prepared to take him into the business. While he was waiting for his visa to Canada, we explained to the manager, Arye wanted to obtain whatever experience he could within a bakery – even if it was without pay. We wanted him to be mobile within the unit so that we could use him wherever necessary, either in the stores, the delivery department, or the bakery itself.

At first, the manager refused to buy our story. So we tried a second time, bringing all kinds of sweeteners – the usual supplies of cigarettes, alcohol, and chocolates. This time he took Arye into his firm. Arye started work almost immediately in the storeroom which was an important and strategic position for us.

Meanwhile, we also needed to know exactly what the procedures inside Stalag 13 were. When the bread was delivered. How it was distributed. And in what quantities. Who delivered it? Where was it stored? Were the deliveries once a day or twice a day? Who ate what? After all, it was not only the former SS inmates of the camp who ate the bread, but also the American guards.

We managed to place two people inside the camp as administrative assistants: Jasiek and Bartek. They got the jobs posing as foreigners for, at this time, there were a lot of people who had been brought to Germany for forced labour, and at the end of the war, few wanted to return to the East. It was a common situation and they explained they had family in the west who were supporting them while they waited for visas to the United States or Canada.

As a result of the investigations of our plants within the camp, we learned that on Sundays, the Americans received a special delivery of white bread, while the Germans took their regular black bread. Therefore, when the time came, we decided we would carry out our plan on a Saturday night.

During this entire period, the War Crimes Trials were being held in Nuremberg. We observed what was happening, and were disturbed by the slow progress, how the procedure demanded evidence of Streicher's villainy; how they had to prove that Rosenberg was the initiator of the Nuremberg laws; how they had had to find proof against Frank, the Governor of Poland, Ribbentrop, Keitel, the Chief of Staff of the German Army. Each had his team of defence lawyers. The whole process frustrated us enormously and so we made plans to find a way into the courtroom – if only to protest publicly.

We would have liked to break into that courtroom, but the security was too tight. So we tried to befriend some officers of the First American Division who were in charge of courtroom security, to get them to help us – or 'not to see us' – enter the court chamber.

We did not succeed.

* * *

Life in Nuremberg during this entire period meant collecting and coordinating information, reporting regularly to headquarters in Munich and Paris, travelling frequently to Munich to meet with people from other cities; comparing how they were managing, consulting with them on their experiences. Each of the five people responsible for the different cities had to know how far the other four had progressed. Timing was important, since the plan was to hit all five cities on the same day. Waiting for the go-ahead was often frustrating and many of us became nihilistic. Life was not important, neither your own life nor anyone else's.

From my notebook: December 15th 1945:

'I am suffering from a terrible migraine. The doctor told me I have meningitis. Some days I can hardly see anything. I feel a terrible pressure on my head. I have it all the time, especially in winter, in the rain and snow, and even in spring, it was very difficult. I have to lie down for hours. It attacks me day and night and keeps me awake for hours. I think a lot about my mother. How is she managing in the strange surroundings and climate of her newly adopted country of Palestine? She's alone – she's lost everybody – and was probably counting on my support, and here I am far away – once again "underground", surrounded by people in a strange environment.

'Here, we are a circle of acquaintances who become closer the longer we live and work together on our project, but the closer we become, the further removed becomes my own mother. I am smitten by conscience at leaving her to start up life alone in such strange surroundings. After all she is the only one in the world who cares for me – really. I often wonder whether she understands, whether she'll ever forgive me.'

'December 20th: My migraine is unbearable. I can hardly go up the stairs, certainly can't walk down. *Nietzsche:* "I want nothing – I want everything to end". When he was in a bad mood and suffering, he, too, saw the only way out as death.'

'It is Christmas 1945 – I've received an invitation to come to Munich and they say that Abba might be there – back from Palestine. Two years ago at Christmas we were blowing up a train in a village not far from our base. Danka was with us then – but a week later he was dead. On December 31st, he was killed.

'We had gone into a village called Dainova to prepare an operation – we were targeting three German agents. I was in charge of one of the groups – and Danka came into the house where we were hiding and asked me how long we would have to stay there. It was obvious that we might be surrounded. That was the last time I saw him because that's where he was killed. We carried his body back to our base in the forest and the next day we held a funeral. I could not go. Chiena Borowska apparently fainted. Danka was the best of us – a good friend, bright, intelligent and responsible, and very brave. He had often spoken about death – about wanting to die – about the family he had lost, and about having had enough of this terrible life.

'It seems to me here today, in Germany, I am in the same psychological frame of mind. Well, Danka, I want to tell you – I am here because of people like you – the memory of friends like you push me towards the deed we are here to carry out. It was a matter of fate that you had to die – killed probably by the bullet of one of our own friends. The bullet was not meant for you – it was meant for the enemy – what a cruel irony. I will remember you to the end of my life. The night of December 30/31, 1943. I will remember you as a hero – all honour to you – my friend.'

* * *

Why were we told to freeze Project A and direct our efforts towards Project B?

Back in July/August, when we had discussed the various plans with the people in the Jewish Brigade, it was clear that if we wanted the blessing of the authorities of the Yishuv (the Jewish leadership in Palestine), Abba Kovner, as head of the organisation, had to go to Palestine to convince the Jewish leadership of the importance of our plan, to make a guilty nation pay for its crimes, and equally important, to establish a warning for the future.

We did not want to become pariahs, so we wanted this approval, and we also needed the operational materials. So Abba sailed to Palestine in late August, and there he met with various people, including the high command of the Haganah. As I learned later, what he presented to the Haganah command was the viability of Project B. Only a limited number of individuals knew of Project A. Even on Project B – the less destructive plan – individual members of the Haganah command were divided. Abba soon learned that the leadership did not agree with the pursuit of vengeance, but were devoted to other priorities, mainly bringing in as many Jews as possible, strengthening their own structure. They probably had not yet fully grasped the enormity of the tragedy, and like everyone else, they still cherished hopes that many families, including their own, had survived.

Abba was extremely disappointed during his first few weeks in Palestine, and wrote to Pasha Avidov in September 1945 that it looked as though the only way of proceeding was, first to rely only on ourselves, and second to devote all efforts to create the necessary materials locally, i.e., in Europe. However, the reaction of one of the major leaders of the emerging nation was of enormous and surprising satisfaction to Abba. This figure, 'an elder' of the nascent state, identified strongly with the suffering of the Jews in Europe. Less politically pragmatic, and more sentimental, he was willing to help and made sure that Abba obtained the materials we so urgently needed.

Wearing the uniform of the Palestinian Brigade and bearing this material, Abba returned to Europe on a military ship that sailed from Alexandria, Egypt, on December 14, 1945, for Toulon, France. On the fourth day of the journey, as the boat approached its destination, Abba was summoned to the captain's quarters, where he was arrested by the military police on board. But before he left his cabin, he jettisoned half of the precious material he was carrying, leaving the other half in his bag with orders to his companion to hand it over to certain people in Paris; however, when he learned he was to be detained, that too, was thrown into the sea.

Abba was taken to Cairo where he spent the next two months in prison; from Cairo, he was sent to a prison in Jerusalem. Never was he told why he had been arrested; nor did he ever learn who had betrayed him. Back in Germany, we learned about all this from Pasha and Vitka in Paris.

A Footnote:
Colonel Shimon Avidan was at that time head of the 'German' regiment of the Palmach (the elite unit of the Haganah). This was a regiment established by the Jewish Agency during the time Rommel threatened to enter Palestine, and in case of a German occupation, the unit was intended to serve as an underground movement, an intelligence unit to fight the Germans from within. Later, during the War of Independence, Shimon Avidan served as Commander of the Givati Brigade, which fought the Egyptians in the south and repelled their advance at Ashdod, an overwhelming triumph over the Egyptian armies.

When we were active in Europe, Shimon Avidan performed certain functions related to vengeance. In his biography he is quoted as saying that the initiative to arrest Abba Kovner on his way back to Europe came through the intervention of the Jewish Agency which, at the time, was the leading authority of the Jewish people in Palestine and 'if anyone comes up with a different explanation or interpretation, it should be ignored'.

Abba never came back to Europe and the execution of the operations was left to the people in the field, led by the headquarters in Paris.

* * *

The date chosen to implement Project B was the Saturday night of April 13 1946. There were three reasons for this choice. First, there was to be a full moon that night and the plan required many night-time hours of work; second, the 'material' provided was going to have to be spread on the base of thousands of loaves of black rye bread. Normally, that bread was distributed to the German inmates of Stalag 13 and to their American guards; but on Sundays the American guards received only plain white bread. Third, there were fewer guards on duty on the weekend.

The 'substance' was delivered to me in Nuremberg a few days before April 13 by a gentleman in uniform who carried it in rubber hot water bottles strapped round his body. One of the chemical engineers in Paris had produced the arsenic mixture, experimenting with it on a cat. The cat had died instantly. The man who brought it was a tall strong man, but on arrival, he collapsed from the weight of the material he was carrying. The bottles were immediately taken into the bakery by Arye and hidden under the wooden floorboards until the night of April 13. A hiding place had also been prepared for those who were to carry out the task, in case they were interrupted.

Five people were supposed to carry out our plan that night. Three were smuggled in on Saturday morning, when people came to work. Willek (the waterman) and I were supposed to come in at two in the afternoon, when the morning shift ended. For some reason, they stopped working two hours earlier that day. So it was impossible for us to get in, since the entrance was always under guard.

We had been told to arrive there at two and when Arye came out at twelve, as the shift ended, we had not yet arrived. When we did, there were guards at the entrance. Thus there were only three of them inside to carry out the entire job. They started as soon as night fell. The mixture had to be stirred constantly so it wouldn't separate and the three of them succeeded in smearing the mixture on three thousand loaves, until they were interrupted.

One of the window shutters had somehow become loose in the wind and banged against the wall, making a terrific noise. Naturally the guards came to investigate, turned on the lights and immediately saw that something was up. We had, of course, foreseen the possibility of some kind of interruption. The contingency plan was to simulate a theft. There was a widespread shortage of bread and other provisions, and theft was quite common. Loaves had been put into bags and placed on the area approaching the window and on the window ledge itself. When the guards approached, Arye immediately hid the bottles and brushes under the floorboards, and he, too, climbed into the hideout. The other two jumped through the windows. The guards called the police and Arye could hear from under the floorboards that they concluded that there had been a robbery.

Meanwhile, Willek and I waited in the car outside until Arye crawled out of the hiding place after the police left.

Next morning, 3,000 loaves of contaminated bread destined for some 12,000 German inmates were delivered to the camp, distributed and eaten.

We know that some died – it is not sure just how many. We also know that many hundreds were saved at the American military hospital where they had their stomachs pumped.

If we had had the right material, the outcome might have been different, as it might have been had Abba succeeded in delivering the material he had obtained in Palestine instead of being arrested and forced to discard it into the sea.

* * *

Kennedy Airport 1987

Forty-one years later, I was flying from London to New York. At Kennedy airport, I ran into an old friend, one of Israel's leading scientists, and we shared a cab to the city. In the cab, my friend invited me to dine with him that evening. I told him that I had to attend a conference, but had kept the time free to visit Abba Kovner, my dear old friend, who had recently had his vocal chords removed at the Memorial Sloan Kettering Hospital.

'Oh,' he said, 'I know Abba Kovner very well. You know, there is a story I'm reluctant to tell, but maybe since so many decades have passed I can risk repeating it.'

'What's the story?' I asked. We always like to hear stories about old friends, and I thought I could tell Abba when I saw him later that evening.

My friend proceeded to tell me the following:

'Many years ago, some forty or so – when Israel was still Palestine, Abba appeared at the scientific institute where I was conducting research, requesting a certain substance. He was very tense and in a great hurry, saying that he needed this material urgently because there were some people waiting for it in Europe and time was of the essence.'

I looked at him, and said:

'You know, my friend, this is a story I know very well, and I have known it for many years.'

'How come?' was the response.

Quite calmly, I said: 'Because I was the one who was waiting for that stuff.'

Just then, we reached his hotel, and as he said goodbye, he added: 'Really? I would never have connected that episode with you!'

That evening, when I visited Abba in hospital, I told him the story. Abba looked pensive as he reflected on the past, and a bittersweet smile crossed his face.

* * *

From Fürth/Nuremberg, Arye, Jasiek, Willek and I made it to the German/Czech border where Willek and Jasiek crossed over. Manik came a day later. Arye and I were arrested by German border police, but since our papers showed we were foreigners and they had no right to apprehend us, they handed us over to the American military police who released us next morning.

We crossed the border the following night and were awaited and received by our own people in the Bricha. They took us to Prague where we were the guests of the *Sheliach* of the Haganah, Levi Argov.

We were each placed in different rooms in Prague, which had not suffered much damage during the war, except for the odd shelling here and there. By then, it was almost a year since the war had ended and the city was more or less intact. It was approaching May, and people were exceptionally good-humoured as the city prepared for a week of festivities. May 1 had always been a public holiday, May 4 marked the first anniversary of the liberation of the city of Prague and May 8 – the anniversary of the end of the war (by the Western powers), while the Soviet Union celebrated it on May 9. The Czechs were so thrilled to be freed of German domination that the jubilation over those ten days was unforgettable.

Everyone was singing and dancing day and night, flags were flying everywhere. A huge dais was erected at the end of the Boulevard Waclavsky Nemesti and there sat Benesh, the President, with Jan Massaryk, Foreign Minister, General Svoboda, Minister of Defence, with Furlinger representing the Communists, as well as ambassadors and military attachés of the allied command. From the top of the boulevard approaching from the National Museum came two huge open limousines: in one stood the Soviet Marshall Koniev, who had led the front that liberated Prague, and in the second stood General Rybalko who had commanded the tank division that entered Prague and ultimately drove out the Germans.

Thousands of people lined both sides of the boulevard; they stood on the ground, on chairs, on balconies, on the rooftops, all throwing red and white flowers into the two limousines. By the time they reached the dais, the two generals were completely covered with red and white blooms.

* * *

Meanwhile Pasha Reichman, who was in charge of Operations and was at the time moving from Paris to Marseille with other members of our group, sent me a note through a messenger, saying:

'My dear Menachem (my pseudonym): I want you to know that I am tremendously proud of what you have done with your people and now believe that we are able to accomplish further challenges. I do hope that we will be able to come back and proceed with our original targets. And if not, others will do it for us, on our behalf. Give my best wishes to your people; I love you, respect you and hold you in high esteem.'

Letter from Sorrento

Sorrento, February 17, 1995

Dear Dorka and Pasha,

I was in Paris last week for one of those annual international meetings I am invited to, and there I took the opportunity to see Ze'ev. We met, he, Renée his wife, and I, at the Café de la Paix just like in the good old days. I was delighted to find him in quite good shape. He is not entirely his old self, the way we knew him and the way we would like him to be, but after all, who is these days? Yet, we were able to discuss issues we remembered from the past, and spoke a little of the future. How much future can you discuss when you're already seventy? People normally think that history started on the day they were born, but at our age, we have had enough time and experience to conclude that the history of the future should be left to others. This probably arises from the fact that there really is no other choice.

Right now, I am sitting in a charming hotel here in Sorrento, just south of Naples. It is a sunny day, although last night a storm raged like the end of the world. But today, all is calm and serene; my balcony faces the island of Ischia, to the left is Capri, and to the right is Mount Vesuvius giving the impression that it has calmed down and will, for the time being, remain peaceful. The steep rocks of Sorrento descend abruptly some one hundred metres into the still, deep blue-green sea whose mirror-like surface is disturbed only now and again by the gentle ripples of a small fishing boat or the hydrofoil taking curious tourists across the waters to Capri.

Now and again I leaf through the book written on the isle of Capri in the 1930s by the Swedish author, Axel Munthe, called *The Story of San Michele*, which I read sometime during the 1940s and which impressed me even then. And in between, I glance through the international newspapers to keep in touch with the world around us – and today, with all the talk of the fiftieth anniversary of VE Day, it suddenly dawned on me that it is now fifty years since you and I first met.

I remember arriving in Lublin on January 17, 1945, and by February 12 I was already in Bucharest. For some reason, we did not come across one another in Lublin, but I do recall very clearly that we first encountered one another in Bucharest and it must be exactly fifty years this week. Our first meeting took place in the bathroom of the house where we were all based, at 9 Maria Rossetti Street. We were washing our hands and you asked me if I was Julik. I said I was and immediately realised that you were the Pasha I had heard so much about in Lublin. It was the beginning of a fine, deep friendship. And a long one. Fifty plus fifty makes a hundred, and if you add fifty for Dorka and some 40 for Gina, you get almost two hundred years of friendship. When speaking of friendship, you have to add the years of your friends; after all, you cannot be a friend to yourself.

What preoccupies me these days more than the politics of the future is memories of the past. And these have been provoked by a series of articles in the newspapers on the bombing of Dresden fifty years ago. We, in those days, fifty years ago, knew nothing of the bombardment and if we had known, we would probably have taken no notice of it, since we were engrossed in other matters. We were gathering information from the newly liberated survivors of the concentration camps.

Most of us, like you and me, knew about the horrible persecution in the ghettos, the murder of hundreds and thousands of Jews in the small and larger villages and towns of Eastern Europe; we knew how people had suffered, but we also had experience of fighting the Germans, in the ghettos, in the forests. All this gave us some satisfaction that we had contributed to the punishment of those animals and had thereby executed some kind of vengeance for what had been done to our own people.

As we met people liberated from the camps, including my own mother, we also learned how other members of our families had met their deaths, how they had been executed and burned, how they destroyed the inmates of the camps, body and soul, primarily how they tried to remove their human dignity before they took them to the gas chambers. We learned first-hand from the victims and the witnesses of that carnage. We heard how children had been tortured and burned, how the elderly, the sick and the infirm had been treated. We counted six million dead, and we decided that that act of barbarity, that savage destruction must be paid for.

It is fifty years since we decided not to leave that cursed continent until we had let the Germans and everyone else know that what had happened could not pass into history without being avenged.

We know what we planned to do, we know the obstacles and handicaps we had to overcome, and we know what we did.

They say that in Dresden 35,000 civilians were killed in two days of bombing. In an article written by two Germans, Donald Koblitz and Christian Habbe in the New York Times, a story is unfolding that this burning of Dresden was not the first dramatic fire the city endured. 'On the morning of November 10, 1938,' they write, 'the people of Dresden came out to see what they had done the night before – on Krystallnacht, the best organised nationwide pogrom against the Jews. Among the many establishments destroyed by the fire was the central synagogue.' Koblitz and Habbe tell us that the painter, Otto Griebel, later wrote of viewing the rubble with Franz Hackel, an eccentric well known in Dresden as something of a prophet. 'This fire will come back,' said Hackel, 'it will make a great arch and return to us.'

'It took six and a half years to fulfil that prophesy. Shortly after 10pm on February 13, 1945, Dresden citizens heard, as survivors later described it, sounds like "falling trees" and "onrushing locomotives". Britain's Fifth Bomber Squadron was starting the two-day bombing campaign. Within 23 minutes, 3,000 heavy fragmentation bombs, 250 incendiary bombs, and 400,000 small incendiary "fire sticks", fell on the city.

'The next day a second wave of bombers, mostly American, followed. They turned the centre of the city, already engulfed in flames, into a fire storm with hurricane winds. The heat at ground level reached 1,000 degrees centigrade; glass bottles stored in drugstore basements melted. Some 1,600 hectares, largely apartment buildings, were obliterated – along with the men, women and children who inhabited them.

'For days afterward, many buildings gutted by fire – including the Frauenkirche, the Baroque church that was the symbol of the city – remained standing as their embers cooled, only to suddenly collapse in on themselves.

'The peace of the dead settled over the city, broken by an eagle that escaped from the zoo, circling over the ashes.

'There were no military targets in Dresden. According to British archives, the city was chosen largely because it was still intact, a necessary prerequisite for the elaborate bombing pattern designed to spark a firestorm, a technique never before used on such a monstrous scale.'

Was it vengeance? Or justice? Revenge relates to the past, justice to the future.

The American, Hebert C Pell, a former US representative at the United Nations War Crimes Commission spoke in 1945 at the Conference of American Jews and said: 'At least ten million died indirectly as a result of the war. Is it too much to ask that one man should hang for ten murders?'

To tell you the truth, all these articles on the bombing of Dresden gave me not only a lot of information, but also quite a lot of gratification. I remember gaining some satisfaction when, in 1992, Queen Elizabeth the Queen Mother of Britain dedicated the statue outside the church of St Clements Dane near the Aldwych in the City of London, to the general who planned and executed the bombing of Dresden, Arthur (Bomber) Harris. You might recall that I was based in London at that time and I watched this great lady unveil the statue to this fine British general.

I also remember that she and her late husband, King George VI, were right there in London together with their subjects, the British people, when the Germans bombed London and set it alight. Britain was the only country that stood against Germany when Europe was occupied, when the Soviets signed the peace treaty with Hitler and America was still far away and well outside the war. The Queen Mother was, and still is a great lady, loved by one and all, and it was appropriate that she should unveil that statue.

It is true that the statue was smeared with red paint by all kinds of hyper left-wing radicals such as exist everywhere. But when you see the British of those wartime days marching in London's Whitehall on November 11 each year, the day of Remembrance, the invalids in their wheelchairs, all proudly displaying their medals of honour and saluting the Cenotaph, the memorial to the unknown soldier, you know what part Britain played in that terrible struggle for freedom.

The survivors of the concentration camps have also been commemorating their liberation these days, in particular the liberation of the camp at Auschwitz-Birkenau.

A Jew from New York writes to the editor of the Herald Tribune that Hitler and his lieutenants were clever enough to dispatch Europe's Jews mostly to the camps and gas chambers located in Poland to achieve their purpose of keeping Germany cleansed of Jews. The articles written about the fiftieth anniversary of the liberations of Auschwitz focus on the differences and animosities between Poles and Jews only. Rudy Rosenberg writes that it is his belief that Germany is getting off too easily. He is concerned that years from now other generations will only learn and remember that Jews were exterminated by Nazis. 'The Nazis having disappeared,' he writes, 'it will be assumed that they were extra-terrestrial creatures who appeared from nowhere and disappeared after 1945.

'As a Jew born in Belgium,' continues Rudy Rosenberg, 'I spent nearly five years under German occupation and 27 months hiding from the Germans in a Brussels basement. It was the German army that invaded Belgium. It was the Germans who occupied Belgium. It was the German troops who terrorised the population. I was hiding from the Germans. When the Germans were defeated and driven out of Belgium by the allies, we were liberated from the German occupation. We never referred to the Nazis. I never saw one. The people who occupied Belgium wore German uniforms of various colours – blue, green, navy, brown and black – we feared them all.

'It was only upon arriving in the United States in 1949 that I began to hear the word Nazi used continuously and exclusively with reference to the Holocaust. Germany was somehow exonerated; the Nazis took the blame.

'It is time to put the proper perspective on the Holocaust and to remember that without Germany there would have been no Nazis and no Holocaust. To focus the Holocaust on Poland and the Nazis is a perversion of history that should be corrected.'

As you see, my dear friend, there is still a lot to learn, to study and probably to do as yet, but you can think of that only if you are not preoccupied with many other problems and you spend a few quiet days here in Southern Italy, in peaceful surroundings. Such days stimulate philosophical thoughts such as comparing the destruction of nearby Pompei by natural forces 2,000 years ago with the destruction of our own people fifty years ago by the barbaric deeds of human beings in the twentieth century.

Forgive my rambling thoughts, dear Pasha, but you are one of the few with whom I can share these sentiments.

Yours, in friendship,

Joseph

To the Promised Land

The Haganah took care of the practical and organisational matters and our move towards Italy went smoothly. We were covered at all border crossings, the Czech/Austrian and Austrian Italian frontiers, borders at which only a year earlier, we, the initiators of Bricha, had prepared; now we were reaping the benefit of the 'system'. After all, with the reputation gained as a result of our most recent activities in Germany, they were all eager to see us gone as quickly as possible.

We reached the region north of Milan, where we were placed in a huge building in Tradate, a lush green, picturesque setting and there we rested for about two weeks before the next leg of our journey. This was the end of vengeance. At least we had tried. It was time to move on.

* * *

Meanwhile, yet another illegal boat to take us to Palestine was being prepared at Vado, near Savonna in the Gulf of Genoa. With the quota allowed into Palestine by the British authorities still at 15,000 per year, and the number of people coming out of the DP camps and the stream from Eastern Europe constantly escalating, the battle for immigration was now at its peak.

The Haganah bought boats, rebuilt and converted them, providing accommodation for as many souls as possible for each sailing. We were packed so tightly into four level bunk beds, that sardines were comfortable by comparison. There was not enough to eat or drink, there were no washing facilities, people vomited constantly as heavy waves tossed the boat from side to side. Our group tried to make some kind of order in the chaos on that ship. They did what they could to help the sick and the elderly. Only I could do nothing – I had one of my migraine attacks.

Our boat, formerly the *Beaumarchais*, was renamed the *Wedgwood*, and bearing a Panamanian flag and the Union Jack and carrying 1,257 illegal immigrants, we entered the port of Haifa on June 26, 1946, in an intense heat which none of us had ever experienced. British soldiers came on board, we mounted a symbolic resistance, which was quickly overcome, and we were herded into buses waiting for us in the port of Haifa. On the boat we had been accompanied by two members of the Haganah whose task was to supervise our group. These two were wanted by the British, so when we were pushed into those buses, they too found themselves on the bus guarded by two British soldiers. On the quay were dozens of women eagerly offering drinks to the new immigrants, and more important, seeking news of relatives who might have survived in Europe. They would shout out the names of towns and villages: 'Warsaw, Krakow, Lublin.'

And as they did, from within the bus, we suddenly created a huge commotion and shouted: 'Yes, here, Warsaw.' Meanwhile, we pushed out the two Haganah men *and* the British soldiers. In a flash, I gave my sunglasses to Berchik, so he would not be recognised, and years later, when I saw him lunching on the Champs d'Elysée I reminded him that he still owed me a pair of sunglasses.

The mood was also exceptionally tense in Palestine that day, for it was just three days before what was known as Black Sabbath, when the British arrested and imprisoned leaders of the Jewish Agency, a reprisal for the Etzel bombing of the King David Hotel in Jerusalem, the headquarters of the British High Command. Thousands of members of the Haganah and Palmach had been arrested by the British Army for arms searches, especially among the Kibbutzim, in an effort to break the Haganah.

On the way to Atlit, the British camp for illegal immigrants, my good friend Grisha Gurwicz stood next to me in the bus. A popular character and an excellent machine-gunner, he had fought with me in the partisan group in the forests outside Vilna, and I met him again in Milan and persuaded him to join our ship to Palestine. Grisha had been working in Milan for the Jewish Agency dealing with the transportation of immigrants to the illegal boats. There he had at his disposal a beautiful shiny Lancia car to which he was very attached, and he needed a lot of convincing to leave his car behind for a new country and a new life.

On that hot dusty journey from the port of Haifa, the long convoy of buses stopped for a few moments before turning off the Tel Aviv road towards Atlit; as we looked through the window, we both saw an elderly Arab, dressed in white pantaloons, riding his donkey, his legs dragging along the ground, and Grisha turned to me and let out a profoundly explicit Russian curse. 'So, this is where you have brought me, you *!*!! You took me away from my trusty Lancia to a place with this kind of transportation.' Still, we all enjoyed his company in the camp at Atlit, where he cheered everyone up with his good humour and wide repertoire of provocative jokes.

At the British military camp of Atlit we were placed in tents and barracks, and our group managed to stick together.

Mother came to visit me, happy to see her only remaining son again, even behind barbed wire.

Then we were released.

Most of those who came with me went to Kibbutz Ein Hachoresh, but a few like me already had family in Palestine. I set about doing what I could to take care of my mother who had been living and working with Rachel and Zalman Rubashov, who later became Shazar, the third President of the State.

I picked up whatever work I could: first on a construction site in Holon, and then, because I wanted to do manual and not office work, some friends told me to learn textiles as a trade. I joined a textile factory as an apprentice with no salary, but the noise was so unbearable I would come back to my mother's room at night and complain bitterly, since I still suffered from terrible migraines. After a short time, I was told there was a crisis in the textile industry and little chance of getting a job, so I quit.

Another acquaintance arranged for me to work six days a week at a gas station. There was no question of filling cars with petrol, that was luxury. My job was to carry oil drums from one area to another, and to clean the toilets; the British were very strict about cleanliness, all the edges had to be whitewashed. On Friday and Saturday nights, to make extra money, I worked as the nightwatchman.

Back in Ponteba, in Northern Italy, when we had been deliberating our future in Palestine and were immersed in the conflict of ideologies – one of the young soldiers tried, in the nicest possible way, to tell me that all these discussions were fine in theory, but there was a reality to be faced when we eventually reached Palestine – a reality of forging a life. One day, in that gas station, that fellow came by for petrol in his little beat-up jalopy. I was delighted to see him.

'You see,' he said, 'what did I tell you back there in Italy. It's not exactly how it sounded there, is it?'

Soon I found somewhere for my mother and me to live. All the large apartment houses had laundry rooms; we washed in the yard and in that room there was a bath. I slept on a board on top of the bath and mother had a bed for herself. That's where we lived, until her brother arrived from Rhodesia in 1947 and decided to help buy an apartment for mother and myself. He found a house still under construction on Hayarkon Street with an apartment for sale for the sum of three thousand pounds. He gave us one thousand and the other two thousand came from my aunt Fanya, my father's sister in America.

Immediately after arriving in Palestine, some of us still hoped to return to Germany to complete our unfinished business. But most of us, including myself, decided to stay in Palestine: I really wanted to do what we had set out to do, but I could never leave my mother again. A small group did go back but did not carry out their plans. It was too late, they did not have the right infrastructure, or the financing.

* * *

Abba

Ten years after arriving in Palestine, I was working for the Jewish Agency in Geneva when Abba Kovner came to visit me. Sitting in our apartment in Geneva, Abba told me how aggrieved he felt because no real punishment had ever really been meted out to the Germans. The world, he said, was overlooking the whole episode and he had come to the conclusion that something had to be done along the lines we had planned ten years earlier. He had arrived in Geneva after visiting other places in Europe and he had a list of people he had talked to about his assessment of the situation, most of them former victims of the Holocaust.

Meanwhile the State of Israel was already negotiating with Germany for reparations and there was a sense that the Germans wanted to buy their way out of their crimes.

Abba asked if I would participate in his plan, his new concept. I listened to him, but even though I still shared the same ideals, I had to decline, for two reasons:

First, I was in Geneva on behalf of the Israeli authorities which obliged me to undertake certain very responsible functions and all my time was devoted to these tasks. I did not consider it correct for me to split my time and effort in different directions, while I was so overburdened with work requiring deep concentration and skilled management.

Second, I had heard rumours that the Israeli authorities had changed their policies and were now actively focusing on the search for prominent Germans who had personally played a major part in the annihilation of the Jewish people. If that was true, I explained to Abba, it was exactly what we had wanted and were unable to achieve ten or fifteen years earlier, that is, the appropriate authorities would make it their priority, and they were certainly better equipped to carry out such deeds than we were or could ever be.

Abba left disappointed.

On May 2, 1960, Adolf Eichmann, living in Buenos Aires under an assumed name, was tracked down by Israeli secret agents, and on May 11 he was brought to Israel for trial. The trial began on April 2, 1961, and lasted until August 14 when Eichmann was sentenced to death for crimes against the Jewish people and crimes against humanity, and on May 31, 1962, he was hanged.

Although Eichmann's capture was an individual case, the drama of his arrest and re-patriation to Israel, the high-profile trial, and the massive worldwide coverage it received, the controversy it aroused, made it a momentous symbol, which raised the spectre of the Holocaust once again.

The fact that Abba himself was called as a witness at the trial – and his testimony was one of the most dramatic – compensated us in a certain way, if we can use that expression, and I believe that Abba understood what I meant when he had come to me a few years earlier in Geneva.

I first met Abba Kovner in the Vilna Ghetto. Abba was then a leading member of the FPO and I was called to a meeting to report and be briefed on possible future activities for my group in the coming months. My group was composed of members of the Jewish police in the ghetto, and as such, and as tension in the ghetto rose, my communications with Abba became increasingly frequent. Abba became commander of the entire FPO after the death of Wittenberg and was based at the headquarters inside the ghetto. I reported to him on events at the gates of the ghetto, the Germans' activities and movements, and since he and his officers were confined to headquarters, he was dependant upon our information. This was how I first got to know Abba well, learned how he would react, what he expected of the people he worked with. We became closer during the last few weeks of the liquidation of the ghetto, and shared the same tragedy of leaving our mothers behind when we left through the sewers. Our friendship grew even more profound when we served as partisans in the forests of Rudnitski. He was a commander of a battalion, not mine, although we were based in the same area.

Several times I was able to help Abba, particularly when the authorities in the forests did not see eye to eye with him. Crises often arose out of differences of opinion; I was fortunate enough to be in a position to smooth out some of them. I was appointed head of the department of intelligence when Abba and other officers were asked to resign from their positions, as a result of an unfortunate incident.

Moscow had dropped parachutes with arms and explosives, and as so often happened in such cases, some of the parachutes had been caught and left suspended in the trees. The supplies which had been delivered fell to the ground and some of the soldiers in Abba's battalion had picked them up and taken them back to their bases. This was, of course, strictly against regulations and was a crime in the eyes of the High Command. All such supplies had to be delivered to headquarters, but the battalion commanders kept the matter quiet and did not report that these arms had been kept by the soldiers. Either they did not want them court-martialled or, as was later explained, they felt they did not have enough arms to fulfil their duties and that it was their right to keep these weapons. Nevertheless, when they were discovered, the decision was that all officers of the battalions involved were to be dismissed, and were court-martialled. A critical situation arose and some of us who had key positions and authority, spoke up for them, and thus the matter was resolved.

In another case, the head of intelligence of the Lithuanian Partisan Movement came to me to complain that Abba had been seen in the forests constantly writing. Since Abba was known as a Zionist, they were suspicious of him and questioned what was he up to. So I went to Vitka and told her to do us all a favour, and tell Abba to either go deeper into the forests so that no-one could see him writing there, or to postpone his writing for better times. Officially, what I did was out of order, but as a friend, I could not do otherwise.

The early years in Palestine and the newly-born State of Israel were a struggle, and although our daily lives took us in different directions, we always shared our respective problems, our joys and disappointments, failures and successes, and we remained in constant touch with one another. Whenever there was an important decision to be made, I would always consult Abba first. Abba's opinion and judgement was an essential part of my future working life. In good times and in bad, my family and I were sustained by his friendship and there is no doubt that he enriched all our lives.

Above all Abba Kovner was a great writer, a great poet, a great philosopher. He won all the major cultural and literary prizes, and was awarded several honorary doctorates. He was also a great soldier, fighting in the Israeli War of Independence, as an officer in the Givati brigade.

Years later, Abba was asked to contribute to many publications and organisations, but perhaps his most remarkable achievement was the Diaspora Museum.

When Abba Kovner passed away on the eve of Rosh Hashanah 1987, Israel, literature, and the Jewish world, lost a great man. They say there is no justice in the world – such a creative spirit, such a loving, lovable personality, such an achiever, should endure for eternity. But we do not live in a Utopia or a never-never land where life is everlasting. We are fortunate to have been left with a tremendous legacy in the works and words of Abba Kovner and for that I and all his friends are grateful. To have known and worked with him was a great privilege.

Benjamin Franklin once said:

If you do not want to be forgotten when you die, either write things worth reading, or do things worth writing about'.

Abba did both.

Abba Kovner 1918–1987

With Valia Pshevalska and Avraham Sabrin on the day of liberation of Vilna, 1944

Tevya Rubin, Sergeant Major, 1944

With ex-partisans in Bucharest, 1945: left Baruch Goldstein, and 2nd right: Welvel (Ze'ev) Rabinovich

Former partisans, right to left: Schmulke Kaplinski, Vitek and Josef Kronik

A reinforced underground shelter re-visited in 1994

Core of the Vengeance group, Bucharest 1945

Some of the Vengeance group in the camp of Atlit following arrest by the British Navy of illegal immigrants on the 'Wedgewood', June 26 1946

Illegal immigrants on the high seas, en route for Palestine, 1946

VI

ISRAEL 1947–1956

The Palestine Electric Corporation

All I wanted after those war-torn years was to be a simple labourer – to work with my hands and to earn enough to support my mother and myself, but mother wanted me to be engaged in a more serious career.

I was reminded of how she went about this during a chance meeting I had some 45 years later with the head gardener in the grounds of the ORT Braude Institute of Technology at Karmiel, where a garden was being planted to be known as the Minnie Wingate Rose Garden, a dear friend of ours. The gardener had always been friendly to me whenever I visited the college to observe its development, and he had an excellent sense of humour. I remember the two signs he placed on the lawns: one read: 'Please don't walk on the grass' and the other immediately behind it: 'Why did you?'

On that occasion he took me aside saying, 'I believe you might know my grandmother.' I asked who his grandmother was. 'She is Genia Pilnik-Shoham,' he replied. It turned out his grandfather had married Genia, who was now actually his step-grandmother. She had been a great friend of our family back in Lithuania, where the Pilniks and Harmatzs were amongst the most respected families in the community. Genia had come to Palestine in the 20s as one of the early pioneers and settled on Kibbutz Tel Josef, where she had worked with Golda Meir.

When my mother arrived in Palestine in 1945, Genia was thrilled to learn that member of the Harmatz family was still alive. She was working then as head of the Employment Office in Tel Aviv, and another friend of hers, Rachel Katznelson-Shazar, the wife of Zalman Shazar called Genia to say that one Dvora Harmatz had been recommended to take care of her severely handicapped daughter. Genia rushed round immediately to see her old friend, my mother.

So my mother, unhappy that her son was working in a petrol station, discussed the matter with Genia; at the earliest opportunity, Genia informed mother that the Palestine Electric Corporation, one of the most prestigious, solidly-based institutions of pre-State Palestine, was looking for employees and suggested that I take the entrance exam. Mother put enough pressure on me, and somewhat reluctantly, wearing a dirty overall and reeking of petrol, I went straight from the gas station to the examination hall where I found 30 serious-looking youngsters, sitting at desks, clean, presentable, concentrating on the task ahead of them; I sat down and wrote the exam.

The invigilator, Dr Rothstein, who was in charge of staff recruitment for the Palestine Electric Corporation, paced up and down the aisles looking over the candidates' shoulders to see how they were getting on. It was probably my good fortune that whenever he passed by my desk, I was on the right track with my answers. Since the room was crowded, he allowed a few people he had already passed to leave early. I was one of the four candidates selected and much to my mother's delight, I started work there almost immediately.

When the young gardener from Karmiel told me about Genia all those years later, I asked cautiously whether she was still alive. The answer came that she was living in a home for the elderly in Ramat Gan, and at the earliest opportunity, together with my son Ronny, I paid her a visit. She was very frail, her hearing was poor and her eyes were weak, but as soon as she realised who I was, she was overcome with joy.

'You see, Joseph,' she said, 'how right I was to recommend you to join the Palestine Electric Company! I knew already a year later because I called them to see how you were getting on the company. "Oh, Joseph Harmatz?" they said to me, "he is surely going to be the Director of the Company."'

When I mentioned to Genia that ORT was at that time about to open a centre in Moscow to re-train emigrants waiting to come to Israel, in spite of her infirmity and fragility, she said, 'You see, if only I were younger, I could have helped absorb the Russians today!'

At the Palestine Electric Corporation, I worked diligently in the domestic consumer accounts department. By nature, I was conscientious about any task assigned to me, but here I kept my nose to the grindstone, my head permanently bent over the books, as I checked and rechecked the endless columns of figures. There were never any errors in my work and I gained a reputation for being a fastidious, hardworking employee. As a result, I was promoted to the position of Comptroller and was offered a post in the commercial consumers department which was far more complicated, with many different rates requiring logarithmic calculations. I coped easily with this aspect, as well as answering customers' queries with clear explanations of how the charges were made. The reason I kept my head down – quite literally – was that I still suffered from the most excruciating migraines – a legacy from the bout of meningitis I had had in Germany – and the only way I could get through the day was to keep my head still and move it neither right nor left: I took no coffee or lunch breaks to chat with colleagues and just got on with my work until it was time to go home at the end of the day. It was a routine, some would say, boring existence, but it was what I wanted and needed at that time of my life.

Later that year, in November 1947, after the United Nations Resolution was passed to declare Israel a State, there followed a series of uprisings among the Palestinian Arabs – particularly around the area of Jaffa, and many of us volunteered to help resist these uprisings and protect our settlements. The Palestine Electric Corporation however, asked me to return to work as soon as possible, which I did until May of the following year. With the declaration of the State of Israel, the five surrounding Arab states attacked immediately and the newborn state was immediately plunged into war. I was mobilised into the Tel Aviv District division of the Infantry, and later posted to the Taggart Police Station in Sefad, in the Galilee. From there, our unit attacked the Syrians, and succeeded in maintaining control of the Galilee, and despite heavy losses, the unit was responsible for retaining the borders at their original positions when an armistice was eventually reached.

Meanwhile, my mother had intervened once again through different channels. She appealed on the grounds that, as a widow who had lost two sons in the Holocaust, she was desperate for her only remaining son to stay alive and thought it more reasonable that he should be moved from a fighting unit to a desk job. So after several months I was moved to the manpower headquarters in Jaffa, where I served in a unit which dealt with all the infantry units in the army, recording their movements and supplying headquarters with relevant statistics. I was specifically in charge of the registration of the three Palmach brigades of the army, selected fighting units, but as far as the Administration was concerned, this was not their forte.

When fighting ceased towards the end of 1949 and armistice talks began between all the neighbouring Arab states and Israel, some soldiers were released, mainly those who were older and had large families. At the same time, a commission was established at army headquarters to deal with applications from various large corporations for their employees to be returned to them on the basis that they were urgently needed back in their respective jobs. If such a release was granted it was conditional upon the approval of the commanding officer in charge of the soldier.

The Palestine Electric Corporation applied to the commission for my release as soon as it possibly could, but my commanding officer, Lt Col L, refused to give permission for my release. When I approached him, he replied: 'We will go together.' 'Colonel L, you are probably keen on a military career,' I appealed to him, 'but I am not in the slightest bit interested in staying in the army. I have a job at the Palestine Electric Corporation, a mother to support, I'm a pretty new immigrant and I need to get on with my life.'

'No, young man, when I leave, you leave,' came the reply. He was a fine officer, but as stubborn as a mule.

A few months later the PEC presented a second request. Now, it is true that L. was my commanding officer in the professional sense, but it was my administrative camp commander who officially received the application. I knew when it would reach him, and at the appropriate time I implored him to deal with it rather than pass it to Lt Col L. I explained my position once again, and he was compassionate enough to sign my release.

In the meantime, more and more people were being released from the army and all this was organised at camp 751 just outside Tel Aviv, where I had been sent by my commanding officer to set up the administrative procedure for the general release of army personnel; it was here that the reserve units were organised and it was Lt Col L himself who sent me there to deal with the matter. While I was handling releases, my own documents came through and I actually signed my own final release along with all the others. The law was that within two weeks of being released, the army had the right to request a soldier back. I continued to work, wishing the time away, and when the two weeks were up, I went to see Lt Col L.

The general pattern of discharge had increased, and more and more troops were being released. 'Look Colonel, everything at base 751 is properly organised; you'll have no problem replacing me; it is such a waste of time for me to stay when there is no longer an emergency; it is ruining all my chances of promotion at work.'

'I won't discharge you; I've told you: we will go together,' he repeated.

'What if I told you I have a way of leaving?,' I said.

'I understand what you have in mind, but remember I can still bring you back within two weeks.'

Then I could hold back no longer. 'The two weeks have already passed, Colonel,' I told him. I can still see the dirty look he gave me.

I was out. I returned to the Palestine Electric Corporation, and continued to do my job.

By 1950 I was disappointed that I had not been properly promoted. It was not the management who opposed my promotion, but the unions. I could see no justification for this and so, having received an invitation from my uncle in Rhodesia to visit him there, I asked for a few months leave of absence.

The few months in Rhodesia were pleasant, and there was talk of assisting my uncle in his business, since his four children were much too young to help. Still, life in Rhodesia did not appeal to me, even though it was a prosperous life, compared with conditions in Israel, which was undergoing a difficult period of extreme shortages and rationing. I had already made a few good friends back home, my mother was there, and I was corresponding with a young girl named Gina whom I had met shortly before my departure.

I decided to return.

Gina

Shortly after being released from the army, I was invited to a party of mostly young married couples. Since everyone was coming in pairs, I invited a girl I had known for a while, though we had no romantic attachment. I immediately noticed another girl sitting off to the side, and no-one seemed to be speaking to her. She had recently come from France and spoke French and German; since nobody there spoke either language, my hostess asked if I minded taking care of her. Her name was Regina Kerszenfeld and she had come to Israel as a tourist from France; if she liked it, she planned to stay.

That evening, Gina told me only that she was living in Paris with her father and that her mother was no longer alive. We chatted some more, and when it was time to leave, I had a dilemma: whom should I take home first. I decided to take my date home first, and then I accompanied Gina to her aunt's home and invited her for coffee some day. She agreed, and a few days later we met again and chatted for hours.

She had dark brown hair, brown eyes, was neatly dressed, had tremendous poise, and spoke directly and to the point. But most of all, I was entranced by her eyes – they were so sad. She hardly smiled and always seemed serious.

Gina's father, Oskar, was originally from Eastern Poland, her mother from somewhere in the heart of the Austro-Hungarian empire, more Hungarian than Austrian. Gina was one of seven children and when Hitler came to power in 1933 her parents moved from Frankfurt to Paris. Evidently the family were stateless and France was hospitable to refugees. The family had a hard time in Paris. The oldest child was Edith and then came Gina, their second daughter born in 1923. Two more daughters followed: Rachel born in 1925, and Sarah in 1927. There were also two boys: Siegfried born in 1933 and Henri in 1929. Charlotte the youngest, was born in Paris in 1935.

Gina had lost her mother, five brothers and sisters – all younger than her, on July 16, 1942 when she was staying with good friends, the Kaminskis. That night masses of Jews were arrested. Two days later, when she returned home, no-one else was left.

Gina stayed with the Kaminskis as one of their family. A couple of months later, as the Germans cracked down, they made their way to Switzerland. In October 1942, Estelle Kaminski, her brother Marcel and three others managed to get to Thonon-les-Bains on the southern shore of Lac Leman (Lake Geneva) near Evian. There they were caught by the Swiss police, who refused to let them in. Estelle convinced them at least to let Gina into Switzerland since she was recovering from a serious kidney operation and was very weak. Estelle agreed that, if they let Gina in, the rest of them would stay behind. They returned to Chambery where Estelle remained with her parents, hidden by a priest in a monastery.

As for Gina, she lived in Switzerland from November 9, 1942, to June 28, 1945, as a refugee, first at Camp Charmilles, a suburb of Geneva, then with family Wolf-Nobs in Zurich, and then with the Sorokin family in Geneva; from there she was sent to the Saint Nikolaus home for refugees in Luzerne, and finally to another refugee camp in Finhaut in the Valais (a place we visited together many years later). At the end of the war in 1945, Gina returned to Paris.

In Paris, she found her older sister Edith, the only other one who survived, who was married and had a son and daughter. Her father had remarried Adèle, a divorced lady with a son. They had opened a shop together, with father as buyer, the wife as the saleswoman. Her father had always been a Zionist with a warm spot for Israel, while his new wife was more of a Bundist.

We went out often and soon after I returned from Rhodesia, we decided to get married. Our wedding took place on June 28, 1951, in the 'German' synagogue on Ben Yehuda Street. Gina's sister, Edith, came from Paris; Shazar (Rubashov) was best man.

At first we lived in my mother's apartment in Hayarkon Street, but that was too much for mother. Since she could not rent out the rooms we occupied, we decided to rent our own flat on Ibn Gvirol Street.

* * *

So Gina and I, newlyweds, settled into the third floor flat on Ibn Gvirol Street, which was not even a proper road then, just a sandy cul-de-sac at the northern tip of Tel Aviv. It was not ideal but we were young with plenty of spirit and hope for the future.

Our son was born on July 10, 1952, and we named him Zvi, after my older brother who had himself been named after his uncle who died serving as an army doctor in the First World War. He was a lovely baby who grew up during a difficult time of rationing. We worried about rickets, for food was scarce and you had to make do with whatever you could. We were not as fortunate as some who had friends on farms who helped their families with home grown produce.

From the Palestine Electric Corporation, I moved to the Jewish Agency, where I later managed the Supply and Equipment Division of the Settlement Department. Gina and I moved back to mother's flat on Hayarkon Street. Mother was happy to watch Zvika growing up and it suited us to live closer to the centre of Tel Aviv for the next few years.

Gina in the meantime became involved in Israeli life, and having lost almost her entire family so tragically, she now immersed herself in the creation of a new family of her own which all of us who had similar experiences were proud to do. She was a full partner in everything I did and would participate whenever appropriate, always had her own independent point of view, offering it only when asked. On the whole, she was quiet and reserved, but her advice to me during critical times or moments of decision, was invaluable.

In 1956, I was appointed to the Jewish Agency office in Geneva. Zvika went to a French-speaking school, while Gina blossomed in this genteel Swiss environment, returning to the country where she spent three years as a refugee, now she was the wife of an official representative of the Jewish Agency, representing the State of Israel. To come from having been a stateless refugee in Paris as a citizen of an independent Jewish state made her fiercely proud.

Mother decided to spend some time with her brother in Rhodesia and although we had originally intended to return to Israel after two years, my assignment was extended for a further two years. In 1957, on a mission in Budapest, I received a telegram to go immediately to Salisbury where mother lay gravely ill. Leaving Hungary quickly was a problem in those days. Not only did you need an entry visa, but you also required an exit visa. The Israeli Embassy in Budapest did everything possible to give me a car to drive to Vienna where tickets and visas for Rhodesia were waiting for me.

By the time I arrived, Mother was barely conscious. I held her hand and she could hardly speak. Summoning whatever strength she had left, she first asked how Zvika was. I told her he was growing into a fine boy, what he was doing at school, and explained whatever news I had. Then she asked about Gina whom she had grown to love. Her strength was failing and when I came to the hospital the next morning, I learned that she had passed away during the night. Somehow she had held on until I arrived from Europe, but the struggle of those tormented years had taken their toll on her heart. She was only 59 years old.

At the end of 1960, we returned home to Israel, where I had accepted an appointment as Comptroller of ORT Israel. We sold my mother's apartment in Tel Aviv and settled into our new home in Kfar Shmaryahu. In general, these were wonderfully happy years; Zvika went to the local school, we had good friends in the neighbourhood, people came to visit us from abroad. Gina wanted another child, and on July 20, 1961, a second beautiful blond baby boy was born in the Beilinson Hospital. We named him Ronel Ephraim, this time after my younger brother.

In the 1960s, with some French colleagues, we established a shipping line – a Franco/Israeli company – which operated all over the Mediterranean. Then, of course, Gina and I would take the children on holiday – either joining one of the cruises to various Mediterranean ports, or we would put our car on one of the boats, sail to the continent and tour Europe.

Life looked beautiful and promising for all of us, until the late 60s. In 1966 Gina started complaining of pain. She had check-ups and tests, and all doctors came up with nothing, all of them claiming that it was psychosomatic. But the pain did not subside, and it was only in 1968 that we consulted the head of the gynaecological department at Beilinson Hospital. After examining Gina, he announced that she would have to be operated on immediately, and performed the operation himself the next morning. He emerged from the operating room and told me that Gina had cancer, that it was already widespread, that he believed he had removed all of it and had treated the surrounding area to prevent any further metastasis. But, in a solemn voice, he told me that there was no hope, and he gave her one month to live.

I immediately called my closest friend, Abba Kovner, and we decided to consult Professor Trainin of the Weizmann Institute, who was doing cancer research. He sent us to Harry Brenner, a young doctor at Sheba Hospital. Abba and I consulted Dr Brenner and he accepted her as a patient. The only other problem was how to keep Gina from knowing that she had cancer, since Harry Brenner's treatment was immediate heavy doses of chemo- and radiotherapy. In consultation with Dr Schonfeld we told her that as a result of a previous operation on her kidney, a certain, possibly harmful growth had developed and had to be treated.

Of course, all this changed the course of our lives significantly. We had to stop our active hospitality, receiving guests from Israel and all over the world, lest someone break down the wall of secrecy I had created around us to protect her from the truth of her illness. By nature, Gina never wanted many friends, she was always content with one or two close friends. After about four years, by the early 1970s, life returned to normal, and her illness seemed a thing of the past.

Settling new immigrants

A time to cast away stones and a time to gather stones together
                                                              Ecclesiastes 3.5

Back at the PEC, I continued in my old job, but it was no longer the same. I decided that if anything came up, I would leave. Something did indeed come up, in the form of Hillel Giladi, who had known our family from the time when he visited us in Rokishkis, as *sheliach* of the Zionist movement. Giladi came to our apartment and asked to chat with me. At that time he was head of the Supply and Equipment Division of the Settlement Department of the Jewish Agency. The management of the Jewish Agency was under serious attack by its Comptroller for incompetence. Levi Eshkol, in charge of the Settlement Department, decided to clean up by recruiting new, more reliable, younger staff. So, Giladi offered me a position in his department of spare parts and heavy agricultural machinery, which served the new settlements for the massive influx of immigrants, and involved importing large quantities of heavy equipment. All this was funded by the first loan of 10 million dollars – a vast amount for those days – from the Import/Export Bank of America (Exim).

I accepted Giladi's offer on three conditions: first, that I receive the salary of a senior officer; second that I receive appropriate housing; and third that I receive a car. They gave me the salary, a Landrover, and I was promised a Swedish-style house in Yazur which I never lived in, but which remained available for me. I found housing in town and preferred to live there.

By 1951, the Settlement Department had to deal with masses of immigrants, survivors from the Displaced Persons camps, newcomers from Northern Africa, and from the surrounding Arab states of Iraq and Yemen. The Jewish Agency wanted to settle as many as possible on the land, extending settlements over as wide an area as possible, while simultaneously making them productive and self-sufficient.

Industry in those days was not very sophisticated – the principle was to focus on agriculture as the main industry; while the philosophy was that, by forging a link between the human being and the soil by people working the land, the newcomers would be more likely to feel that they belonged to the country. Certainly the second generation would feel that way. Settling people on the land also meant securing the borders of the new State. To achieve all this, we had to train the immigrants, who had no experience of agriculture, and this required a vast infrastructure of agricultural experts throughout the country, to cope with the various climatic and geographical conditions.

The immigrants were not oriented toward the collective, so it was decided to establish Moshavim rather than Kibbutzim. In the Moshav, each family had its own plot of land close to the residence, while all the principal products of the Moshav were produced collectively. It was a major task to teach some of these immigrants about machinery and it took time; at one stage, we had to switch from motorised machinery back to basics: a tractor was too much of a shock to the system at first, for a Moroccan from the Atlas mountains, whose only known form of transport had been a mule. So we brought mules from Cyprus, donkeys from Turkey, and horses from Europe. We gave them a cart for a temporary period, until we had time to train them in the use of tractors and harvesters.

The immigrants had big families, and with so many children, milk was an important part of their nutrition. At first we brought Friesland cows from Holland to provide the necessary quantities of rich milk. Experts would choose them, accompany them to Israel, control the quarantine regulations, and place them in the agricultural settlements; but then we encountered a new problem. Since there was rationing in the whole country, the new immigrants would slaughter their cows for meat instead of keeping them for milk. Meat was scarce and in great demand, and therefore very expensive. To combat this problem, we brought in white goats, that are less aggressive than the tree-eating black ones. These white goats produced good quality milk but the meat was good for nothing. These goats were brought over in DC3 planes and it was a sight to behold as the animal experts dashed off the planes at Lod airport faster than a missile to get away from the stench.

The people who worked in the Settlement Department were the elite of the workforce – dedicated in their mission to create a new society in a new country. They identified wholeheartedly with the tasks and challenges they faced, believed in their contribution to the future strength of the state – a new and modern state which would one day serve as a model to all others.

There are several examples of these successes: two Belgian cotton experts, for instance, were brought in to determine whether cotton plantations could be developed in Israel. Their report was negative, there was no way that cotton would grow successfully in this climate and on this soil. Later an American Jew, a successful cotton-grower in the United States, told us to ignore the Belgian report, and he set up cotton plantations, which ultimately produced five times the amount of cotton produced by Egypt, *the* manufacturers of the finest cotton in the world at that time. Then there was the dripping irrigation system which is very economical in its use of water. It was introduced and developed by Israel and it became world famous and widespread. Today Holland and Britain import flowers from Israel, something inconceivable to the early pioneers. My specific task in the Supply And Equipment Division was to deal with spare parts. We had bought agricultural machinery from all the major manufacturers and when the machinery was originally purchased, spare parts hadn't seemed necessary, but these essential elements soon wore out regularly, and it turned out that there was an urgent need for spare parts. The immigrants often poured water instead of oil onto machinery, or poured oil into the radiator. Costly equipment was ruined for lack of experience and training. There were genuine and non-genuine spare parts. The latter were less expensive, usually just as good, but needed proper specifications. Some spares could also be produced locally.

The quantity of stocks held by the Supply and Equipment Department was huge, amounting to thousands of items which required vast warehouses, and that led to a risk of theft, safety and security. At weekends we regularly inspected the Moshavim to make sure that goods had been delivered as promised; and my wife, Gina was not happy to spend her weekends driving around the settlements with me, checking all this out.

Eventually I became Secretary-General of the Supply and Equipment Division, in charge of all operational aspects.

While Eshkol was Treasurer of the Jewish Agency and Head of the Settlement Division, he was also Minister of Agriculture. When he became Minister of Finance, replacing Avraham Kaplan (the first Minister of Finance of the State), Dr Giora Josephtal became Treasurer of the Agency, and also continued to serve as Head of the Absorption Department. It was at this time that the Supply and Equipment Division was moved from the Settlement Department to the Treasury, and served all departments of the Agency, including Absorption; thus I came under the umbrella of the Treasury.

Giladi's post was taken by Nachman Vidan. When Vidan was sent to Germany as part of the Reparations programme, his place was taken by

Izzy Reiss. Vidan was an excellent administrator, a former colonel in army depots; while Izzy Reiss who, in pre-State years had been Treasurer of the Illegal Immigration, was also an actor and a theatrical director. A member of Kibbutz Givat Brenner, he was a cheerful character, always smiling, who possessed a unique combination of competence in arts and computation. Constantly on the go, he neglected his heart-condition until it defeated him. He left behind his widow, Paula, three sons and an enormous circle of bereaved friends.

At Izzy's funeral, I was told that Dr Josephtal was looking for me. He had been a close friend of Izzy's ever since they both belonged to the Zionist movement in Germany before the War and both had settled in Kibbutzim. Josephthal told me then and there that he was appointing a management of three to the Supply and Equipment Division: Eliezer Shavit, Mordechai Paran, and myself. 'But,' boomed Josephtal, 'I only want to see you in my office'. Thus, indirectly, I became first among equals. By 1955 the functions of the Division began to decline, mainly as a result of the decline in immigration, although there was still plenty to be done.

During this time, Gina and I and our son, Zvi were living with my mother, and I was trying to increase my salary so we could buy our own home. The only way I saw to do this was to take a post abroad, and I had been offered a position with the Israeli Mission in Germany for Reparations to the State. Germany certainly had no appeal, so, when Dr Josephtal heard that I had received such an offer, he made a counter-offer, proposing that I wait another year, and he would assign me to the European and North African Treasury office in Geneva. I accepted and continued to run the Supply and Equipment Division for another year.

In the summer of 1956 we moved to Switzerland. My new assignment was certainly a challenge, an unknown field. The posting was as one of two deputies to the representative of the Executive of the Agency and its Treasury for Europe and North Africa, whose headquarters were in Geneva.

Gina Harmatz, née Kerzenfeld

Our wedding day, Tel Aviv June 28 1951

Gina with Zvi and Ronny

VII

BACK TO EUROPE 1956–1960

Geneva

The office coordinated all activities of the various departments of the Agency in Europe and North Africa. The tasks were extensive: emigration, transportation, education and culture, Youth Aliya, financing operations, control of expenditure, sourcing finance (either from contributions, bank loans, or individual donations), currency dealing, overseeing purchasing in Europe for the Supply and Equipment Division back in Israel, and the general administration of all the *schlichim* in Europe and North Africa, some of whom were permanently based in Geneva and some were there only temporarily.

I found myself in a new environment. The contrast between the rationing of Tel Aviv in the 1950s and the wealth and extravagance of Switzerland was a shock to the system. French was, of course, to be my working language, and was almost entirely strange to me. I had studied it in Lithuania, but our teacher had been so delightful that she allowed us to play around instead of paying attention to our lessons. So the only support I had as far as language was concerned was from Gina who, having been brought up mainly in Paris, was fluent in French. My English was also not exactly Shakespearean and German, in which I was fluent was not readily accepted in French-speaking Switzerland. My predecessor had spoken all three languages perfectly as did my boss and all the secretaries.

Thus I arrived in Geneva with a ready-made handicap.

My immediate boss was Eran Laor, formerly Erich Landstein; he was born in Slovakia/Hungary in the era when Franz Josef was Kaiser of the Austro-Hungarian Empire. He was a perfectionist, a diplomat, a financier, a poet, a writer, an intellectual par excellence, at least a generation older than I, with a rich experience in Jewish life and Jewish communities in Europe. As a collector of Judaica, primarily old maps, and renowned as the foremost authority and collector of these maps, he devoted great energy to that hobby. Laor was then a 56-year-old bachelor with all the capricious characteristics of a single man. I was only 31.

My duties under Laor included budgetary control of all expenditure, the financing of all operations in cooperation with the Treasury in Jerusalem. The overall budget was set by Jerusalem, but the Geneva office had to approve each and every expenditure to maintain the budget. So we were granted managerial status, both because we were the representative office of the Agency, and also because we had to finance the operations when money was short and still balance the budget.

One of my earliest tasks was to go to Köln to inspect a divisional office that dealt with Reparations from Germany to Israel, and purchased equipment and supplies in Germany. The functions of this office had, however, long ago been taken over by our office. In Köln I found an entire house with a garden and its own caretaker, and a woman who had been dealing with all this, but whose function was now redundant. Rows of purchasing files also seemed redundant and I made an instant decision to light a fire in the garden and burn the lot. Then I took Mrs Blumenfeld back with me to Geneva where I made her comptroller of purchasing and budgets throughout Europe and North Africa, a function she performed splendidly.

In Geneva we worked mainly with the Immigration Department which had to obtain approval for every detail. The same financial approval and operational involvement also applied to two important additional activities: emigration from Eastern Europe, and emigration from North Africa. These areas had to be handled discreetly, since although they were sometimes legal, they were often considered illegal: this included the organisation of a self-defence body in North Africa, in light of extreme national movements in Morocco, Tunisia and Algeria.

The first few months in my new post were relatively peaceful, but things gradually became more problematic and even turbulent. In June 1956 emigration from Morocco was stopped when Isteclal, the national Socialist party, came into power, diminishing the authority of King Mohammed V, as control passed to the military and the police. The offices of the Agency were closed down and emigration was declared illegal. After months of negotiation and intervention, some eight thousand emigrants who had been held in a camp in Casablanca were transferred to another camp – Grand Arenas – in Marseilles, and eventually sailed to Haifa. A new organisation had to be established to help the remaining Jewish community, both in emigration and in self-defence.

There were some 350,000 in Morocco, while in Algeria and Tunisia there were a lot less.

With the help of French paratroopers, we rescued more than one thousand emigrants from Algeria, via the port of Phillipville, after an attack by the FLN – Front Liberation Nationale, a bitter enemy of the Jews. Despite promises that two of our men, whom they had captured, were both alive and would be turned over to us, Hassan and Ben Guera were both killed by the 5th Brigade of the FLN and all we could recover was the burned out wreckage of their bullet-spattered car.

In October 1956, the Hungarians staged a revolution against the Soviet regime as the Russians invaded Hungary, and thousands of Jews escaped. Here again we had to assist, although many wanted to emigrate to the United States and Canada.

And it was also at this time that Gomulka was returned to power in Poland, having signed an agreement with Krushchev who had agreed to allow Polish immigrants, gentiles and Jews who had been trapped during the war years all over Russia, to leave the Soviet Union. That became the third surge of repatriation – Jews who came to Poland – to Silesia, an area the Russians had taken from the Germans and then handed over to the Poles against the territories they had annexed from Poland for themselves, in the east.

The Geneva office was flooded by these tides of immigration, which involved chartering boats and planes, organising train transportation, agreements with ship-owners, moving boats from one European port to another, financing operations in different currencies, providing emigrants with cash to buy tickets and transport their belongings, and collecting their belongings from the ports of Gdansk and Trieste, among others.

Financing was sometimes straightforward, but was often complicated; and those who were financially competent and familiar with the money markets, local conditions, and variable rates of exchange could either lose or make money. The usual way of raising finance applied particularly to France and countries within the French franc zone, such as North Africa. France was short of dollars and it was possible to buy French francs for dollars at a preferential rate (dollar *titres*), on condition that the francs were spent in France or in their ex-colonies. Since many of our activities were connected with those countries, we would naturally take advantage of this. This was especially so in chartering the Argentinian boats – the *Salta* and the *Santa Fé* – from the Argentinian shipping company, the Dodero line, within the Franco/Argentinian trade agreement, when the French franc was strong against the Argentinian currency. Thus we benefited twice: on the French franc, and on the Argentinian peso. Since the cost of hiring boats was exceptionally high as a result of the blockade on the Suez Canal, this was very important.

In other countries, especially in East European countries, the official rate of exchange in local currencies was artificial and totally unrelated to sterling, dollars or Swiss francs. Those countries were desperate for such currencies and they threw their money onto the international financial markets by the billions. The critical problem was how to get hold of these quantities of money and use them inside the countries to pay for transportation, either for passengers moving from there to western European ports, or sending their belongings from East European ports, partly on their cargo ships, and partly by Western shipping companies. These countries seemed to be losing money on such transactions, since we gained significantly; but the truth was that they were so desperate for foreign currency, that they would pay any amount of their currency for dollars. We would always have to consider how far we could go with such transactions, because we never knew whether certain elements within these countries might use the situation for political purposes.

We stayed within the limits, and in general, it could be said that, as a result of these transactions, the Agency had more funds available than it might otherwise have. This enabled us to pay the governments of these East European countries, allowing many more thousands of Jews to leave than might otherwise have been the case.

Once I was summoned to a meeting in Vienna with the head of the Agency's Treasury where the issue of currency dealing was raised. After a heated exchange of opinion, I was asked for details. My immediate superior expressed his complete trust in the way this matter was handled, but the 'super boss' insisted on hearing the precise nature of these transactions, and then ordered us to 'stop it at once'. It was late, and before too many tempers flared, we decided to retire for the night.

Next morning we resumed our discussions over breakfast. The Treasury boss asked me what the difference would amount to if we hadn't engaged in playing the currency markets. When I explained that if emigration were to continue at the same rate it would be somewhere in the region of 16 to 18 million dollars, he was amazed. 'OK,' he said, 'so we didn't say what we said last night'.

'All right, Sir,' I replied, 'last night you did not know it, but today, you do!'

Cutting the Mast – The Charlton Star

Many years later – about thirty-seven to be precise, I was visiting London and, anxious to see a good play, I went with a friend to the Savoy Theatre. Susan Hampshire was starring in a Noel Coward play, and having always been a fan of hers, especially since I learned about the good work she was doing in the field of dyslexia, I figured this would be worthwhile seeing. The play was, in fact, rather mediocre, although Susan Hampshire's performance was superb. My companion for the evening and I both agreed that one act was enough and so during the interval we slipped away to a restaurant opposite the Savoy.

Sitting over dinner and a good bottle of wine, I recounted to my friend the story of another dinner I had had thirty-seven years earlier at the Savoy Hotel with two gentlemen: one a shipowner and the other a maritime expert.

In 1957, the Nikita Krushchev and Vladislav Gomulka agreement resulted in tens of thousands of Polish Jews moving back into Poland and it included thousands more who had married Soviet nationals, their spouses and of course the children of such unions.

Since Poland under Gomulka was a relatively liberal regime, the authorities permitted the returning Jews to leave Poland for the Jewish State, and they were even allowed to take their belongings with them, property they had either brought from Russia or had acquired in Poland before leaving.

Based as I was in Switzerland at this time, I was deeply involved in the supervision of this exodus. At first it proceeded quite smoothly: people would leave by the only train departing from Warsaw for the West, which left at midnight, crossed the Czechoslovakian border into Austria, and arrived in Vienna at three o'clock the following afternoon. The emigrants would be taken from Ostbahnhof to a restaurant in the suburbs of Vienna so as not to cause too much disturbance to the locals; there they would rest and after a meal, were taken to the Westbahnhof to continue their journey, either to Genoa in Northern Italy or to Naples in the south, from which point they would leave on scheduled shipping routes, or on chartered boats, for Haifa.

All this proceeded well as long as the numbers remained manageable, and while the existing means of transportation could cope with the masses wishing to leave. But two things happened.

The numbers of applicants for visas to leave Poland increased dramatically and could no longer be handled by the once-a-day rail departure, the number of wagons on the train being limited.

The four-fold exodus, from Poland, Hungary, Morocco and Egypt, created a huge bottleneck. With the Suez Canal blocked by sunken ships as a result of the Anglo-French-Israeli assault, the greatest problem lay in the field of shipping. The supply of available ships worldwide had shrunk almost to zero, since all vessels, both cargo and passenger liners, now had to circumnavigate the Cape of Good Hope in South Africa. Finding good ships was a problem. Not only did the price of transportation escalate incredibly, but it was virtually impossible to find a free-floating vessel anywhere.

I explored every possibility and started travelling between London and Paris, from Piraeus to Marseilles, from Southampton to Le Havre, to Stetin and Trieste. I had to find the most practical and effective solution to transport tens of thousands of Jews from countries which either did not want to keep them, or from those countries where, for politics and morale, the Jews no longer wished to remain.

There did not seem to be any adequate means of transporting these huge numbers of refugees, so we called for a meeting in Geneva. Four people participated: my boss, Eran Laor, as the Jewish Agency's representative and head of the department for European and North African Affairs; the Israeli Ambassador to Warsaw; a gentleman in charge of East European Affairs representing the Israeli Prime Minister's Office, and myself. The objective was to find a solution to this problem, and we concluded that our Ambassador in Warsaw should intervene with the Polish authorities to allow boats into Gdansk, the Northern Polish port, to transport substantial numbers of Jews to relieve the pressure. We were talking of 8–12,000 people to be transported in ships with large capacities in ten or twelve crossings. The Ambassador was doubtful that the Poles would agree, yet we had to insist on this line of action. I pointed out that at the present rate it would take four years to get them out, and if he thought the Poles, or any other communist government, would keep the doors open that long, he was mistaken, and should push a little harder. I remember my boss kicking me hard under the table.

Fortunately, a few days later, the Ambassador came back to us with a positive response. And yet, along with this approval came a condition. The Poles did not agree to Gdansk as the exit point, but offered us the port of Stetin, a quiet little port, not as highly developed as Gdansk; it did not function at night because it lacked the appropriate naval equipment, and as such, was of little importance. This was precisely why they chose Stetin; they thought any large-scale shipping manoeuvres there would be less likely to attract the attention of the population, i.e., it would not irritate 'Big Brother' in the East, for that might have resulted in closing the gates between Poland and Russia for those who were still waiting to return. We accepted the decision on Stetin, and soon discovered the problematic nature of those restrictions.

Our next task was to find ships. With such huge numbers of immigrants to transport, we needed all the options open to us. To move the migrants from Warsaw to Vienna or Athens, from Bucharest to Athens, from Gibraltar to Marseilles, and then from Athens to Tel Aviv, we also chartered planes employing Bal-Air, Tarom, Lot, El Al and the Flying Tigers, a US company based in Zurich which flew from Athens. In spite of using air transport and the European train network, we still needed more ships.

We managed to obtain, for one trip only, the Italian *Aurelia*; there was a break in its regular schedule which allowed us just enough time to transport 1,000 emigrants out of Stetin to Le Havre. It was then that we were also offered the opportunity to charter the Egyptian ship *Misr*, but we were obliged to tell the naïve broker that this was not an appropriate vessel for us.

In due course, one of our shipping brokers offered us a bargain. 'There is a large boat', he said. 'It's not modern, in fact, it's quite antiquated but she floats well in the water; she was bought for the experiment in the Pacific when the first submarine atomic bomb was exploded on July 24, 1946 in the lagoon of Bikini.' The *Charlton Star* was one of the few which survived the experiment which involved 75 boats.

This *Star* was our bargain! It had been lying in the port of Southampton waiting for better days. Nobody had the chutzpah to touch it, because rumour had it that the boat might have been radioactively contaminated. So, we sent out experts with Geiger counters who reported no radioactivity. We chartered the boat for six months with the help of the representative of the Israeli National Shipping Line, an expert in maritime affairs based in London. It was indeed an old ship but it was refurbished at our request by the owners, a renowned ship-owning family of Greek origin, who were also based in London.

We decided to bring the *Charlton Star* into Stetin to ferry the immigrants to Le Havre. It would take only a few days and from there they would take the train to Marseilles. This allowed us to gain time and to avoid having to negotiate the Bay of Biscay and the Straits of Gibraltar, which would have taken two weeks longer. Between 1,000 and 1,200 people would be transported on each of these trips. Because of the huge numbers waiting to leave we had to unlock the blockage in Poland as quickly as possible before the emigration process was stopped.

Stetin was a port with restricted hours of operation, and it was also very difficult to manoeuvre ships there because of the high walls around its harbour. Boats had to be in and out between dawn and dusk, and to meet the time constraints, ships had to pass through the Kiel Canal, and the arrival and departure times had to be calculated correctly. On our first voyage, the captain encountered a problem we had not reckoned with. Because of the exceptionally high tide and the sudden turn in the tide, the ship, which had a very tall mast, could not pass under the Kiel Canal Bridge.

Our representative, Greenman, called me at night in Geneva. 'Harmatz? I hope I am not calling you too late'.

'Not at all,' I replied, 'what's the problem?'

'Look,' he said, 'I had no choice but to call you. What with the tide and the bridge, we're not going to make it through the Canal tonight – so would you please call our people in Warsaw and tell them we'll be late into Stetin?' Then he added in a kind of undertone: 'The only alternative I can suggest is to cut the mast – that way, we'd make it under the bridge before the tide turns'.

I believe he offered this solution as a sort of joke. I hesitated for a few moments, and then said to him: 'Go ahead, cut it down, but first, clear it with the captain; either talk him into it, or give him a few good drinks so he agrees'. Greenman, with all his tact and diplomacy probably did both, and the deed was done.

* * *

Several more successful voyages were made in and out of Stetin and our objective was accomplished. After these exercises, the *Charlton Star* was brought to the Mediterranean, where it was used on journeys from all the South European exit ports to Haifa within the six month period left under the terms of the time-charter. When the six-month contract had expired, Toni X, a member of the family who owned the

Charlton Star, presented us with a bill of £42,000 for extra costs – a vast amount of money in those days. There was no way I would accept it. And so, Toni sent over his 'Captain of Captains' to negotiate with us in Switzerland. This so-called naval expert, more of a hardened drunken seaman, was so far gone when he staggered off the plane at Geneva, that it would have been impossible to discuss the weather conditions, let alone serious financial matters. He was sent back home and I called Toni X to fix an appointment with him personally in London.

London was an ideal place for such a meeting. The representative of the Israeli national shipping line was based there, an expert in maritime matters, and with him as arbiter, we started our negotiations at nine in the morning. The dispute was complex, but the meeting was conducted in a civil manner. I explained that as a non-commercial enterprise, the price for the charter was already more than we had expected to pay and that in fact, the shipping company would have earned nothing from the *Charlton Star* had we not agreed to take it on for those six months. Of the £42,000 they were claiming, I offered to settle for £6,000. By four o'clock in the afternoon I was still stuck on six, while they had come down to nine. My expert colleague called me outside and said that he had never been involved in such tough negotiations. As a member of the Shipowners Club he thought I might need these people in the future for other chartering purposes; he thought we should not spoil our chances and that I should compromise. Back we went into the room and I announced that I was ready for conciliation. Toni X offered to settle at £7,500.

'OK', I said, 'but since I still don't believe I owe you anything and I intend to stick to my principles, I am deducting one hundred pounds symbolically and offer you £7,400.'

Before I left for London, I had called headquarters in Jerusalem to advise them of the possibility of a substantial claim against us. I had been given leave to go up to a maximum commitment of £21,000 in my negotiations. When I eventually cabled to inform them that I had settled at £7,400, I received a telegram from the Treasurer himself with warm congratulations on my success.

Toni invited us to dinner at the Savoy Hotel that night – an evening spent in a spirit of friendship and courtesy, and at a certain point during the meal he turned to me, smiling, and said: 'You know, Joe, I come from a family of navigators and shipowners; my whole family has been involved in the world of shipping, my father, my brother and I are all naval people. We've had many experiences over the years, but one thing is certain: I do not recall that in any of our charter agreements we have had a mast cut down off one of our ships'.

Vitek

When the problems began with the emigration of Jews from Poland, I had resolved to go to Warsaw to see what could be done. However, that was an awkward situation since Poland was an Eastern Bloc country and I had left the Soviet Union in 1945 under dubious circumstances and if the Soviet authorities in the 1950s wanted to give me trouble, I could have easily been branded a deserter. But as I was deeply involved in the migration of Jews to Israel, I risked going to Warsaw whenever necessary.

There, through Israel Kronik, a former comrade-in-arms from my battalion, I got in touch with Vitek. Vitek was born in Vilna; he was either a Lithuanian Pole or a Polish Lithuanian and was one of the paratroopers who joined the underground partisans in the forests south of Vilna under the German occupation. He was an officer at the headquarters of the Lithuanian Partisan Movement, a young man, who spoke Lithuanian, Russian, Polish, and even understood Yiddish. When Abba Kovner describes Vilna in his book *On the Narrow Bridge*, he writes that the Jews in Vilna were *real* Jews and that even the non-Jews in certain quarters were sometimes very Jewish. Vitek was one of them. He was brought up among Jews in a very Jewish environment and always felt comfortable in their company. As an officer in the forest, he dealt with important matters of intelligence, contact with the local population, and the printing and distribution of propaganda, a vital aspect of our work. Since I was Head of the Department of Special Operations in the partisan battalion *To Victory*, we had a close working relationship.

After the war, we parted company. He attended the school of intelligence and we lost contact. I left Lithuania and eventually, of course, settled in Israel, while Vitek made a career in the security forces and then, when Marshall Rokosovky was sent by the Soviet regime to Poland to strengthen their influence there, he came with an entire entourage, including Vitek. Having a knowledge of languages, and a fine reputation as an underground officer, he continued to make a distinguished career for himself, and by the time I came to Warsaw late in 1957, he was Deputy Minister of the Interior and Head of the KGB system.

I decided to try to see him. Perhaps he would tell me why the authorities had curtailed the movement of Jews out of Poland and whether there was any prospect of the standstill ending, and if so, when. First I had to consult our people at the Embassy. A meeting between four people was arranged to discuss the issue. The Israeli Ambassador, Katriel Katz, was one participant; then there was a man who dealt with immigration problems, Zvi Netzer; the third was a man in charge of security, and the fourth was myself. We discussed whether or not I should go to see Vitek. The ambassador was non-committal, he knew my past and did not want to risk any diplomatic embarrassment. The security man was reserved.

'I cannot take responsibility for your personal safety,' he said. 'You could find yourself in a trap. It's true that this Vitek has a high position and is a person of influence. If it works out OK, it could be just the contact we need, but it could turn sour. If you reach him and it turns out well, great!'

Zvi Netzer, in charge of immigration, said: 'Joe, go, just go ahead, nothing terrible will happen, you'll have a great meeting and you'll feel good about it in the future'. The verdict was 50:50.

I called Vitek the very next day and when I finally got through to him, I addressed him by the code name he had used in the forests: Margis.

'Margis', I said, 'It's Julian here (Julian was my nickname), I'm in Warsaw.'

'I know you're in Warsaw,' came the reply.

'Listen, if it's not too inconvenient, I'd like to meet you.'

'It's certainly not inconvenient for me.'

I said, 'Let's meet in a cafe or in a restaurant.'

'No, no, no way', said Vitek, 'if you're here in Warsaw, I insist you come to my home. Come over around eight o'clock tonight. I'm looking forward to seeing you and welcoming you to my home.'

So Kronik and I went to his apartment and as we entered some kind of party was in progress which seemed to be nearing its end. I learned later that it was his wedding anniversary. Gradually people left and eventually he asked his wife to withdraw. Finally we were alone. He kept putting records on his gramophone – they were old scratchy records – and he asked me if I remembered the tunes. Of course I remembered them, but I don't know whether he was just being sentimental, or whether by putting on this music he was trying to muffle any bugging devices. A bottle of French cognac stood on the table with a lot of food, and as we ate and drank into the early hours of the morning, we caught up on the intervening years; I told him what I had done; how I moved south and started to deal with the illegal immigration, how I had gone to Germany in search of vengeance, how I arrived illegally in Palestine, was arrested by the British, fought in the Israeli War of Independence and so on.

'You know,' he said to me, 'you were crazy ever to leave the Soviet Union. Why on earth didn't you stay, Julik?; you would have made a great career for yourself within the Party. Today, you and I would be sitting on the same side of the desk, not on opposite sides.'

'OK, Vitek,' I said, 'what's done is done, but tell me, we have heard so many terrible stories about the regime, how on earth did you survive? So many of your comrades seem to have just disappeared.'

'Look, it's quite simple: it's true there have been many changes of leadership within the regime, but I am an expert in my field. I don't deal in politics. I confine myself to my expertise and just get on with my job. And you know what, every time there is a change of leadership, I get promoted! The bureaucracy doesn't worry me.'

Then we chatted about other things and in passing, he made it clear that he was not going to give away any information. Then I asked him two things: first I wanted to now why they had stopped the Jews from leaving Poland. I learned that it was not the Poles but the Soviets who had stopped the process. 'Look', he said, 'under their agreement with Gomulka they let ex-Polish citizens out and what happened? Their relatives, either in Vilna, or Moscow, or Leningrad, received letters from Tel Aviv telling them that they have arrived there safely. That was never the idea. The Soviets didn't make the agreement because they support Zionism. That's not what they had in mind when they granted permits to leave. They didn't intend to send people from the Soviet Union to Jerusalem via Poland. Since there has been one such incident after another, they could not let this continue; after all, news travels. And because there are also Soviet citizens marrying Poles just to benefit from the agreement, the situation has gotten out of hand. There are whole families – children and mothers who are not always the legitimate relatives they claim to be, they were leaving in droves.'

And Vitek continued: 'We don't mind if the Jews decide to leave Poland. We actually want to have good relations with the West. And, you know, Julik, we're not so eager for them to stay anyway; if they do, we may face yet another problem; they may expect to get their homes back – although, with Eastern Poland belonging to Russia today and the Western Zone being part of Germany, they wouldn't stand a chance. But still, in the meantime they're in camps all over the place, in Silesia, and so on. And there's also a problem of jobs; there are severe economic conditions; what are we to do with these people?'

Vitek believed the situation would improve, and offered to help if he could. Within a couple of months permission for Jews to leave was once again granted.

The other subject I raised with him – privately – was the question of a forum of the heads of security of all the Eastern European countries. I asked him whether he had knowledge of any such forum and if one did exist, if he had access to it. I asked if his relations with the Romanian representative were good and if he would be willing to ask if the authorities would consider a similar agreement to the one in Poland: that is, to let the Jews leave Romania.

He said he was prepared to approach the appropriate people. 'I believe in this,' said Vitek, 'I believe since the Jews did not have a state of their own until a few years ago, the reason that Gomulka let the Jews leave and not the Ukrainians and the White Russians was just because the Ukrainians and the White Russians have their own republics right there. And now the Jews have their own State too, even though it is far away. Ideologically there is good reason to let them leave.

'I believe the Romanians will listen and will react sympathetically to such a request. I'm ready to speak to the appropriate people on this matter,' said Vitek. I have no proof, but I believe that he did. A year later emigration from Romania began.

Before I left Vitek's apartment that night, he asked me if there were any people I was personally interested in helping to leave Warsaw. I gave him a list, mostly people who had been with us in the underground, whom we had seen queuing up for their permits at the Israeli embassy. Vitek looked at the list and suddenly said: 'What, Isca Gordon also wants to leave?' Isca Gordon was the youngest of three brothers, two of whom had been with us in the underground. Both had been killed. Isca was married to a girl who was also in the underground. Within a few weeks he, and all the others on the list were out of Poland, on their way to Israel.

Years later, after changes in the political regime of Poland, Vitek was relieved of his post, and appointed Chairman of their Military and Security Sports Association. One day, out of the blue, he arrived in Israel with the Polish basketball team, and I was able to reciprocate his hospitality.

Later I heard that he was sick, that he had difficulty moving, and, no longer a youngster and having lived through difficult times in Poland, he was finding life rather tough. I sent money to help him out, and from time to time I would try to speak to him on the telephone from London; whenever I did, after two or three sentences, our conversation was cut off. This came, I imagined, from his end; the authorities were undoubtedly monitoring his calls; after all he had had quite a past and they knew what his connections were, so they still kept track of his every move. Again I sent him money and he thanked me. Our last conversation was about a book he said had been published about the Underground, and he told me proudly that he had sent me a copy. I never received it.

In January 1990 as Director General of the World ORT Union, I travelled to Warsaw with a colleague from the London headquarters to discuss a potential collaboration with the Polish authorities on manpower training. I planned to contact Vitek.

At Warsaw airport, I asked Simon Feldman if there were any engagements that evening. He said there were none till the next morning and so, as soon as I reached the hotel, I picked up the phone and called Vitek. A woman answered and I asked if I could speak to him.

'No, I'm afraid not,' came the reply.

'Will he be at home later?' I asked.

'Who is speaking?' I explained that I was an old friend of Vitek's. Then came the devastating news.

'He won't be home later. he won't be home at all again. I'm afraid he's no longer with us.'

I was stunned. I could hardly speak but managed to ask when it had happened.

'Ten days ago,' said the woman. 'He died on January 13.' I muttered my condolences in my rather rusty Polish and put down the telephone.

Here I was in Warsaw after all these years, and I had come just ten days too late.

Horses from Transylvania

By the late 1950s there had been some emigration from Romania, but conditions for obtaining an exit visa were strict. Only certain people were permitted to emigrate; those in key positions, engineers, scientists, military personnel were absolutely prohibited from leaving. Those who were allowed, were restricted in what they could take with them: 30 kilograms of belongings, no cash, no gold, diamonds or furs.

And then suddenly, one day, out of the blue, even those who had already applied for visas were refused. No-one knew exactly why this sudden change had come about, but rumours of all kinds were circulating, including one supposition that the reason was a speech given in Tel Aviv by David Ben-Gurion, Prime Minister of Israel at the time, during which, in his usual excited manner, he had declared that not only the Jews of Romania, but also those from the Soviet Union would soon be coming to Israel. So when the Romanian Jews came to the authorities to apply for exit visas, they were told 'Ask Ben-Gurion, he's been promising everyone that Romanians will be let out!'

From that moment on, the Romanian Jews faced a difficult situation: thousands who had applied for their exit visas were fired from their jobs, forced out of their apartments, and their children were expelled from school. Nobody wanted to have anything to do with them. They were branded as traitors.

These people were left penniless, they had spent their final salaries on refurbishing their apartments; one condition set by the authorities was, that if they wanted to give up their apartments and fulfil the stipulation for an exit visa, they had to restore them to perfect condition: every light-bulb had to be replaced, every surface repainted, every missing door handle or light switch supplied, and it was almost impossible to find spare parts for certain electrical or plumbing fixtures in those times, and if they could be found they cost a small fortune. The authorities used every excuse not to grant the appropriate certificate of approval, and that was only one of the requisite documents; you had to prove that all taxes had been paid up to date, municipal and governmental; that the children's tuition fees had been paid; students who had graduated from university had to repay the cost of their studies. To supply all these certificates to the Ministry of Interior which supervised the issue of exit visas, families had to appear repeatedly at these offices because the bureaucrats would always find something not quite in order.

The Jewish Agency tried to help those unfortunates to ease their plight and get them out of Romania as soon as possible. The Agency was responsible for financing their departure – because they had to pay for their tickets themselves plus taxes. Since they had no money – that too became our responsibility. If there were debts to pay, there, too, we had to assist. The Agency had no offices of their own in Bucharest so it was the Israeli Embassy staff who worked day and night to help the emigrants on our behalf.

Based in Geneva, the Agency's Division for Europe and North Africa received regular accounts on the emigration process, and related difficulties, as well as financial reports on expenditure. Yet, at a certain stage, I resolved to go personally to see for myself how matters were progressing, how we could help improve the situation, to try to open wider the exit gates and to discuss future procedures with the Ambassador and Embassy staff.

I applied for a visa to Romania at the Embassy in Berne, and was immediately refused. A very good friend of mine told me that the Settlement Department of the Agency was sending a delegation to Romania to buy horses. Why?

As I described earlier, Israel in those days was blessed with huge waves of immigrants from all over the Middle East, principally Muslim countries. These people were not trained for agriculture and those who were, were used to very primitive methods and standards. They had no idea what to do with a tractor, not to mention a combine harvester. Supplying them with this kind of machinery was a disaster and without proper training it could not work. It was decided therefore to return to the old-fashioned methods – to the horse and cart, the mule and donkey, in short, the methods they were used to. Mules could be obtained from Cyprus and Turkey, but the source for horses, they were informed, was Romania, specifically, Transylvania. Two experts were appointed to discover if there was a possibility of exporting mares to Israel from Romania. Amichai Kroll was an agronomist by training, and the other expert was Professor Komorov – Kimron, head of the Veterinary Institute of Israel, and *the* authority in the country on horses. The two were preparing for this trip when I learned of their intention to travel to Bucharest. I cabled the Treasurer of the Agency, explained my reasons for wishing to visit Romania and asked permission to be appointed to the delegation to Romania. Since the Romanians were interested in export orders and collecting dollars, the visa was immediately granted and I was told I could pick it up at the Embassy in Berne. The title in my service passport – Chargé de Mission par le gouvernement d'Israel – sounded impressive, and I was therefore appointed head of the delegation – of horse experts!

I met my colleagues in Belgrade and we took a Tarom flight to Bucharest, with a stop over in Sofia, where we were invited for coffee in the airport lounge and then for some reason rushed back to the plane at the last minute. I was the last passenger to board and there was a frightening moment when the plane steps were whisked away from under my feet. While I had one foot just inside the airplane, the other was left dangling in mid-air and once again I wondered if I'd make it to Romania after all.

But we did, and the First Secretary of the Israeli Embassy picked us up and took us to the hotel – the Palace Athenée, the hotel reserved for foreigners. There wasn't a single corner that wasn't bugged. Suddenly I saw the First Secretary leafing through all our belongings, all our papers, everything. When we looked a little perplexed, he explained – in Hebrew: 'Look, when you go down to dinner, they're going to look over every single thing here, so I might as well do it for you – and if there is anything that might be compromising, I better be the one to find it and remove it!'

Sitting downstairs at dinner, I observed three 'gentlemen' who had certainly been appointed to watch us. When I mentioned this, my two colleagues refused to believe me, so I told one of them to go to the bathroom, and promised that one of the three would follow, so he would discover which one was to shadow *him*. They both did as I suggested and sure enough, when they returned to the table they were paler and wiser than before. The three guards did not leave us for a moment until we left Romania.

At dinner we were entertained by a small first-class orchestra. I was surprised to find a small replica of the East German flag on our table – and I was even more astonished when they made a point of playing one German melody after another. At the end of one of these pieces, the conductor came to our table and asked if we were enjoying the music. When we said we were not that fond of German music, he asked: 'But aren't you German?' 'No, we're from Israel.' we replied. There was a flurry of agitation around the table and the East German flag was whisked away and replaced by an Israeli flag. The orchestra struck up once again and started to play all kinds of Israeli and Jewish melodies.

The guy who was on percussion took up the musical saw and gave a rendition of the Iddische Mamma such as I had never ever, and have never since, heard. That saw sang out with such emotion that to this day I can still hear its melancholy tones. After dinner, we thanked the musicians for their beautiful performance. The chap who had played the saw stayed behind and it turned out he was a Jew. We asked him what was going on; he looked at us with sad eyes, and said:

'Listen, I am not going to tell you too much, but I will tell you a story that is going around Bucharest these days:

'At three o'clock in the morning somebody knocks on the door of a Jewish family's home. "Who's there," asks the father.

"It's the Post Office, we have some mail for you."

'The father opens the door and three officers of the Secret Police walk in.

"Did you ask for an exit visa?" they demand. "We did," comes the answer.

"Why do you want to leave the country? The country has given you everything you needed, a job, an apartment, education for your children, don't you understand that this is treason against the state, aren't you ashamed that you show no gratitude to the regime which has looked after you so well? Where do you want to go to? To Israel? To a capitalist state where you will be exploited by those who just want to use you? Tell us, why, why are you going there?"

'The head of the family pauses a moment, and then looks his questioner in the eye, and says: "We want to go to Israel because we have heard that mail there is not delivered at three o'clock in the morning."

Those first few hours in Romania set the mood and made clear to us what we could expect.

Next morning I met with the Ambassador – but not before my documents were checked over and over again at the gates until they finally let me in. I followed up the problems the Embassy staff were facing by assisting those persecuted people and tried to ease the hardships they faced before they could leave. There were many family problems and the Israeli Embassy staff were limited by strict guidelines about what they could and could not permit.

There was one case of a family who had been granted an exit visa but came to ask for help. A mother appeared at the Embassy with her two children, a boy and a girl while I was there, and the Embassy official asked her where her husband was.

'He died two weeks ago', she replied.

'But your exit visa is about to expire,' explained the official, 'you must go as soon as possible'.

'I will not go,' said the wife, 'until I have placed a headstone on my husband's grave'.

'So do it, and go,' said the official impatiently.

'But I have no money for the stone,' explained the young widow. The embassy official had authority to grant money only for certain expenditures and headstones did not fit any of the categories. It was just fortuitous that I was there at that time and was able to step in and authorise the payment so this poor family could fulfil its obligations and leave as quickly as possible for Israel. The money was granted, the proper arrangements made and the family was able to leave Bucharest on the next available transport.

Then I joined my friends, Kroll and Komorov for the official part of our visit – meetings with the Ministry of Commerce and Trade in connection with our desire to purchase and export some three to five hundred horses to Israel. The Ministry arranged for us to go to Karei in the heart of Transylvania – an area where many local farms bred the kind of horses we were looking for. It was deepest winter and the local peasants brought their stock for our inspection. As my colleagues and I stood in the centre of a compound, the horsebreeders walked the horses around us in a circle, stopping now and again to allow Professor Komorov to look into the mouths of these animals, inspect their general appearance, and ask the relevant questions.

The experts seemed satisfied with what they saw and so our next visit was to Constanza, the Black Sea port where the horses would be shipped. There we were to make inquiries about insurance and transport, meet the people who would accompany the shipment, and inspect the quarantine facilities since this was a necessary precaution before the horses could be imported into Israel. We were handsomely received by the authorities in Constanza, for Professor Komorov had a worldwide reputation as the inventor of Serum K – for Komorov – to prevent disease – and all veterinarians were anxious to meet this highly respected member of their profession.

I split my time between the affairs of the delegation and seeing what could be done at the Embassy. Once we had finalised details of the purchase of the horses, timing, currency conversion, transportation, insurance and quarantine arrangements, my colleagues left for Israel, while I decided to take the train to Switzerland with a group of emigrants. I was interested in the general conditions of transport and border procedures, and this was an ideal way to observe them. From Bucharest the emigrants travelled by train via Hungary to Austria, but it was at the Romanian border that the guards behaved in what one can only term a cruel and inhuman fashion. I watched horrified as one official ripped the fur collar from the coat of a frightened elderly woman and another tore a child's necklace off her throat, practically strangling her. They made everyone get off the train while they searched through their cases, and behind and under the seats of each carriage to see if anything was hidden.

I reported in detail to my superiors on the situation in Romania and an initiative was launched to pressure the Romanian authorities to let the Jews go.

This is where we believe Vitek stepped in.

Eventually permission to leave was granted but a restriction remained on emigrating to Israel. Romanian Jews were allowed to go to any other country that was prepared to accept them. The European governments, primarily in Italy, Austria, France, Switzerland and Germany, were requested to ask their embassies in Bucharest to grant transit visas to the Romanian Jews. The plan worked, and the governments of those countries did indeed issue transit visas, while the Israeli authorities, assuring them that they would not remain in those countries for any length of time, guaranteed to cover all expenses while they were in transit.

But, while a nation can help its people collectively, an individual can often rely only on himself when faced with danger. On that train from Bucharest to Vienna, I witnessed an example of such ingenuity.

I was travelling in the same compartment as an elderly Jew, his wife, son and daughter-in-law and their two children. When he left Bucharest, this Jew had managed to smuggle out a rough diamond, the only item of value which he could salvage from his belongings. He knew that once they reached the border, the Romanian guards would use every possible means to find anything he was hiding. Well before the frontier with Hungary, he stared to chew a piece of gum, took it out of his mouth and pushed the gem into the sticky gum. Then he opened the carriage window and stuck it hard against the outside of the train. He shut the window and later watched, amused as the border guards searched every nook and cranny of the train carriage. I watched incredulously as, once the train passed through Hungary and crossed the border into Austria, the old man opened the window once again and smiled, as he pulled the gum off the side of the train and pulled it apart to reveal the diamond – his family's entire fortune.

The Straits of Gibraltar

In Morocco, the situation was no less delicate than in Romania or Poland. In 1956 the Isteclal government came to power and with it came the end of officially-sanctioned emigration of the Jews. Here, too, we faced problems of rescue.

As the Party became more aggressive towards the Jews and the King, who was more liberal and a friend of France, grew weaker, a special organisation had to be established to help Jews escape from the country, and to set up a self-defence group of local people, in case of an emergency, to protect the community from hostile elements or provocation.

It was, after all, only ten years since the Holocaust and the Israeli authorities were acutely aware of the possibility – God forbid – of a repetition. Nasser had become the leader of the Arab world. There was an anti-Zionist bias since Israel had joined France and Great Britain during the Suez crisis and every national organisation in the Arab world became pro-Nasser with his legendary speeches after the nationalisation of the Suez Canal. Together with Marshal Tito and Nehru, they formed the so-called bloc of the non-aligned nations.

The Tunisian and Algerian Jewish communities had already more or less dispersed, but in Morocco, the Jewish Agency office – Kadima – had been closed, while some 350,000 Jews, mostly poorer families, remained in the cities and outlying areas. There were already 8,000 in a camp waiting to leave for France and ultimately Israel.

The first task was to smuggle youngsters from former Jewish Youth movements out of Morocco via France into Israel, to train them there in military institutions and then sneak them back into Morocco, where they were organised into small groups which were armed.

My office dealt with the budgets of this operation; since I knew the people involved and because I was always eager to observe what was happening in the field, by default I became deeply involved in the details of the execution of this mission. There was close cooperation between all the parties and an admirable working relationship developed.

Tangiers was crucial, both because of its political standing (it had previously been a free-port) and for its geographical situation, facing Gibraltar – another free-port. Even at this time, under Moroccan national independence, it still maintained this status. There were also two

Spanish enclaves, Melia and Ceuta, which were a part of Morocco/North Africa geographically, but politically belonged to Spain.

The Agency had a bank account in Tangiers, where the manager was a friend of mine. He was an American citizen, had been an intelligence officer in the US airforce during the war. This bank manager knew of our activities and was very helpful. When the time came to rescue the Moroccan Jews and take them to the coast of Spain and Gibraltar in small boats, we bought a Cessna plane. It was a 50:50 partnership between him and the Agency. The plane was used partly for short trips to meet with him, but mainly to identify quiet shores where we could launch small groups in little boats. When I told him that I needed to bring 'equipment' into Morocco he considered a few moments, and then told me he had an idea. There was a large multi-national enterprise which the authorities treated liberally when it came to importing light and heavy equipment. He knew one of the engineers and would introduce him to me.

The next day, the gentleman came to meet me, in the bank manager's splendid two-storey villa with a courtyard and surrounded by pillars. There was also a huge garage with a ping-pong table in it, and there he invited me to play table tennis to cover our conversation. Whenever the ball dropped to the ground and we had to fetch it, we would interrupt our conversation. I told him who I was, the issue at stake, and the danger in which the Jewish community found itself; I spoke of the Holocaust, of my own past in the underground during the Second World War. I told him of our fears for the community, and the responsibility we felt towards them, and then I asked for his assistance.

He listened and his reaction seemed favourable.

I stayed in Tangiers another day, and that evening the bank manager visited me at my hotel and told me that his acquaintance was prepared to help, but he wanted a vast amount of money. I was shocked. I thought I had convinced him of the importance of the operation and the fact that he was demanding money, and an enormous sum at that, came as a huge surprise.

The situation had become urgent and I had no-one to consult at that moment.

Next morning when we met, I asked him a question:

'Why are you asking for this huge sum of money?'

'Because,' he replied, 'when I go back home, I, too, want to fly around in a Cessna, just like you'.

I gave the bank manager instructions to issue the cheque.

It does not matter how we finally brought in our 'equipment'. What is significant is that the cheque was never cashed!

The Treasurer

The entire Moroccan project required huge financial resources and as the situation became more dangerous the plan had to be implemented as fast as possible. Back in Geneva, we had long submitted a budgetary request, but didn't get an answer from Jerusalem. Since time was of the essence, I could no longer delay in approving an advance of a significant amount of money. I believed that the authorities in Jerusalem would see the importance of the project, as my colleagues and I did, and would understand the urgency of the decision.

I was called to a meeting in Paris, which had a considerable effect. The Treasurer of the Agency flew in from Jerusalem, while my immediate boss, Eran Laor, and I arrived from Geneva.

The Treasurer opened the meeting.

'I have called you both here,' he boomed, addressing Eran and myself, 'to discuss the matter of increasing the budget for the special unit.'

As he continued his voice gradually grew louder and more agitated.

'How could you approve this kind of expenditure without prior approval from Jerusalem?' he exclaimed. 'You had absolutely no authority to take such action!'

As an experienced lawyer he knew exactly how to go on the offensive. The fact that the European office had sanctioned the expenditure in advance without official approval had probably placed him in a compromising position with his fellow Executive members in Jerusalem. Money after all, was short as always, and to sanction such a figure was unusual and it had made him nervous.

At this point, Eran started to fidget uncomfortably in his seat. He was not accustomed to being spoken to in this tone. He gradually turned his head away, cast his eyes downward, took out his Swiss Army pocket-knife, and started fiddling with his nails. At this point, the storm clouds blew right over his head and settled firmly above the real culprit: me.

Sitting in that plush Parisian office, and listening to his rebuke, I recalled an incident at the beginning of 1944, after the battle of Stalingrad and the battle for Moscow. The Red Army was advancing westwards and depended on the partisans destroying as many trains and bridges, telegraph poles and railways lines as possible to help prevent Germans delivering reinforcements to the front. At this stage, the partisans started to receive massive support from Moscow. DC3 planes flew overhead and dropped all the vital supplies we fighters needed – antitank and machine guns, as well as explosives and ammunition. Everything had been packed in propaganda paper in many languages aimed at the different ethnic groups in that area. Although our brigade was known as the Lithuanian Brigade, most of the fighters, including many of the officers, were Jews. We were so happy when we discovered even more packages containing Camel cigarettes, chocolates and cocoa. Each of these little presents was accompanied by a note saying: 'To our brothers in the Lithuanian Partisans, who are fighting against the Nazi occupiers. From your Lithuanian brothers in America'.

For years I wondered how many Lithuanians there could possibly have been in America, compared with the number of Jews there. I thought of how difficult it must have been to transport these goods from America to Russia when German U-boats were doing whatever they could to sink everything en route from America to Murmansk, the northernmost inward port in Russia. And yet, these caring people far from their homeland, found a way, the goods, the space, the time, they had the idea, and they understood the importance of identifying themselves with those fighting the Germans; they understood how isolated we felt behind the lines, cut off from our families and from all normal life. The goods had been properly packed, put onto planes that had to cross enemy lines, and not all of them made it. But these precious supplies did arrive with their heartwarming message and, as I recalled, we suddenly felt that someone, somewhere was thinking of us, that they knew of our existence, knew we were fighting and that encouraged us. We believed that there were at last people, however far off, who were behind us.

So when all those years later, when I took this post in Europe on behalf of the Agency, I felt a profound sense of duty, of responsibility towards any Jewish community in danger or under seige. It surely did not matter what it cost; what was vital was to make the people in those countries aware that someone cared about them and would help them. I thought, if after everything that happened during the Second World War, the Jewish leadership did not understand that, they had learned nothing.

The Treasurer was still talking and explaining the delineation of authority, and when he finished I looked up at him and said, slowly and sincerely: 'I have been listening to everything you said, and I understand that I am accused of some kind of misdemeanour, but I want you to know something.'

And I explained to him my thoughts, my sentiments, how we all felt, what it meant to be abandoned, helpless and without support, unable to communicate, with no-one stretching out a helping hand. And I concluded thus:

'But many did survive and I believe that those who were fortunate enough to survive should do everything in their power to rescue and help Jewish communities that are still in danger; I believe that they should endeavour to do what, much to our regret, others failed to do in any significant manner when we were in that situation.'

Silence prevailed. For some time nobody moved, nobody spoke. Suddenly there seemed to be no sides, there was a common, unspoken but deeply felt bond among all those in that room that day.

After a while, The Treasurer broke the silence. 'I understand you very well, young man,' he said, 'but procedurally, you were wrong.' I paused, thought for a moment and, drawing a deep breath replied: 'I don't know whether or not you will recall me to Israel and if you do, I will, of course, go – with a heavy heart, but I will accept your decision. However, please remember that if you leave me here and, should I face another similar situation, I will have no choice – because of my past, because of my experiences, because of my feelings – but to take the same course of action. I hope you understand.'

The meeting concluded.

I was not recalled to Jerusalem, but when I terminated my contract with the Agency the following year and returned to Israel, the Treasurer approached me with a proposition to work for him at the headquarters of the organisation in Jerusalem. I declined the offer – firmly but politely.

Marcel

My work with the Agency took me to Paris frequently, since much of the organisation's activities were centred in or channelled through Paris. When I came to Paris in the late fifties, I would visit Gina's family as often as possible and they would greet me warmly in their modest but cosy apartment near the Daumesnil district.

One day when I went there to visit them I arrived a little late. Along with my father-in-law and his wife Adèle, another gentleman was at the table. He was of medium height, slim, with strong blue eyes, and he chatted fluently in French – with a hint of Polish and Yiddish here and there. He was introduced to me as Adèle's cousin and he told us all that he was on his way back to Warsaw from the Far East. Adèle added rather vaguely that he was a diplomat acting as the Polish representative in Indo-China and on his return, had taken the opportunity of passing through Paris to renew contact with his cousin. We had no reason to doubt him.

It was 1954, the year of Tien Wen Puh, that bloody battle between the French and the Vietmin in Northern Indo China and the last siege lasted for almost 60 days, until they fell into the hands of the Vietmin. As a result of the victory of the Vietmin, and negotiations between the East and West, an armistice commission was established with Poland representing the Eastern Communist Bloc, and the gentleman at our lunch table was that Polish representative. He was an eager idealist, believing that Communism would solve all the problems of humanity, including those of the Jewish people. I told him my view that the solution for the Jewish people was a stable and democratic State of their own. I told him that just as he was faithful to his ideology, I too, was working for my country and trying to bring as many Jews as possible safely to Israel, and like him, I was doing all I could to achieve my goals.

When we parted, I gave him my calling card that said: *Chargé de Mission par la gouvernement d'Israel*. 'Take it,' I said, 'you never know.'

He was reluctant, but eventually he did, perhaps out of courtesy, or, maybe he had other ideas. He went to Poland, I went about my business; now and again I asked his cousin Adèle how he was, and who exactly he was. She kept telling me that he was a fine man, from a fine home, but she always added as a footnote that he was, after all, an ardent communist devoted to the service of his government and a strict believer in communist ideals. He had had a colourful past, full of problems, beset with danger, but she was never eager to go into detail. Perhaps she did not know them, or perhaps she was just being discreet.

She mentioned another brother somewhere in France to whom he was closely attached, particularly since the entire family had been wiped out during the Holocaust and whenever he could, she said, he came to France to renew contact with the little family he had left.

* * *

Ten years later, in 1967, just after the Six Day War, I had, of course, forgotten all about the wars in Indo-China and my meeting with the Armistice Commission representative in Paris. I had been back in Israel for seven years, having left the Agency I had worked for, and had moved to another organisation. My life-style had changed. I was working for an educational organisation and, seated in my office one day, I took a telephone call from somebody named Shlomo L in the Prime Minister's Office, an office I had had regular dealings with years before.

'Joe,' said Shlomo, 'listen, I've had a call from the Immigration Office and they tell me that a couple with a child of 13 or 14 has just landed at Tel Aviv Airport from Rome. According to the immigration officer, their passports are not actually their passports, but they say they are prepared to explain everything. We've asked them whom they know – and they gave us your name. They've even got your visiting card with your former title. Their name is X. What do you suggest we do?'

At first the name meant nothing to me. But after a few moments something clicked and I managed somehow to connect the name with a face.

'Shlomo,' I said, 'I believe I do know them. Let them in.'

A few days later they arrived in my office, he, his wife and their son, then called Jessi, later known as Joshua; in time they visited our home on several occasions. Both of them were bright people, fluent in several languages, but they were disappointed, discouraged, and disillusioned. Israel was foreign to them. They did not know the language – they were looking for work so they could make a living for their little family, and I did what I could to help. Somehow I felt a strange sense of responsibility – perhaps because of our meeting in Paris – after all, he may never have come to Israel if he had not had my visiting card from that day. Since I had dealt with immigration and the absorption of new immigrants, I could recommend these people as reliable, worthy citizens of the State, even though in some cases people could not be so freely trusted, particularly when they came from the Eastern bloc with that kind of background.

So I resolved to help them and went to one of the directors of the educational network I headed and found him a job as administrative officer in a school. To his credit he took everything seriously, studied the language diligently, and both he and his wife applied themselves to their absorption with dedication and zealousness. Together with other people of similar background, many of whom they had known from the war, and who were also talented and proficient in languages, he and his wife formed a cooperative, providing technical translations; they themselves were fluent in French, German, Spanish, Russian, Polish and English; as an agency they covered dozens of languages and, in addition to his more mundane day job, M assisted his wife with the translations; thus together they supplemented their income through this work in the evenings, creating for themselves and their son a comfortable existence.

* * *

I had always been intrigued to know what M's background really was. Years later, when I was retired and had more free time, I turned my attention to this extraordinary character.

His father had come from Kielce in Poland, a town some 180 kms south of Warsaw, with a population of about 30,000, including a fine Jewish community. Later his father, Moshe, moved to Warsaw, married one Sarah Buzin, and they built up a successful wholesale business. They were a typical middle-class family with five children, four sons and one daughter.

Our hero, born Menachem Mendel in 1914, later known as Marcel, was the third child and was followed by two younger brothers: Leon, born in 1916 and Jerzy Jossel. The family was brought up in a strict Jewish tradition – and the three youngest brothers were sent to a Mizrachi school, the orthodox Zionist movement, where they studied Hebrew and religion. Father Moshe was a committed Zionist and contributed money to the Land of Israel. Marcel was very close to his mother but in 1927 she died of cancer when he was barely 13. From the age of 14 to 17 he attended a commercial school in Warsaw. It was difficult for young Jews to integrate into Polish society – there was much anti-semitism and discrimination in higher education and so at the age of 19, in 1933 Marcel was sent to France. He had an uncle in Paris in the upholstery business and Marcel worked and learned the trade.

Two years later, in 1935, he returned to Poland to arrange his military service. Meantime, his younger brother Leon, had joined the illegal communist youth movement and as a committed party member was involved in the distribution of political material. When Leon tried to bring in some Czech communist publications, he was caught. The police searched his home and found more incriminating material and both brothers were arrested. Shocked by these events, the father did his best to have them released; he paid their bail and made rapid arrangements to get them back to France at once.

So in 1936 Marcel found himself once again in Paris, living with Leon who also learned the upholstery trade. With their communist inclination they were naturally in sympathy with the opponents of the fast-rising Fascist regimes throughout Europe, and were specifically drawn towards the cause of the Republicans in Spain at that time. The two brothers volunteered as freedom fighters in Spain, and in 1937 crossed the border illegally near Perpignan in the Pyrenees with other comrades in arms and reached Figueras.

From there, Marcel and Leon joined a training camp where they were taught to handle machine guns and in July 1938 they participated in what was known as the Ebro offensive intended to hold back Franco's military units. The campaign failed and young Leon was wounded during the attack. Marcel took him to a hospital where he remained for some months, and the brothers did not meet again until the end of 1938 before the evacuation was announced. The defeat of the International Brigade which had come from all over the world, with a great many Jews among them, meant that they had failed to hold back the forces of General Franco. They were taken into camps having crossed the border to France, and moved from place to place, conditions were abysmal; to survive as a human being you had to be extremely strong physically and morally. The two brothers eventually escaped from the camp at Gurs in the unoccupied zone of Southern France. Arrested by the French police, they presented themselves as Spanish refugees, and since their Spanish was first-class, the French did not suspect them as anything else. They were given Spanish papers with Spanish names they created for themselves and continued their lives.

By this time, Marcel had been recruited by the communist movement and became a member of the French underground. The Second World War had broken out in September 1939, and while France was largely occupied, the southern area, although under supervision of the

Germans, was not strictly under occupation. Leon also joined the underground movement and remained an active member until the liberation of France in 1944.

Back in 1941, since Marcel had been selected to work for the military intelligence of the Soviet authorities, and because of his excellent knowledge of French, he was asked to take charge of radio communications between France and Moscow. This link was vital and was maintained by the underground movement throughout the years of the Nazi regime. The information he provided was essentially concerned with German military movements, airfields and French institutions which cooperated with the Germans, the morale of the French people, what was happening on the Franco/Spanish border; but his activities did not include sabotage. With his warm personality and excellent command of the language, he successfully infiltrated every echelon of French society. The 'NET', as those concerned with providing this information were known, also produced false documents and had technicians within the movement who were experts in every field of forgery.

The two brothers met again after the end of the war in Paris, where they learned that they were the only two members of their family to survive.

With war over, the younger brother Leon married Jeanette, settled in Southern France, and resumed a normal life. Marcel remained in Paris for a while, active in his old workshop but he was restless and sought a more meaningful existence in the socialist world he longed for. So he returned to Poland where he renewed contact with many old friends; he separated from his wartime girlfriend and married Miriam – Mimi.

Mimi had been born in Hamburg in 1924 and she had a disrupted, difficult and tragic youth; in 1926 her parents left for Belgium. In 1940 when war broke out she joined the underground; in 1943 she was caught by the Germans while printing some illegal material, and then imprisoned in Waldheim in Saxony. She was taken from one camp to another and spent two and a half years doing hard labour.

Mimi was liberated on May 7, 1945. In 1947 she returned to Belgium and worked in an organisation called Solidarité which provided assistance to Jews. It was here in 1948 that Mimi was approached by a gentleman who asked her to work for the Polish intelligence in Paris. Later this gentleman was replaced by Marcel. They fell in love and when Marcel decided to return to Poland from Paris, Mimi gladly joined him.

Marcel was given the rank of major and appointed head of a special military unit in the Polish army. Later he became political editor for Spanish and French languages on Polish national radio; he worked there until 1955, when, following the war in Indo-China and according to the Geneva agreement of 1954, Poland, together with India and Canada, became members of the Armistice Control Commission. Since he was proficient in French, he joined the delegation in Cambodia where he stayed throughout 1956. Then he returned to Poland and became an adviser in the Foreign Office on Far East problems.

When Gomulka returned to power later that year, Marcel and his colleagues, the Spanish Civil War veterans, started hoping that things would change for the better and tried to promote their cause; at the same time he was offered the post of cultural press attaché in the Polish Embassy in Hanoi, Vietnam, where he remained for two years from 1957 to 1959. Then he returned to Warsaw and joined the Polish Red Cross. He loved the humanitarian nature of this welfare organisation which suited his character and was actively involved in the aftermath of the earthquake in Yugoslavia which almost entirely destroyed the city of Skopje in 1963.

Miriam, his wife, who had meanwhile learned Polish, formed a cooperative with friends to translate various technical publications and books for Polish export companies. Marcel joined this organisation soon afterwards and there he met many of his former friends, and since this was more lucrative, he concentrated his efforts on that. He had kept in touch with his brother in Marseilles throughout, and now and then they would meet, either in Warsaw or Budapest. As he became more and more disillusioned with the regime he had once felt so passionate about, Marcel gradually started doubting, but despite the many disappointments, his optimistic nature, humanitarian approach and sense of humour prevailed and helped him overcome adversity. Anti-semitism became rife once again, freedom was more theory than practice, and as he watched the West developing and observed all that the West had to offer, he concluded that it was time for him and his family to leave Communist Poland.

They went to Yugoslavia where they were permitted to travel with a *laissez passer* and there he met his brother Leon, who helped him plot an escape route for himself and his family. The story is shrouded in mystery, but they travelled to Italy with certain documents whose authenticity was dubious; from Rome he, his wife and son boarded an

El Al plane to Tel Aviv, and that was when I received the surprise phone call.

Marcel and his wife Mimi and son Jessi created a comfortable life for themselves in Israel; but in 1983, Marcel was diagnosed as suffering from lung cancer. His wife nursed him at home for as long as possible and that December, he died in his sleep.

* * *

Almost thirty years after that phone call in 1967, I was sitting in a lovely little house in Ra'anana, a suburb of Tel Aviv, with Marcel's son Joshua, the little boy who arrived in Ben Gurion airport at the age of 14 with his parents on that El Al plane. Since then he made his way through school, served in the Israeli army, and was severely wounded in the battle with the Syrians in 1973. The medics managed to put him back on his feet, and he went on to study business administration at Tel Aviv University. Today he works as a senior officer of a major Israeli export company. His wife, a computer expert, serves us a drink as their younger daughter studies for exams. The bell rings, and a young woman in the uniform of the Israeli airforce enters.

'Who is this lovely young sergeant?' I ask Joshua.

'That's my older daughter'.

Four generations – war upon war in between – so many deaths – and many fewer births. Passion and devotion to ideologies, ultimately shattered.

A helping hand

Many international bodies were based in Geneva during the late 1950s, including several Jewish organisations, which had been set up there in the Second World War to assist Jews during the Holocaust and immediately afterwards. Their functions included rehabilitation, emigration and aliyah, which became the most important issue of the surviving remnants of the Jewish people. Thus, the principal organisations of the Jewish Agency, the AJDC (American Jewish Joint Distribution Committee, known as the Joint), ORT and HIAS operated out of Geneva, which was also the centre of the United Nations, ILO, the Red Cross, and many other international bodies.

When I was appointed to Geneva I came across all these organisations and immediately established a working relationship with them. Naturally, we cooperated and on many occasions I met their executive officers, primarily those of the Joint and of ORT. The Joint's overseas headquarters for Europe was directed by Charlie Jordan, and the Director-General of the World ORT Union was Max Braude. Both were exceptionally fine people, who became good friends, as did Dr Vladimir Halperin, who was second in command at ORT, a descendant of the Baron de Ginzburg family, one of the founding fathers of ORT in Tsarist Russia in 1880. We were all involved in problems concerning Jews, and we met regularly to share information, to try to assist each other wherever and whenever possible. The goodwill shown by all concerned was remarkable, probably due both to the nature of the times, and the background and experience of the personalities involved.

When I met Max Braude in Geneva for the first time, he looked at me curiously and then said: 'I believe we have met before – could it have been in Nuremberg in the forties?' Max Braude was an American, the son of Latvian parents, who had been a chaplain in the US Army during the war, stationed in Germany at the time. He was an interesting personality: he dealt with international bodies and had a liberal approach towards Jews and non-Jews alike, while at the same time caring deeply for all Jewish matters; above all, he felt profoundly about the Holocaust, and tried to assist anyone who needed help. He had been actively involved with the Bricha movement, and many years later was presented with the Distinction of the Independence of Israel for his contribution to the State before its establishment, an honour accorded to very few non-Israelis.

Within my work with the Jewish Agency, if I had a problem, as in the late fifties in Morocco, it was natural for me to appeal to Max Braude for help. A group of more than 100 Jews, families with young children, had been arrested by the Moroccan authorities in Tetuan, formerly Spanish Morocco, for trying to leave the country illegally. After the intervention of the community leadership in Tetuan, the authorities agreed to let them out of prison, on condition that they be housed and kept together under supervision in one public building.

At that time ORT had a school in Tetuan and since this incident took place during the summer, I asked Max Braude to put the school at the disposal of these unfortunate people; he asked how long we would need it and I replied that it would take about ten to fifteen days to clear the matter with the authorities. He agreed immediately.

It so happened that we were not able to release them within the fifteen days as we had hoped, and the group was stuck there for many months, which in the event, ruined the entire school year for ORT. Max would call me periodically and in his deep husky voice would ask 'Nu?', and I would reply, 'Sorry, we're not ready yet.' Ultimately, he understood that the safety of the Jews was sometimes an even greater priority than education.

Eventually the matter was resolved and the group was transported safely to Israel.

* * *

Charlie Jordan was the charismatic head of the Joint and another of those giant leaders of the major Jewish organisations with whom I worked closely, and who became a great friend during those years of intense activity in Europe.

While ORT worked only in Poland during the 1950s to provide Jewish survivors with skills before they left the DP camps for Israel, the Joint was indirectly involved in almost all Jewish communities in Eastern Europe and Russia, helping them in every possible way. The Jewish Agency's cooperation with the Joint was therefore on a wider level than that with ORT.

Both Max Braude and Charlie Jordan were genuine leaders, in the right place at the right time, whenever Jewish communities were in need or in crisis.

That spirit is what brought Charlie Jordan to Israel during those tense weeks preceding the Six-Day War in 1967, and that is what took him immediately to Romania under the horrors of the Ceaucescu dictatorship. Charlie Jordan was worried about the fate of the Jewish communities in the Eastern bloc when relations with Israel were cut there as a result of the six-day War. Passing through Geneva en route to Bucharest, he stopped in Prague, where he met his tragic fate. He was killed and his body mysteriously thrown into the river, later recovered, and brought for burial accompanied by Max Braude and Hy Wachtel, who had served together in the American Army rescuing Jewish survivors in Europe after the war. Years later the Czech authorities insisted that Charlie Jordan was assassinated by Egyptian Intelligence.

I last saw Charlie Jordan the night before he left Israel for Romania, the night before the outbreak of the Six-Day War. We were sitting in our home in Kfar Shmaryahu, and Charlie insisted that as Director-General of ORT in Israel, I should write a report on how ORT institutions had prepared themselves for whatever might happen in case of war. I did write that report, on how schools were partly mobilised, giving a picture of how students dug trenches, and describing the general atmosphere that prevailed. He took that report with him to Geneva, delivered it to Max Braude, and it was later published and distributed all over the ORT world.

I will never forget how, before he left late at night, Charlie entered the bedroom of our two sons who were fast asleep; he looked at them with pity in his eyes. Gina and I accompanied him to the front door and said goodbye, and as we did so, he turned back, his eyes brimming with tears. Like many people in those days, he clearly thought that Israel was facing another Jewish catastrophe.

* * *

In 1956, my assignment to Europe had been for two years; it was extended for a third year and then a fourth. At the end of the fourth year, Gina and I decided to return home to Israel. It took another half year to do so since I had to spend a period overlapping with my successor.

As I have mentioned, the Treasurer of the Agency urged me to come to work with him in Jerusalem, but Gina and I had no wish to live in Jerusalem.

At that time, the role of the Jewish Agency had diminished. The waves of immigration had subsided, private companies had taken over many of the functions previously carried out by the Agency, and I could foresee the organisation's operations continuing to diminish in scale as time went on. Meanwhile, several organisations, banks and other private companies, had approached me with various offers.

I had a choice, or rather Gina, my life partner, had the choice; the four and a half years had been a restless, demanding, and tense period during which I spent little time at home, and it took its toll. Gina was firm and insisted we settle down to a calm and peaceful life in Israel, without tension or pressure. I declined offers to manage a bank in Lugano or in London or to join a shipping organisation in Geneva, and accepted a position offered by Max Braude, Director General of the World ORT Union, as comptroller of an educational network: ORT Israel. This was a newly-created post, but Braude hinted that there was a strong chance of my taking over the general management of ORT in Israel, when the incumbent Director General, Jacob Oleiski, retired.

Max told me that if I accepted his offer, he would have to write to the President of ORT Israel, Josef Shapira, for his agreement. Josef Shapira was a well-known personality, respected in economic and industrial circles in Israel, as President of the Israeli Foreign Trade Bank; he had also been the Director-General of the Palestine Electric Corporation, which I had left to join the Jewish Agency, and he may have remembered me from there.

Shortly after Max had made his offer, he called me to ask if I could drop by his office. He took out a piece of paper – Shapira's answer to his request – and showed it to me: 'If Josef Harmatz agrees, chupp!' (grab him).

Thus I left my hectic, sometimes dramatic life in Geneva and entered a new chapter which was intended to be calm, quiet, and uneventful. Little did I know that this was to be the start of a career spanning thirty-three years, which were far from uneventful.

VIII

ISRAEL 1960

Back to School

'Train up a child in the way he should go: and when he is old he will not depart from it'

Proverbs 6

ORT Israel had been established in 1949, eleven years earlier as a branch of World ORT Union, to promote professional education among youngsters and adults. It started with the transference to Israel of the teachers and students of the former school in Sofia, Bulgaria, who were initially accommodated in a dilapidated building in Jaffa; ORT Israel appointed Jacob Oleiski as its director after he had served for some time as a director of the ORT school in Prophets Street, Jerusalem, which now bears his name.

Jacob Oleiski was born in Lithuania, studied agriculture in Germany, returned to Lithuania, and was appointed director of the ORT school in Kovno. During the German occupation, Oleiski created a professional school inside the Kovno Ghetto, and when it was finally liquidated, he was taken to Dachau concentration camp. He was a tall man with impressive features and a beautiful baritone voice, which rose and fell according to the mood of discussion. When he started to shout at high pitch, the entire three floors of the office would almost vibrate. It did not mean that he was really angry, but it was his way of convincing people: it meant either stay in or get out. Oleiski had a sharp mind and was a splendid judge of character, having been involved for so many years with people: as director of schools, director of an organisation, and in particular, the years of the German occupation in the ghetto of Kovno, and in Dachau, had sharpened all his human senses: you could see in his eyes his quick reaction and fast comprehension of any given situation. Immediately after the war he had been empowered by ORT's leadership to create professional training centres in the DP camps. This was one of his greatest achievements: to rebuild the lives and existence of a depressed and broken people and provide them with a new beginning was an act of immeasurable importance, a heroic deed, and one he continued to fulfil in Israel.

Oleiski created a finely-tuned ORT organisation in Israel and gave it a sound and healthy foundation for others to build on. He had to cooperate with the government, the municipalities and other organisations on a political level, which was a strange environment for him. He had not been a Zionist before he came to ORT Israel, nor was ORT a Zionist organisation in the diaspora. By the year it started to function in Israel, ORT was already 70 years old.

When Oleiski took over the management of ORT Israel, he appointed as principals and directors of the first phase of schools established, those people who had assisted him in the DP camps in Germany immediately after the war. As educators or engineers, or both, they had extensive experience in setting up and running professional and technical courses in all fields and at all different levels. Oleiski's energy was inexhaustible; if anybody can be described as a bulldozer, it was Jacob Oleiski.

In 1951 Oleiski came to our home in Israel and invited me to visit two of ORT's schools: one in Safed, and the other in Ein Harod. Our dedicated driver Nick, drove us there in a Ford station wagon and when we returned to Tel Aviv late at night Oleiski asked me if I would join ORT, but at that time, I turned him down. In 1960 when I finally agreed to work with ORT in the newly-established post of Comptroller, I think he was pleased.

My job was primarily to tackle the administrative and financial aspects of the organisation. Once I had visited the schools around the country and learned all there was to know about the system, I recommended certain organisational changes so that the organisation would function more efficiently both practically and economically. It was not that the organisation was in bad shape, but I felt it was important to prepare a framework for what was likely to be a chaotic period of mass immigration.

For example, in the schools, lunches had been regularly provided. These were often schools with between 600 and 800 pupils, which meant that the running of each canteen was a major undertaking involving the employment of large numbers of domestic staff, the purchase, storage, and cooking of food, which in turn brought with it problems of hygiene and theft. In addition, with children from vastly differing backgrounds with diverse tastes in food, be it North African, Yemenite or European, parents would complain that their children were not being appropriately catered for. My proposal was to hand over the canteens to professional caterers, and we appointed a parents' committee to supervise the standard and quality of the meals which they provided. This had the added advantage of making the parents feel more involved in their children's school. The canteens were left to the caterers on the basis of quality and price. If the service they provided did not meet the principal's satisfaction, they could appoint a competitor. Thus we no longer had catering staff problems, nor industrial/union involvement as far as this area was concerned.

The same applied to the cleaning staff, when we handed over the entire function to a domestic contractor. Before that, we had been forced to hire staff from a rehabilitation network which would engage people unable to obtain any other kind of employment. This domestic operation was not quite so straightforward at first because the organisation was obliged to employ staff who were often sick or elderly, and when I introduced this change, the unions intervened immediately. Yet, the premises still remained dirty. The teachers did not even want to enter the classrooms or labs. It became a real problem, and I pressed hard for a change, until gradually we dismissed all the cleaners and decided to pay by the square metre cleaned. The contractors were then forced to hire good staff to do a good job and the principal of each school had to approve the quality of their work.

Changing the way these functions were carried out gave the organisation a basis with which to cope with the astonishing development of the State. The basic principle of my recommendations was that the Director and his staff should only have to deal with education, while all the administrative functions would be handed over to professional companies specialising in the relevant field. In this way, the principal and the teachers could focus on teaching the students, and were not bothered with feeding them or dealing with domestic matters.

I gradually got to know the people, learned about the functions of the organisation and its future potential. I was a member of the board of management, would meet with the president and director general from time to time, and soon became one who belonged. There were also other issues related to World ORT which I would discuss with Max

Braude, during his frequent visits to Israel. Having been involved in financial matters in Switzerland, I was also looking at foreign currency rates and was astonished to discover that the foreign currency transferred to Israel from the headquarters in Geneva was being exchanged at a reduced rate (20 per cent). There were at that time two rates in Israel: a tourist rate, which was preferential, and the lower rate which was applied to ORT. I raised the issue with banker-friends and we found a solution. Everybody was delighted, no-one more so than Max Braude. It meant that ORT Israel obtained 20 per cent more of the Geneva subvention. Over the years, that ran into millions.

Yet, there came a time when I felt quite bored with my functions as comptroller and really wanted to leave the organisation, but Max Braude persuaded me to stay. He had probably decided, together with others, that I was a strong contender for the post of Director General of ORT Israel.

Meanwhile, fate intervened, to help solve the problem of boredom.

Shipping

During my posting to Geneva with the Jewish Agency, when one of the major problems was the transportation of immigrants, I had developed a close cooperation with the various shipping and airline companies. Most prominent among these were ZIM, the Israeli national shipping line, and EL AL for air transport (which was less desirable as a mode of transporting immigrants since it did not allow for time during which to interview them en route as on the ships).

There were, however, for obvious reasons, routes which neither ZIM nor EL AL were able to service, such as the ports of North Africa, and the Arab states. The French Compagnie Paquet was the only shipping company which covered the route to North Africa; they were keen to fill their ships, had no interest in politics, and my organisation had developed good relations with the company's agents, Oceania. This was a Jewish agency led by well known figures in Paris and Marseilles, who had proved their dedication throughout the wartime years by trying, whenever possible, to channel groups and individual survivors through Spain, Portugal and Vichy France. They were also active in the illegal emigration during the pre-state years in Palestine.

Compagnie Paquet agreed to our request for permission to post two of our people to their offices in North Africa. The two, who had outstanding Franco-Jewish backgrounds, did an excellent job of supervising the port of Casablanca, and created first-class relations with the local staff. It was vital to our operation in Morocco. I remember one of the directors of the company asking me on one occasion: 'Who is actually running your country, if you can afford to send such people to act as clerks in the ports?' It was hard to explain to French businessmen that Israel's first priority in those turbulent days of the fifties was immigration. The relationship was one of close cooperation and understanding: on several occasions our camp at Grand Arenas in Marseilles was full to capacity because of the shortage of ships for transporting the immigrants to Israel; so the management of the shipping company even agreed to delay the entry of their boats into the port of Marseilles, by a day or so, bringing yet more immigrants into the port, in order to allow time to empty the camp of the existing immigrants. We would just pack as many as possible onto boats to Haifa before bringing in more and more emigrants from North Africa as we sped up the evacuation of Jews from that country.

One day, around the time of such an exercise, during one of our regular lunchtime meetings in Marseilles, having enjoyed a first-class meal and a good bottle of French wine, one of the company's directors suddenly approached me with the following query:

'Why on earth do we do these things for you? We must be crazy?'

Maybe I had had just a little too much red wine, or I was tired and irritable, but whatever it was, I replied:

'Listen, old chap, one day, when you decide to create a route to Haifa, I can promise you, we'll let you in.'

So who was I to promise them an entry to Haifa, when they would require no such permission anyway? Anyone could enter the port of Haifa in those days, particularly the French who, politically, were enjoying a honeymoon period with Israel.

Now in 1960 in Israel, having just committed myself to work as comptroller for ORT, suddenly, out-of-the-blue, I received a cable from Paris to say that a delegation of the Compagnie Paquet would be arriving in Tel Aviv to discuss the opening of a French line to Israel.

Heading the delegation was André Chadell, the commercial director of the company, a charming personality, who subsequently became a great friend. He was accompanied by Jules Jeffroykin, the proprietor of the travel agency, Oceania, Compagnie Paquet's representatives, and Marcel Navarro, a co-owner based in Marseilles.

They came to inform me that the management had decided to establish the route from Marseilles to Haifa and that they were keen to set up a separate company to run this line. Moreover they wanted me to become a partner and director, and to act as their representative in Israel, offering me shares in the newly-established company.

The meetings took place at the King David Hotel in Jerusalem but I was obliged to tell them that I had just accepted a post with ORT and doubted whether I could join them *and* fulfil my obligations to ORT. I assured them, however, that I would introduce them to the right people who could help and would even guarantee their credentials.

While Messrs Jeffroykin, Chadell and Navarro were all stubborn, it was Chadell who was particularly determined that I should join them, and as such he declared that if I did not, he would recommend that head office altogether abandon the idea of establishing this subsidiary company.

These were good reliable people, whose credibility was unquestioned. I had known and worked with them for so many years and I was seriously tempted by their offer. My instant reaction was to take a plane to Geneva and meet with Max Braude, tell him of the offer and ask his advice. Max listened attentively, thought for a few moments, and in his deep bass-baritone voice asked me: 'Reb Yossl,' (his usual form of addressing me), 'to tell you the truth, you can do both jobs. I don't mind at all. I don't suppose you are going to be selling tickets. I understand that basically you're going to represent the company. I'm in favour of the American way of doing things; there's nothing wrong with this kind of arrangement; on the contrary, I would like to know that we have among our managerial staff, people who are involved in Israel's development. I even think it would add a certain prestige to ORT.'

It did not really fit into the mentality of most Israelis of those days, but frankly, it suited me down to the ground.

My return journey to Israel took me via Paris. There I met with my French friends and told them that the way was open for me to join them. They were delighted. It presented me with a challenge and made me realise that the years of hard work in Geneva had given me the opportunity of meeting fine people who became good friends and who had remembered me.

Thus the Compagnie Francaise de Navigation (in Israel it was known as the French Line) was set up, agents were appointed, all experts in the field of shipping. In France, Leo Stern joined the company. He was formerly deputy commercial manager of ZIM in Europe, and an expert in the field of passenger transport. Ships previously used for the North African route, were re-named – the Caesarea, the Galilée – to appeal to those travelling to Israel. Meanwhile, cargo shipping began to increase significantly as relations between Israel and France continued to improve.

An office was established in Tel Aviv and another, naturally, in Haifa, while our staff worked closely with the various travel agencies to promote the line which very quickly became a great success. In due course, as air travel grew more popular, the trend was to move from regular crossings towards luxury cruises in the Mediterranean. Slowly several ships were taken out of service, while some were converted into luxury liners, and a superb new ship, which we named Renaissance, was specially commissioned and built in St Lazaire to take passengers from France to the Greek Islands, Greece, Italy, Turkey and Israel.

Relations with France continued to flourish and since the company over the years had created an import and export division representing

French heavy and light industries in North Africa, the French parent company decided to expand its activities with the Israeli branch. A separate trading company was established between CFN and other Israeli companies for this purpose and the whole enterprise served to bring about a sounder relationship between Israel and France (not only militarily and politically, but commercially and socially). French personalities who were well-placed in political and economic circles, helped to create a more cordial entente, even during the years when De Gaulle returned to power and turned France's policies in favour of the Arab world.

As a record of this development, I have among my souvenirs the Ordre Nationale de Merite signed by Charles de Gaulle, which was presented to me in Tel Aviv by the French Ambassador, de Sablier.

By 1965, ORT Israel's Executive and World ORT Union announced that I was their candidate to take over the directorship of ORT Israel. At this point, I had to make a decision between the French shipping company and ORT. It would not have been appropriate for a director of ORT Israel to be involved in other enterprises and developments. I finally decided to accept the appointment as Director General of ORT Israel, and relinquished all my commitments: towards CFN, towards the people with whom I had become involved in the establishment of a stained glass company, and others.

The day I took over the management of ORT Israel I was free of all other constraints and I dedicated myself totally to the educational network I had been charged to run.

INDEX OF PEOPLE

Abramovich, Adèle 167
Anolick, Benjamin 30ff, 35–36
Argov, Levi 142
Avidan, Shimon 139

Baron, Yithak-Eliezer 19
Bartek 135
Ben-Gurion, David 117, 192
Ben-Zur, Jasiek 135, 142
Benjamin, Brigadier General 116
Bernstein, Mira 68
Bichunas 73
Bick, Asia 81
Borowska, Chiena 69, 90, 137
Braude, Max 212, 213, 215, 223
Brenner, Professor Harry 169

Chadell, André 222
Chwoinik, Abrasha 81

Daiches, Musia 54, 56, 61
Debeltov, Dobka 134ff
Distel, Arie 135ff, 140

Eichmann, Adolf 142
Eshkol, Levi 152, 153
Ettingof, Mark 21

Feldman, Simon 191

Gens, Ada 76
Gens, Jacob 76, 77
Gevissar, Menasche 92
Giladi, Hillel 171
Goldstein, Baruch 77, 78
Gomulka, Vladislav 179, 181
Gorbachev, Mikhail xiii

Grumberg, Genadi 28, 29, 30

Halperin, Vladimir 212
Harmatz, Abraham (Abrasha) 10, 73ff
Harmatz, Dvora (Dora) 10, 53, 112, 113, 161, 168
Harmatz, Ephraim 30, 36ff
Harmatz, Ronel Ephraim 1, 21, 36, 67, 79, 91, 169
Harmatz, Gina (née Kerszenfeld) 165ff, 214, 215
Harmatz, Zvi 1, 167, 168
Harmatz, Zvi-Hirsch 2, 21
Hitler, Adolf 43, 71, 118

Jeffroykin, Jules 222
Jordan, Charlie 212, 213
Josephtal, Giora 173

Kaminski, Marcel 166
Kaplan, Jankel 81
Kaplinski, Shmulke 67, 80, 83
Kark, Meir 3
Katcherginsky, Shmerke 105
Kerszenfeld, Edith 166 167
Kerszenfeld, Oskar 166
Komorov-Kimron, Professor 193, 196
Korchak, Rushka 80
Kovner, Abba 80ff, 105, 115, 129, 137ff, 150ff, 169
Kovner, Vitka (Kempner) 81, 98, 105
Krou, Amichai 193
Kronik, Josef 187
Krushchev, Nikita 181

Laor, Eran 177
Lazor, Chaim 68, 75, 76, 97, 115
Levin, Ilya and Sasha 41, 50
Levin, Josef and Sanna 41ff
Levine, Benik 106
Lubotsky, Danka 36ff, 137
Lubotsky, Nusia 113
Lusky, Chaim 64
Lusky, Irena 54, 61, 63
Lusky, Shimon 63, 64

Madeisker, Sonia 75, 98
Manik 119ff, 142
Matskewich, Izka 69
Meir, Golda 161

Navarro, Marcel 222
Netzer, Zvi 188
Nissanelevich, Zelda 98, 105

Oleiski, Jacob 215, 217ff

Rabin, Yitzhak 41
Rabinovich, Ze'ev (Welvel) 110
Reichman (Avidov), Pasha and Dorka 115, 143ff
Reiss, Izzy 174
Rief, Fay 3
Rize, Yitzhak 83
Rosman, Mordechai 110
Rubin, Tevya 87ff

Shapira, Josef 215
Sharet, Moshe 116
Shazar (Rubashov), Zalman and Rachel 150, 161, 167
Shenhar, Willek 131, 140
Sheresnevsky, Bear 69
Shmushkevitch, General 2
Slepp, Henie 70
Slepp, Micha 71, 72
Stalin, Josef 43
Stern, Leo 223
Stuhl, Matla 81
Sternsüss, Marcel and Mimi 207ff
Sutzkever, Avraham 105

Telerant, Tolia 81
Trainin, Professor Nathan 169
Tscherniachovsky, Marshal 100

Vidan, Nachman 173

Wachtel, Hy 214
Weinstein, Grisha 75
Wilensky, Colonel Ze'ev 3
Wingate, Minnie 161
Wittenberg, Itzik 69, 77, 78

Yakubovitch, Liova and Gita 48

Zass, Lena 105, 107
Zeidel, Motl 92ff

INDEX OF PLACE NAMES AND ORGANISATIONS

AJDC – American Jewish Joint Distribution Committee 212
Alexeievka 3, 6, 9
Atlit 149

Barnaul 44, 46
Bricha 148
Byorai 12ff

Comsomol 75
Compagnie Paquet 221

Doron Foundation 52
Drancy 22

Ein Hachoresh Kibbutz 150
Etzel 114, 149

For Victory (Partisan Battalion) 96
FPO – Veraynigte Partisaner Organisatsye 67, 75ff

Ghetto of Vilna 36, 52, 67, 70ff

Haganah 64, 114, 148
HIAS 212

Judenrat 68, 72, 76, 77

Kaiserwald-Riga 52ff
Kaunas 11, 21, 101
Kfar Shmaryahu 67, 169, 214
Klooga 3, 29ff
Krasnoyarsk 45, 48, 145
Kristallnacht 71

Lechi (Stern Group) 114
Lvov 107, 108

Mathausen 111
Memorial Foundation for Jewish Culture 52

Ninth Fort 21, 22
NKVD 102ff
Novosibirsk 45

Obelai 17–20
Oriol 2–5
ORT 52, 90, 212, 217, 224
ORT Braude Institute of Technology 161
Osvientzim (Auschwitz) 53

Palanga 20, 31, 47
Ponar 69, 72, 92
Ponivesh 75
Ponteba 116, 119

Riga 3, 39, 52
Rokishkis 1, 20, 40, 67, 70, 73
Rudnitski Forests 67, 83ff

Shirvintos 19
Siberia 21, 39ff
St Petersburg (Leningrad) 27
Stutthof 3, 53, 54, 61

Tallin 27, 39
Tarvisio 116
Torun 59

Vilna 3, 46ff, 67ff, 100ff